Sursum Corda!
A Collection of Short Works

by

Mother Mary Loyola

edited by
Lisa Bergman

2018
St. Augustine Academy Press
Homer Glen, Illinois

"How to Help the Sick and Dying." *Publications of the Catholic Truth Society*, Volume X. London: Catholic Truth Society, 1900.

Mass Before First Communion: With Some Other Devotions for First Communicants. London: Burns and Oates, 1906.

A Simple Confession Book. London: Catholic Truth Society, 1913.

A Simple Confirmation Book. Brooklyn: International Catholic Truth Society, no date.

A Simple Communion Book. London: Catholic Truth Society, 1912.

What Catholics Believe: A Simple Explanation of the Chief Points of Christian Doctrine. New York: The Paulist Press, 1925.

Holy Mass. New York: The Paulist Press, 1927.

Why Must I Suffer: A Talk with the Toilers. London: Catholic Truth Society, 1911.

"Abba, Father!" London: Burns & Oates, no date.

"Ita Pater!" London: Burns & Oates, no date.

On His Majesty's Service: A Talk with our Wounded. London: Catholic Truth Society, 1916.

Mary Ward (1585-1645): Foundress of the Institute of the Blessed Virgin Mary. London: Catholic Truth Society, 1922.

Maxims of Mary Ward. London: Catholic Truth Society, no date.

"The Time of My Life." *The Loretto Rainbow*, Vol. XXXVII, No. 1, July 1930.

Typesetting and Design Contributor
Regina Rexrode, Point n' Click Publishing

Volume compilation, notes and chronology ©2018
by St. Augustine Academy Press.
All Rights Reserved.

ISBN: 978-1-936639-41-0
Library of Congress Control Number: 2018963054

"Catholic literature, doctrinal and devotional, owes a great deal to Mother Mary Loyola. There is a certain wholesomeness, naturalness, geniality about her spirituality that at once wins a place in the Catholic heart for whatever she writes."
—*The Ecclesiastical Review*, January 1918

About Mother Mary Loyola:

Most Catholics today who have heard the name Mother Mary Loyola know her as the author of *The King of the Golden City*, which has enjoyed a resurgence in popularity in recent years. But few know that she wrote over two dozen works, and that she was once a household name among Catholics of her era. What made her unique among Catholic authors was her ability to draw in her listeners with story after story—and not just any stories, but ones that incorporated current events and brand new inventions of the time. Despite the fact that those events are no longer current, and those inventions no longer brand new, her books scintillate with the appeal of an active mind that could find a moral in the most unusual places. And while the printed word lacks the animated facial expressions and vocal inflections which reveal a gifted storyteller, hers convey her enthusiasm so capably that the reader can easily imagine sitting at the feet of this wise old nun.

About *Sursum Corda!*:

This long-awaited anthology of all the minor works by Mother Mary Loyola is the fruit of many years of seeking. The relatively small size of the many booklets she wrote, mostly for the Catholic Truth Society, seems to have led over the years to the loss of most copies. Therefore it was with the help of libraries and archives around the world that we were finally able to assemble the most complete collection possible, including 13 of her 14 known pamphlets, as well as a bonus selection: a short essay published in a school magazine during the last year of Mother Loyola's life. From her early *How to Help the Sick and Dying* to her biographical preface for the *Maxims of Mary Ward*, they can all be found in this volume. We hope that this will preserve them to future generations.

To learn more about Mother Mary Loyola, visit our website at
www.staugustineacademypress.com.

FOREWORD

Quite a few years ago, our family was introduced to Mother Mary Loyola through her wonderful allegory *The King of the Golden City*. Only later, while helping a dear friend organize her materials for a First Communion class, did I learn that Mother Loyola had written more. A quick internet search soon showed me just how much more, and by now I can state with certainty that at least thirty-three titles can be attributed to her pen, perhaps more. Her work needed no greater recommendation than what we had already read, yet I was amazed to find each work so unique and so appealing, even after 100 years had passed since they were first written. Who was this remarkable nun that could write like this, so prolifically yet with the touch of a skilled story teller?

Thus began a years-long quest for more information that eventually brought me to England twice and caused more than one interlibrary loan specialist to throw up her hands in despair. I still hope and pray to be able to compile a full biography with the treasures I found. For now it is with great pleasure that I present this volume, the most complete anthology of Mother Loyola's shorter works that is likely to be

Sursum Corda!

assembled in this generation. To the extent of my knowledge of what still exists (and I do grieve for manuscripts that have been lost...) there is only one of these minor works missing from this collection, and that is *A Simple First Confession Book.* As we have her two full-length works on the subject, as well as her *Simple Confession Book,* it seemed extraneous to expend the effort it would have required to obtain this, when the material inside was sure to be little different from these three.

It was a surprise to me, then, as this collection was being assembled, to stumble across an article written by Mother Loyola just 6 months before she died, published in a school journal associated with a distant Canadian branch of Mother Loyola's order. It was a thrill to be able to add this before going to press, as its topic of discerning one's vocation in life is not only a wonderful capstone to this opus, but it also shows how vigorously she pursued her own calling in life—that of using her unique talent for wordcraft to bring one and all to Him who has the Words of eternal life.

We give thanks to God for the gift to us that is Mother Mary Loyola.

Yours in Christ,
Lisa Bergman
St. Augustine Academy Press
All Saints Day, 2018

Table of Contents

How to Help the Sick and Dying (1890) 1

Mass Before First Communion (1896) 43

A Simple Confession Book (1901) 71

A Simple Confirmation Book (1901) 113

A Simple Communion Book (1903) 163

What Catholics Believe (1905) 205

Holy Mass (1907) 269

Why Must I Suffer (1911) 319

Abba, Father! (1912) 375

Ita Pater! (1912) 395

On His Majesty's Service (1916) 405

Mary Ward, Foundress of the IBVM (1921) 437

Maxims of Mary Ward (1921) 365

The Time of My Life (1930) 493

HOW TO HELP THE SICK AND DYING

INTRODUCTION

At the time that this short pamphlet for the Catholic Truth Society was written, Mother Mary Loyola had not yet made a name for herself in the Catholic world, and, being a woman religious, it was common practice not to attach one's name to published material. For this reason, it is very difficult, after so many years have passed, to determine with perfect certainty the authorship of this work, much less when or how it came to be written or published.

In spite of these hindrances, I feel quite confident in presenting this text as Mother Loyola's.

First, we know from several sources that she did write a short work by this exact title for the Catholic Truth Society. It can be found among listings of titles by Mother Loyola at the back of several books of the period. It is specifically mentioned in a short biography of Mother Loyola printed in early 1930 in *The Mariale*, a periodical produced by St. Francis Seminary in Loretto, Pennsylvania. And Mother Loyola mentions it herself in one of her letters preserved in the Jesuit Archives in London.

But how can we know that this particular piece is hers? It is possible that someone else might have written a similar work with the same title—after all, it is not a terribly unique one.

The earliest mention we have found of it is around 1890, as one of the CTS "twopenny pamphlets" mentioned in review publications such as *The Month* and *The Dublin Review*. It was later found in a compendium of essays by prominent Catholic authors called *Beautiful Pearls of Catholic Truth*, published in 1897. The version you see in these pages was taken from a printing of it in Volume X of the collected *Publications of the Catholic Truth Society* published in London in 1900. In none of these is the author's name mentioned. An inquiry of the Catholic Truth Society as to its authorship proved fruitless, as no record currently exists.

We do of course know that Mother Loyola wrote a good number of short works for the CTS, most of which populate the current volume. In fact, a close examination of early copies (circa 1888-1918) of the CTS' well-known and very popular *Simple Prayer Book* show a truly remarkable similarity to Mother Loyola's later *Little Children's Prayer Book*—so much so, that if she were not at least in part the author of that earlier book, she must certainly have borrowed from it with surprising alacrity in assembling the latter.

As Mother Loyola would not add her name to any of her published works until *The Child of God* in 1899, one would expect that works like this, published prior to that date, would be unattributed. But the final confirmation of its authorship, in my opinion, is the fact that in many places, the style of address and the structure of the prayers and many scripture quotes matches her later works (and prior works, if my guess is correct that she had a hand in the writing of the *Simple Prayer Book*).

HOW TO HELP THE SICK AND DYING

"Then shall the King say to them that shall be on His Right Hand: Come, ye blessed of My Father, possess you the kingdom prepared for you from the foundation of the world. For...I was sick and you visited Me....Amen, I say to you, as long as you did it to one of My least brethren, you did it to Me." (Matt. 25:34-40.)

Many, encouraged by these words, would gladly serve and console our Lord in His suffering members, *if they knew how*; but a feeling of helplessness holds them back, and thus numberless opportunities of doing good are neglected. Yet to help the sick and dying is a work of charity which may be required of any one of us, for which therefore we should all prepare ourselves. Let us do so without delay. No great skill or experience is necessary: the more simple the assistance the better—a little patience, a little charity and tact, and God's grace will do the rest.

Contents

Part I: How to help the Sick

To those who attend the Sick 7
Morning Prayers for the Sick 9
Night Prayers for the Sick 10
Acts to be suggested to the Sick 11
   1. Contrition 11
   2. Patience and Resignation 16
   3. Faith, Hope, and Charity 20
   4. Preparation for Death 22

Part II: How to help the Dying

To those who attend the Dying 25
The Last Sacraments 28
   1. Penance 28
   2. The Holy Viaticum 29
   3. Extreme Unction 32
The Last Blessing 34
The Last Agony 35
After Death 37
How We May Help Non-Catholics............ 41

I. HOW TO HELP THE SICK

To those who attend the Sick.

1. Keep the room clean and tidy. Open the window sometimes to let in fresh air, but not so as to do any harm to the sick person.

2. Take care to avoid as much as possible the danger of catching the same sickness. For example, if it is a fever, avoid breathing the breath of the sick person.

3. When you have to wash the sick, make their bed, or change their linen, do it with great modesty.

4. Attend carefully to whatever the doctor has said about food, medicine, &c.

5. Be kind and gentle in all you do for the sick and be very patient, for sick people are often irritable and hard to please.

6. Do not be talkative or talk in too loud a voice so as to disturb the sick person. And do not talk about vain, foolish worldly things, especially to those who are dying.

7. When you say prayers or read good books to them, do so in a quiet, gentle voice, and slowly. Notice

what they like, what seems to comfort and encourage them—a favourite prayer or aspiration said two or three times at intervals is often more helpful than much variety. Take care not to tire them by too many prayers or too much reading at a time. Among the acts suggested to them, contrition, patience, faith, hope and charity should be the chief. See that the sick say short morning and night prayers, and, if necessary, say them with them. At night a few minutes should be given to examination of conscience.

8. When the sickness is long, see that the parish priest is told of it, that he may hear the Confession of the sick and give them Holy Communion from time to time.

Morning Prayers for the Sick.

Make the sign of the Cross as soon as you awake and say:

My God, I offer Thee this day
All I may think or do or say;
Uniting it with what was done
On earth by Jesus Christ Thy Son.

Make up your mind to try and keep from anything displeasing to God.

✠ In the Name of the Father, and of the Son, and of the Holy Ghost. Amen.

Our Father ✠ Hail Mary ✠ I believe ✠ Glory be

O my God, I believe in Thee, because Thou art Truth itself.
O my God, I hope in Thee, because of Thy promises to me.
O my God, I love Thee, because Thou art so good: teach me to love Thee daily more and more.
O my God, I offer Thee all my thoughts, words, actions and sufferings; and I beseech Thee to give me Thy grace that I may not offend Thee this day, but faithfully serve Thee and do Thy holy Will in all things.
I desire to gain all the Indulgences that I can.
Holy Mary, be a mother to me.
All ye Angels and Saints of God, pray for me.
May our Lord ✠ bless us, and keep us from all evil, and bring us to life everlasting.
✠ May the souls of the faithful, through the mercy of God, rest in peace. Amen.

Sursum Corda!

Night Prayers for the Sick.

✠ In the Name of the Father, and of the Son and of the Holy Ghost. Amen.

Our Father ✪ Hail Mary ✪ I believe ✪ Glory be

My God, I give Thee thanks for all the benefits which I have ever received from Thee, and particularly this day. Give me light to see what sins I have committed this day, and give me grace to be truly sorry for them.

(Here wait a little, and try to remember the faults you have committed during the day.)

O my God, I am very sorry that I have offended Thee: I love Thee with all my heart, because Thou art so good, and I will not sin again.

O my God, I accept of death as a homage and adoration which I owe to Thy Divine Majesty, in union with the death of my dear Redeemer, and as the only means of coming to Thee, my beginning and last end.

Into Thy hands, O Lord, I commend my spirit: Lord Jesus, receive my soul.

May the Blessed Virgin Mary, St. Joseph, and all the Saints, pray for us to our Lord, that we may be preserved this night from sin and all evils.

O my good Angel, whom God has appointed to be my Guardian, watch over me during this night.

All ye Angels and Saints of God, pray for me.

Jesus, Mary, and Joseph, I give you my heart and my soul; Jesus, Mary, and Joseph, assist me in my last agony; Jesus, Mary, and Joseph, may I die in peace in your blessed company.

May our Lord ✠ bless us, and keep us from all evil, and bring us to life everlasting.

✠ May the souls of the faithful, through the mercy of God, rest in peace. Amen.

Acts that may be suggested to the Sick.

I. Contrition.

Contrition does not consist in tears or any other expression of sorrow. We must *be* sorry for our sins, but we need not necessarily *feel* sorry. It is good to be sorry because we have lost heaven and deserved hell, but the best motive is the love of God, who is infinitely good in Himself and worthy of all love. This is **perfect contrition**. Before our Lord came on earth, before there were any Sacraments, perfect contrition was the only means by which sinners could obtain forgiveness of their actual sins. It is as efficacious now as then. By it mortal sins are forgiven *immediately*, though a person is strictly bound to confess them if he is able. It is of the utmost importance that Catholics should remember what an act of perfect contrition can do for them, if after falling into mortal sin they are delayed or hindered by circumstances from going to confession. And they should bear it in mind for the benefit of others also, so that in cases of sudden and grave accident, before a priest can be had, or when no priest is at hand, they may at once suggest it by short acts to the sufferer:

> My God, I am sorry for all my sins,
> Because Thou art so good.

Suggest such acts even to those who are not Catholics at whose death-bed you may be present, and suggest them often to the sick. The habit of frequently making acts of perfect contrition is a very blessed one, and makes us very dear to God and very safe. And it is not a difficult habit to acquire, for contrition is as easy as it is sweet.

Acts of Contrition.

To think that I have offended Him after being so many times forgiven! To think that I have offended Him whom after all I do love! My God, I am sorry for all my sins: give me a tender, loving, and hearty contrition for them, because they have offended Thee who art so good; and a firm purpose not to offend Thee any more.

Father, I am not worthy to be called Thy child: I have left Thee, I have lost Thee through my own fault: I repent with my whole heart: spare me for the sake of Jesus Christ, my Saviour. Look upon the Face of Thy Christ—look upon the Blood of Thy Christ—look upon the Heart of Thy Christ—and forgive me for His sake.

O sins which have deprived me of my God, I hate you from the bottom of my heart.

Dear Jesus, who didst come to seek and to save that which was lost, have mercy on me.

Good Shepherd, who didst lay down Thy life for Thy sheep, have pity on me. I have gone astray like a sheep that is lost; seek Thy servant, O Lord.

> Jesus, my Lord, behold at length the time,
> When I resolve to turn away from crime;
> O pardon me, Jesus, Thy mercy I implore!
> I will never more offend Thee—no never more.
>
> Since my poor soul Thy Precious Blood hath cost
> Suffer me not for ever to be lost.
> O pardon, &c.
>
> Kneeling in tears, behold me at Thy feet;
> Like Magdalen, forgiveness I entreat.
> O pardon, &c.

I will arise and go to my Father, and say to Him: Father, I have sinned against heaven and before Thee, I am not now worthy to be called Thy son.

O God, merciful and patient, who willest not the death of a sinner—who, when we repent, rememberest our sins no more—have mercy on me and spare me.

Jesus, wounded for our iniquities, and bruised for our sins; I grieve for my sins, which have so grieved Thy Sacred Heart.

Have mercy on me and heal my soul, for I have sinned against Thee.

Give me, my God, the contrite and humble heart which Thou wilt never despise.

O that I had the tears of Peter and Magdalen!

Wash me yet more from my iniquity, and cleanse me from my sin.

O Mary, obtain for me true sorrow for my sins, forgiveness for them, and the grace of final perseverance.

Have mercy on me, O God, according to Thy great mercy: heal my soul for I have sinned against Thee.

O God, be merciful to me a sinner: Thou who hast made me, have mercy on me.

O Lord, I have sinned exceedingly in my life: what shall I do, whither shall I fly, but to Thee, my God.

What can I do for my sins but humbly confess them and lament them: hear me, I beseech Thee, O my God. All my sins displease me now exceedingly: I will never commit them any more: I am sorry for them, and will be sorry for them as long as I live. I am willing to make satisfaction for them to the utmost of my power. Forgive, O my God, forgive me my sins, for Thy holy Name's sake. Save my soul; which Thou hast redeemed with Thy Precious Blood. Behold, I commit myself to Thy mercy: I resign myself into Thy hands. Deal with me according to Thy goodness, not according to my wickedness and iniquity.

Jesus, Son of David, have mercy on me.

My God, what harm hast Thou done me that I should have so greatly offended Thee? O that I had never sinned against Thee! I am sorry for my sins because Thou art so good, and with Thy help I will not sin again. O let neither life nor death nor any creature separate me from Thee any more.

God of mercy and compassion,
    Look with pity upon me;
Father! let me call Thee Father!
    'Tis Thy child returns to Thee.
        Jesus, Lord, I ask for mercy,
            Let me not implore in vain;
        All my sins, I now detest them,
            Never will I sin again.

By my sins I have deserved
    Death and endless misery,
Hell with all its pains and torments,
    And for all eternity.
        Jesus, Lord, &c.

By my sins I have abandoned
    Right and claim to Heaven above;
Where the Saints rejoice for ever,
    In a boundless sea of love.
        Jesus, Lord, &c.

See our Saviour, bleeding, dying,
    On the Cross of Calvary;
To that Cross my sins have nailed Him
    Yet He bleeds and dies for me.
        Jesus, Lord, &c.

II. Patience and Resignation.

What will happen to me to-day, O my God, I know not: all that I know is that nothing will happen but what from all eternity Thy Love has arranged for my good. This is enough for me, my God. I adore Thy holy and blessed Will, and resign myself to it with all my heart for the love of Thee. I desire all Thou shalt send me: I accept all—I make to Thee a sacrifice of all, and unite my sacrifice with that of Jesus Christ my Saviour. I ask of Thee in His Name, and through His infinite merits, patience in my pains, the perfect submission which I owe Thee in all Thou shalt permit to happen to me, and the crown promised to those who persevere to the end. Amen.

Patience, my soul, just for to-day: God will provide for to-morrow. Yesterday has passed away, and the pain of its sufferings no longer remains: the merit will have remained if I offered my sufferings to God. To-day, then, I will try to suffer with merit: after all, today is but one day, and one day is not much. My God, what can I do less than offer Thee the pains and weariness of one day: those of this day shall be borne bravely for love of Thee.

When the Cross first presents itself to us, how hard it looks!—how hard it looks! But bear it bravely, and how bright it will appear when we look back upon it—how bright when we come to the crown!

May the most just, the most high, the most lovable Will of God be in all things done, and praised, and for ever magnified!

My God, I am justly punished by Thee, for I have greatly offended Thee: punish me in this life and not in the next.

My heart is ready, O God, my heart is ready.

Sweet Will of God, I bless Thee: dear Will of God, I love Thee.

As it hath pleased the Lord, so is it done: blessed be the Name of the Lord.

It is the Lord: let Him do what is good in His sight.

O Lord, Thou knowest what is best: do with me as Thou knowest and as best pleaseth Thee. I am in Thy hands, ready to obey Thee in all things: do with me in all things according to Thy Will.

What matter is it how much or what I suffer so I come at length to the haven of salvation? Grant me a good end, grant me a happy passage out of this world; be ever mindful of me, O my God, and direct me by the straight road to Thy Kingdom.

Keep me only from all sin, and I will fear neither death nor hell.

Dear Jesus, accept my sufferings which I desire to unite with Thine: sanctify all I suffer, so that every pain I feel may bring me nearer to Thee.

Lord, I offer and consecrate to Thy glory all that I have ever suffered, all that I now suffer, and all that I shall have to suffer until death. Perfect my pains with Thy love, and grant, O sweet Jesus, that they may be as pleasing to Thee as they are painful to me. I will suffer willingly because Thou wilt have it so, Thou whom I love with my whole heart.

Sursum Corda!

The chalice that my Father hath given me, shall I not drink it? Yea, Father, for so it hath seemed good in Thy sight.

Thy Will be done—Thy Will be done.

Lord, I accept this sickness from Thy hands, and entirely resign myself to Thy blessed Will, whether for life or for death: not my will but Thine be done—Thy Will be done on earth as it is in heaven.

As Thou knowest and willest, Lord.

Jesus, meek and humble of heart, make my heart like unto Thine.

Passion of Christ, strengthen me.

> O Jesu mine, for love of Thee
> I love what Thy Will giveth me
> Whate'er it be:

> O Jesu mine, for love of Thee
> I love what Thy Will giveth me
> Whene'er it be:

> O Jesu mine, for love of Thee
> I love what Thy Will giveth me
> How much it be:

> O Jesu mine, for love of Thee
> I love what Thy Will giveth me
> How long it be.

Blessed be God: Blessed be His Holy Name: Blessed be the Will of God in all things.

Lord, what wilt Thou have me to do?

O Lord God, O Holy Father, be Thou now and for ever blessed: for as Thou wilt so it has happened, and what

Thou dost is always good. To Thee I commit myself and all that is mine: it is better to be chastised here than hereafter.

Give me fortitude that I may stand my ground, patience that I may endure, and constancy that I may persevere.

Grant, me, my God, always to will and desire that which is most acceptable to Thee, and which pleaseth Thee best. Let Thy Will be mine, and let my will always follow Thine, and agree perfectly with it. Let me always will or not will the same with Thee.

O God, may Thy Will be done and be blessed a thousand thousand times.

Father, not my will, but Thine be done.

Teach me to do Thy Will, for Thou art my God.

> I worship thee, sweet Will of God,
>   And all thy ways adore;
> And every day I live, I wish
>   To love thee more and more.

With all my heart I desire whatever God desires. It is all well: blessed be God.

Sickness and sorrow have come to weigh me down: blessed be God in all.

Lord, Thy care over me is greater than all the care I can take of myself. I cast all my care then upon Thee: I cast myself into Thy arms—do with me whatever it shall please Thee, for it cannot but be good whatever Thou shalt do by me. Cast me not off for ever, nor blot me out of the book of life: and what tribulation soever befalls me shall not hurt me.

Lord Jesus, make me faithful to Thee unto death, that Thou mayst give me the crown of life.

Let us rejoice: we shall one day be taken to the bosom of God.

III. Faith, Hope, and Charity.

I believe in God the Father, who created me to His own image and likeness: and in Jesus, Christ my Saviour, who redeemed me with His own Blood: and in the Holy Spirit, who sanctified me in Baptism. Lord, increase my faith.

My God, I believe in Thee: my God, I hope in Thee: my God, I love Thee with my whole heart.

I believe in Thee because Thou art the very Truth: I believe in all Thy Church teaches, because Thou hast bid me hear it: and in this faith I resolve through Thy grace to live and die.

I believe, Lord: help Thou my unbelief.

I hope in Thee, my God, because Thou art so good, and through the sufferings and death of Jesus Christ my Redeemer, I hope for mercy, grace and salvation from Thee, because of Thy mercy, Thy promises, and Thy power. In Thee, O Lord, have I put my trust: I shall not be confounded for ever.

My God, Thou didst not abandon me when I fled from Thee, do not abandon me now that I seek Thee.

Heart of Jesus, Salvation of those who trust in Thee, have mercy on me. My Jesus, mercy.

My sweetest Jesus, be not Thou my Judge, but my Saviour.

Jesus, Jesus, be to me a Jesus, and save me.

> O good Jesus, hear me;
> Within Thy Wounds hide me;
> Never let me be separated from Thee;
> In the hour of my death call me,
> And bid me come to Thee,
> That with Thy Saints I may praise Thee
> For all eternity. Amen.

My God, I love Thee with my whole heart and soul: at least I desire so to love Thee.

I love Thee, who hast loved me from eternity, and hast created me out of love that I may be happy with Thee for ever.

I love Thee, who hast forgiven me so often, and washed me from my sins in Thy Precious Blood.

I love Thee, who hast been so good and kind to me, and given me all that I have and am.

I love Thee, who art so good in Thyself, and so worthy of all my love.

O God, my God, whom shall I love if I love not Thee?

I love Thee—I love Thee: help me to love Thee more.

Give me only Thy love and Thy grace, and I shall be rich enough.

Let me love Thee with all my heart and soul and mind and strength—grant that I may love Thee for ever.

I love my neighbour as myself for Thy sake: I forgive all who have injured me, and ask pardon of all I have injured.

My God, who art Infinite Goodness, I love Thee above all things—I love Thee with my whole heart.

I wish for Heaven, that there I may love Thee with all my strength, and for all eternity.

My God, cast me not into hell as I deserve—there I could not love Thee: let me love Thee and then do with me as Thou wilt.

O my God, make me all Thine before I die.

When shall I be able to say—My God, I can never lose Thee again.

IV. Preparation for Death.

To live for God and then to die: that done, all is done.

If I will take care of my life for God, He will take care of my death for me.

My soul, let us so live, that in Heaven we may rejoice to have lived so.

Let my death colour my life; let me live like one who has to die.

May my soul die the death of the just, and my last end be like unto theirs.

My God, I accept of death as a homage and adoration which I owe to Thy Divine Majesty, in union with the death of my dear Redeemer, and as the only means of coming to Thee, my beginning and last end.

I commend my soul to God my Creator, who made me out of nothing: to Jesus Christ my Saviour, who redeemed me with His Precious Blood: to the Holy Spirit, who sanctified me in Baptism.

Into Thy hands, O Lord, I commend my spirit.

> My God, my Father, and my Friend,
> Do not forsake me in my end.

I desire to die, my God, in order to see Thee.

My crucified Saviour, who to obtain a good death for me didst suffer a most painful death; remember me in my last hour—remember that I am one of Thy sheep, whom Thou hast purchased with Thine own Blood.

> Lord, on the Cross Thine Arms were stretched
> To draw Thy people nigh:
> O grant us then that Cross to love,
> And in those Arms to die.

O Shepherd of my soul, who alone canst guide and comfort me in that hour, when I walk through the dark valley of the shadow of death—when no one of this earth shall stand by me—when no friend shall be able to profit me: be with me then—suffer me not to lose Thee for ever—cast me not off from Thee. O beloved Jesus, since I embrace Thee now, receive me then—hide me in Thy holy Wounds—wash me in Thy Precious Blood.

Jesus, Jesus, trusting myself to the love of Thy Sacred Heart, I give up my soul into Thy hands; receive it unto the bosom of Thy mercy. Say to me in the hour of my death as Thou didst say to the good thief—"This day thou shalt be with Me in Paradise."

My Jesus, Thou art about to judge me, spare and pardon before Thou judgest.

O Jesus, Jesus, Jesus, receive me into the number of Thy chosen.

Blood of Christ, wash me: Passion of Christ, strengthen me: Heart of Jesus, sorrowful even unto death, have mercy on me.

Sursum Corda!

Jesus, dear Jesus, never let me be separated from Thee.

Holy Mary, Mother of God, pray for us sinners—*now* for present graces, *and at the hour of our death* for final perseverance: pray for *me* in the hour of *my* death. Amen.

O most compassionate Mother, show thyself my Mother in the hour of my death—be with me in that last moment of my life on which eternity hangs. As thou didst invite thy Son to thine own blessed departure, so I invite thee now to mine, beseeching thee not to be absent from me then, but to be there and succour me with a mother's tenderness, for without thee I cannot die in peace. Cheer me with thy holy presence, protect me from my enemies, speak for me to thy Son, and obtain for me forgiveness of all my sins, a happy death and life everlasting with Him and with thee. Amen.

Leave me not, my Mother, until thou seest me safe in heaven.

Holy Mary, Mother of grace, Mother of clemency; defend me from the enemy, receive me in the hour of my death.

Refuge of sinners, pray for me.

St. Joseph, Patron of a happy death, pray for me.

O holy Angel, my Guardian, stand by me and help me.

My holy Patron Saints *(name them)*, pray for me.

All ye holy Angels and Saints of God, pray for me.

Jesus, Mary, and Joseph, I give you my heart and my soul:

Jesus, Mary, and Joseph, assist me in my last agony:

Jesus, Mary, and Joseph, may I die in peace in your blessed company.

II. HOW TO HELP THE DYING

To those who attend the Dying

1. In cases of serious accident, or in a sudden and dangerous attack of illness, lose no time in sending for the priest. In other cases he should be sent for as soon as the sickness becomes grave.

2. Tell the sick person gently that his state, though not desperate, is dangerous, and that he would therefore do well to settle the state of his soul without delay—that this will be much better done now than later, when pain, weakness, or the nature of the remedies may render him unfit for so great a work. It is a great mistake to think that the Last Sacraments will make him worse: on the contrary, they will bring him peace, strengthen him against his spiritual enemies, and enable him to bear his sufferings with patience and merit for eternity. What is to be feared is *any delay*, by which he might die without them. If he wishes to put off his Confession till he is better, or shrinks from it because he has been a long time away from his duties, and fears the labour of preparation, tell him that the priest will help him, and if necessary go through the examination of conscience with him. If he still objects, the priest should be told of his state, that he may warn him of the danger there is in delay.

3. If he has a will to make, or any necessary provision, spiritual or temporal, for his family—any debts or other

obligations to discharge, engage him to do this also without delay, that having settled his temporal concerns, he may give his whole attention to the affairs of his soul. If he wishes to leave anything for the benefit of his soul, as a certain sum for Masses, or any other good work, this should also be provided for in good time.

4. Do not flatter the sick person with hopes of life when there are little or no grounds for hope; rather encourage him to make the best use of the time that remains to him, by receiving the Holy Sacraments with fervent dispositions, and accepting his sickness from the Hands of God with perfect resignation to the Divine Will, in union with the sufferings of his dying Saviour and in satisfaction for his sins. Many, through a mistaken affection, are cruel to the dying, and keep from them what it is all important for them to know—or at least fear to speak to them of those things which would prepare them to meet their God. Do not imitate these. Affection at the deathbed must be unselfish—*the first thought of all should be the soul that is soon to appear before God.* How beautiful is the charity of those who help their loved ones to die well, instead of adding to their difficulties and distress by their own unrestrained sorrow!

5. Attend most carefully to the recommendations for the sick room mentioned above. Take out of the room such things as profane pictures, dresses, and anything likely to disturb or tempt the dying person. Place near him, where he may easily see them, a crucifix or picture of Jesus crucified and of His Blessed Mother, that he may be reminded

to commend himself frequently to Jesus and Mary. Holy water should also be near, so that he may easily reach it.

6. Visitors who might disturb or distract the dying person should not be allowed in the room. Keep away therefore all bad, idle and talkative people, any who have been the occasion of sin to him, any who have done him a great injury, any who would talk to him of vain and worldly things, or disturb him by their grief, or make him grieve too much.

7. Bad people should not be left to take care of the dying, above all should not be left *alone* with them. There are instances of bad persons who, being left alone with the dying, ruined the soul instead of saving it. If a woman is dying, and someone has to sit up with her, it should be a woman.

8. Whilst helping the dying, do not forget to say your own prayers. Some people forget their prayers, and so lose the blessing of God on what they do for the dying.

9. The devil is very busy in the room of the dying. He tries to ruin them by fearful temptations, and often makes them see terrible things which frighten them very much. Often therefore suggest to them acts of contrition, confidence, patience and the love of God. As temptations to despair are among the most frequent with which the dying are assailed, it is seldom advisable to speak to them of the Divine Justice, of the pains of hell, or of the grievousness of their sins. Encourage them rather to put all their trust in the mercy of God, in the Passion of Christ, and in the prayers of the Blessed Virgin and the saints. Remind them also that a remedy against all temptations is to make often

Sursum Corda!

the sign of the Cross, and to invoke the holy names of Jesus and Mary. The dying should be sprinkled with holy water, especially during their agony, and when they show signs of fear and trouble.

The Last Sacraments

It is an immense blessing to receive the Last Sacraments. They are given to us by God in His goodness to comfort and strengthen us in our Last Agony, and they help us wonderfully to die a happy death. Try therefore to rouse in the dying person a great desire to receive them, and to prepare carefully for them.

I. Penance

This Sacrament will remit all his sins, restore to him the friendship of God, and open Heaven to him again. His preparation need not be long. Having asked God's grace to know his sins and to be truly sorry for them, let him try to bring to his memory at least the principal sins since his last Confession. If it is a long time since he was at Confession, it may help him in his examination of conscience to remember the places where he has been, the persons with whom he has lived or worked, the work on which he has been employed. Then let him excite in his heart a true sorrow for his sins and a resolution never to commit them again by saying with all his heart:

My God I am sorry for my sins, because by them I have lost heaven and deserved hell; because they have crucified my Saviour Jesus Christ; and most of all because they have offended Thee, who art infinitely good and worthy of all love. I am sorry for them: I wish I had never sinned: with Thy help I will not sin again.

After his Confession, remind the sick person to say his penance, and if necessary say it with him.

II. The Holy Viaticum

When Holy Communion is given to the sick in danger of death, it is called the Holy Viaticum, or food for a journey. A dying person has a long and dangerous journey to take. He has to go from this world to the next, and to pass through many enemies. Our Blessed Lord knows how weak he is, and comes Himself to strengthen him, to protect him from all dangers, and take him safely to Heaven.

Help him to thank so loving and faithful a Friend, who, when all go away will not leave him, but remain with him faithful to the end.

Prayers Before Receiving Holy Viaticum

My God and my Saviour, Thou art coming to visit me: I thank Thee with all my heart. I believe, O Jesus, that Thou art present in the Most Holy Sacrament: I adore Thee, I love Thee, and I desire Thee: come into my poor heart, and never leave me—come, Lord Jesus; come!

Lord, I am not worthy that Thou shouldst enter under my roof; but only say the word, and my soul shall be healed. Come, dear Jesus, into my poor heart: Thou alone canst comfort and help me now: come to strengthen me and comfort me and save me.

O most Sweet and loving Lord, I desire to receive Thee with the greatest love and thankfulness: but I am very weak. Pity me and help me—give Thyself to me, and it is enough. Jesus, Jesus, come to me.

1. Before the priest comes to give the Holy Viaticum, the room should be put in order, and everything made neat. Have a table ready with a white cloth on it, two candles, a crucifix, holy water, and a glass or cup of clean water. Lay a small white cloth for Holy Communion upon the breast and under the chin of the sick person.

2. When the priest comes into the room with the Blessed Sacrament, all present should kneel down. There should be no talking. If it is necessary to speak, do so in few words and in a low voice.

3. After Holy Communion has been given, leave the sick person quiet for a little while to say his prayers, or you may help him to make his thanksgiving, if he cannot do it himself.

Prayers After Receiving Holy Viaticum

Jesus, sweet Jesus, dear Jesus! I believe, O my Saviour, that I have received Thy most holy Body and Blood: I believe that Thou art really present in my heart, I adore Thee—I love Thee—I thank Thee with all my heart, my God and my All. How good, how kind Thou art to me, sweet Jesus: stay with me and never leave me any more; take me to be happy with Thee for ever. Thou hast given Thyself to me: I give myself to Thee for life and death. I love Thee, I love Thee with all my heart. Thou knowest, Lord, that I love Thee.

> Body of Christ, save me;
> Passion of Christ, strengthen me;
> O good Jesus, hear me;
> within Thy Wounds hide me;
> never let me be separated from Thee;
> in the hour of my death, call me;
> and bid me come to Thee;
> that with Thy Saints I may praise Thee;
> for all eternity. Amen.

4. Say some of these prayers, not too many; the sick, and still more the dying, cannot bear much at a time. Say them slowly, pausing a little from time to time. Stop as soon as you see the sick person is tired.

5. The dying can receive Holy Communion as Viaticum without fasting, and they can go on doing so as long as the danger lasts.

6. The sick should be warned not to spit for ten minutes after receiving. If there is danger of their vomiting, the priest should be told of it.

III. Extreme Unction.

1. Extreme Unction, or the Last Anointing, is the special Sacrament of the dying. Our Lord instituted it to give us the grace we need in our last sickness, and the dispositions necessary for a happy death. It strengthened the first Christians as it strengthens us. St. James, writing to them says: "Is any man sick among you? Let him bring in the priests of the Church, and let them pray over him, anointing him with oil in the name of the Lord. And the prayer of faith shall save the sick man, and the Lord shall raise him up, and if he be in sins they shall be forgiven him."

2. The priest anoints with the holy oil the eyes, ears, nostrils, lips, hands and feet, praying that God by that holy anointing, and through His most tender mercy, would forgive the sins committed through each of the senses.

3. Extreme Unction comforts and strengthens the soul in her last agony; forgives venial sins; takes away the evil dispositions left in the soul by sin; and lessens the temporal punishment which we should have to suffer in Purgatory. It makes us patient in the pains of our last sickness. It gives strength against the terrible temptations that assail us at the hour of death. It takes away the fear of death, and makes us willing to die if such be God's will. Extreme Unction, being a sacrament of the living, should be received in a state of grace; but if the sick person is unable to go to Confession, it will take away mortal sins if he is sorry for his sins.

4. This Sacrament can only be received once in the same danger. Its reception should not be put off till the last extremity, or there will be danger of the sick dying without it, and thus being deprived of the special graces which would make them better prepared for death and more fit to meet their Judge. By putting off, they may also lose the blessing of recovery, which God grants by means of this Sacrament when He sees it to be expedient.

Some ill-instructed Catholics have a secret fear of the Sacrament of Extreme Unction, as if death were sure to follow on its reception. This is a great mistake. Its healing power is so often and so wonderfully shown, that many look to it hopefully as the means of saving the life of those they love, and far from deferring it, are eager to secure it in good time.

5. Out of respect for the Sacrament, the eyelids, ears, nose, lips, hands and feet, which are to be anointed, should, if possible, be washed beforehand.

6. The sick person should try to prepare himself well for receiving this great Sacrament. That he may gain its full benefit, let him turn away his mind entirely from the things of this world to think only of God and the salvation of his soul. Let him renew his sorrow for all the sins of his life, trust himself completely to the mercy of God, and resign himself wholly to the Will of God, whether for life or for death.

7. A few fervent aspirations will help him in his preparation, and enable him to unite himself with the beautiful prayers used by the Church in the administration of this Sacrament.

Sursum Corda!

Prayer Before Extreme Unction

My God, I believe that Extreme Unction is a Sacrament, which gives grace to die a happy death. May I receive all the graces of this Sacrament. Give me a true sorrow for all my sins. I grieve for them from the bottom of my heart, because they have offended Thee—who art so good, and with Thy help, I will not sin again. Through this holy Unction, and through Thy most tender mercy, pardon me whatever sins I have committed, by my sight and hearing, by smell and taste and speech, and by my hands and feet. Through this holy Sacrament, make me strong against the pains and temptations of death. Amen.

Prayer After Extreme Unction

My God, I have received the Sacrament of Extreme Unction; may it take away all sin from my soul. May it save me from the punishment due to my sins. I am willing to die that I may gain Thee. Give me grace to persevere to the end. O good Jesus, hear me; within Thy wounds hide me; never let me be separated from Thee; in the hour of my death, call me; and bid me come to Thee; that with thy Saints I may praise Thee; for all eternity. Amen.

The Last Blessing

The Church grants to her Priests the power of giving the Apostolic Blessing with a Plenary Indulgence to her children who are near their end. Though a considerable time may elapse between the granting of this Indulgence and the moment of death, it will produce its effect at this last moment, if the dying person is in a state of grace.

To receive the benefit of this Blessing and Plenary Indulgence, he should renew his sorrow for the sins of his whole life, and his resolution never more to offend God by sin; make an act of faith in all that the Church believes and teaches; unite himself to God by fervent acts of hope and charity; and resign himself entirely to His Most Holy Will.

> My God, I once more renounce and detest all the sins of my whole life. I am sorry for them all, because Thou art so good: I will never commit them any more. I believe in Thee, my God: I believe all Thy Church believes and teaches because Thou hast bid me hear it. I hope in Thee, my God: I love Thee, my God, with all my heart; and for Thy sake I love my neighbour as myself, and I forgive all who have injured me. I love Thy most holy Will: I am willing to die, because it is Thy Will. Father, into Thy hands I commend my spirit, Lord Jesus receive my soul.

The Last Agony

Our Holy Mother the Church has now poured out all her treasures upon her dying child. Let him guard them carefully, and in patience and peace await his last hour and the reward promised to those who persevere to the end.

The few days or hours he has yet to live are very precious, for in them he may lay up great treasures of merit for eternity. Encourage him to lose nothing by impatience, and quickly to efface by contrition any sin or fault he may commit. Should he fall into grievous sin, let him ask for the priest without delay.

Sursum Corda!

Let him pray as well as he is able. Remind him often of the suffering of his dying Saviour, which will sustain his patience, and comfort him in all his pains. Let no long time pass without suggesting to him some short aspiration: though apparently unconscious, he may be able to hear and understand. He will unite with you, and your words will strengthen and encourage him. O how his Guardian Angel will bless you for helping him with that good thought, with that little prayer, at a moment when of himself he could not have made the effort to direct his thoughts to God!

Place the crucifix in his hands, and now and then give it him to kiss, with some short, tender words of love:

> Jesus, sweet Jesus, dear Jesus! My Jesus, mercy. Jesus, I am Thine; save me. Dear Jesus, I kiss Thy Feet; hide me in Thy Wounds.

Guide his hand to make the sign of the Cross, and often repeat the holy names of Jesus and Mary.

When the agony begins, kneel down reverently, and recite with those present the Recommendation for a Departing Soul, part of the Rosary, the Litany of the Blessed Virgin, or any other suitable prayers,—such as:

> We beseech Thee, help Thy servant, whom Thou hast redeemed with Thy Precious Blood.
>
> Mary, Mother of Grace, Mother of Mercy, defend us from the enemy, and receive us at the hour of our death.
>
> Refuge of sinners, pray for him.
>
> Holy Mary, Mother of God, pray for us sinners now, and at the hour of our death.
>
> Jesus, mercy! Mary, help!

During the agony, often sprinkle the bed and the dying person with holy water, especially when he shows signs of fear and trouble. The acts suggested now should be chiefly love and contrition, the simpler the better—and they should be short. When he is near his last moment, repeat them without pausing, and in a louder voice:—

My God, I love Thee, I love Thee.

I am sorry for all my sins.

Lord Jesus, receive my Soul.

My Jesus, mercy!

Holy Mary, pray for me; St. Joseph, pray for me;

St. Michael, pray for me; my good Angel, pray for me.

My dear Patrons (name them) pray for me.

Jesus, Mary, and Joseph, I give you my heart and my soul:

Jesus, Mary, and Joseph, assist me in my last agony:

Jesus, Mary, and Joseph, may I die in peace in your blessed company.

Jesus, Jesus, Jesus.

After Death

As soon as the soul has departed this life, recite Psalm 44 "Out of the depths," for its eternal repose:

Out of the depths have I cried unto Thee, O Lord;
   Lord, hear my voice.
Let Thine ears be attentive to the voice of my supplication.
If Thou, O Lord, wilt mark iniquities; Lord, who shall abide it?
For with Thee there is merciful forgiveness; and by reason of
   Thy law I have waited for Thee, O Lord.

Sursum Corda!

> My soul hath relied on his word; my soul hath hoped in the Lord.
>
> From the morning watch even until night; let Israel hope in the Lord.
>
> Because with the Lord there is mercy; and with Him is plenteous redemption.
>
> And He shall redeem Israel from all his iniquities.
>
> Eternal rest give to them, O Lord, and let perpetual light shine upon them.

Let us pray:

O God, the Creator and Redeemer of all the faithful, grant to the souls of Thy servants departed the remission of all their sins, that through pious supplications they may obtain that pardon which they have always desired; who livest and reignest, world without end. Amen.

May they rest in peace. Amen.

The soul has gone into eternity, but prayers can reach it and help it still. How then can those who loved it in life forsake it now in its extreme need, and leave it to suffer unpitied in the fearful fires of Purgatory! Do not forget it because its voice can no longer reach your bodily ears.

Go down in spirit to the gates of Purgatory and hear its cry: "Have pity on me, have pity on me, at least you my friends—you who watched by me, and cared for me to the last, and promised never to forget me—do not forsake me now." Can you turn a deaf ear to this piteous prayer?

Now is the time to prove your love, not by feasting in the house of death; not by squandering money in costly flowers and outward show of grief when the body is committed to the grave; but by thinking of *the poor soul,* which, unless you come to its help, must suffer so long and so terribly. Send it help continually; you can do it so easily. Many of the short prayers in this little book are indulgenced by the Church. As often as you say them they will find their way to Purgatory, and show the soul you love that you have not forgotten it. They will comfort it, they will ease it in its pains, and hasten the time when it will be freed from them, and go to enjoy God for ever. There, before His Throne, it will remember you, its benefactor, for the Blessed are most grateful. It will pray for you and help you amid the dangers and trials of this life, and will come to your assistance when you too shall have passed the gates of death, and stand in need of the charity you have shown to others. "Blessed are the merciful," says our Divine Lord, "for they shall obtain mercy."

Remember that to have a Mass said for those you love is the greatest proof of affection you can give them. One Mass will help them more than all you could do for them by prayer and good works. A dying child said to her sorrowing parents: "When I am gone give me no flowers, but Masses, Masses."

Let your charity be persevering also. Many souls have to remain long in pain and weary waiting, because those they loved grew tired of praying, and after a few days or weeks forgot them.

And whilst you pray for the soul that is gone, think also of those who have the same journey to make before very long—*To-day for me, to-morrow for thee* is the lesson every death-bed should teach us. Listen to our Lord's solemn words: *"Watch—Be ready."* He does not say *"Be getting ready,"* but *"Be ready."* Then ask yourself—*Am I ready? Shall I be ready? What must I do to be always ready ?*

> Grant we beseech Thee, O Lord, that whilst we lament the departure of this Thy servant we may always remember that we are most certainly to follow him; give us grace to prepare for that last hour by a good life, that we may not be surprised by a sudden and unprovided death, but be ever watching, that when Thou shalt call, we may go forth to meet the Bridegroom and enter with Him into glory everlasting, through Christ our Lord. Amen.

HOW WE MAY HELP NON-CATHOLICS.

Should you ever be with dying Protestants, and have no hope of their reconciliation with the Church, do not speak to them of it, especially if this would irritate them. But say slowly and get them to join you in the following acts:—

My God, I believe in Thee, and in all that Thy Son, our Lord Jesus Christ, came on earth to teach. I believe that there is One God: I believe that in God there are Three Persons—the Father, the Son, and the Holy Ghost: I believe that God the Son was made man, and died to save us: I believe that God will punish the wicked for ever in hell, and make the good happy for ever in Heaven. My God, I believe all Thou wouldst have me believe.

My God, I am sorry, with all my heart for all the sins of my whole life, because they have offended Thee who art infinitely good, and worthy of all love. Help me never to offend Thee again.

My God, if it be Thy blessed Will that I should suffer pain, help me to bear it patiently, because Jesus suffered for me. I resign myself to Thy Will in all things: I am ready to believe and do and suffer whatever Thou wilt. Thy Will be done—Thy Will be done.

MASS BEFORE FIRST COMMUNION

INTRODUCTION

In the long and arduous process of preparing her first full-length work for publication, Mother Loyola was faced with a good deal of hand-wringing over its length. As it was intended to help prepare young people for their First Communion, it naturally needed to cover all the necessary ground, and in that style that would come to be Mother Loyola's unique contribution to the genre, it was chock full of stories and anecdotes to illuminate those lessons. Thus, as a way of decreasing the page count and making the volume less heavy and daunting, a decision was made: that of publishing the prayers of preparation for before, during and after the happy event as a separate small booklet.

This, then was the contents of that booklet.

MASS BEFORE FIRST COMMUNION

Spend well the quarter of an hour before Mass begins. You can make the following Acts:

Faith.—I believe, my God, that You are really present in the Sacred Host I am going to receive—the same Jesus Christ, God and Man, Who was promised in Paradise—and was adored in Bethlehem by the shepherds and the Kings—Who lay in Mary's lap, and worked in Joseph's shop—Who went about doing good—and blessed the little children— Who taught from Peter's boat—and calmed the storm on the Lake—and prayed on the hill-tops—Who gave the Twelve their First Communion at the Last Supper—Who died upon the Cross—and rose again—and ascended into Heaven—Who will come again to judge the living and the dead—and Who has come to us meantime in the Blessed Sacrament to prepare our souls for that coming at the Last Day.

"I believe that Thou art Christ, the Son of the Living God."

"Lord, increase my faith."

Sursum Corda!

Hope.—What can You refuse me, O my Friend and my Brother, when You give me Your very Self? You *cannot* say that anything is impossible or difficult to You. You *will* not say You have no desire to cure what is evil in my soul—and to strengthen what is good—to give me grace to keep free all my life from mortal sin—to persevere to the end—to come safely to Your Feet in Heaven. All these things and all the blessings that You see will be good for me to have in this life—I ask You now—and believe with a firm trust that You will give me. You invite me now to come to You—You *tell* me to come to You—surely I may hope for great things from Your visit.

Love.—I do not know half as much about You, dear Lord, as I shall do some day. But surely I know enough even now to love You with all my heart. I know You are infinitely beautiful and good—tender and gentle and loving—generous and forgiving—and I know that besides being so good in Yourself—You have been wonderfully good and kind to me. In return You ask only my love: "My child, give Me thy heart." Take it, Lord. I give it to You—to be Yours always. Let me love You with all my heart—with all my soul—with all my mind—with all my strength. And help me to love as myself all those whom You invite to share with me this Gift of Your love.

Gratitude.—My God, how good You have been to me. How many things You have given me. How much more You have done for me than for millions and millions of other children who are in the world to-day. I have a good father and mother and a happy home. You have made me a child of Your Holy Catholic Church when I might have been one of the little Protestants I see all around me, who do not know how to get their sins forgiven, who have never heard of Your Real Presence, or of a First Communion Day. Why have You been so very good to me? Why have You loved me so? I cannot think why, for I am sure I have not loved You very much. What can I give You in return? David cried out in the fulness of his heart: "What shall I render to the Lord for all He has given unto me?" Yet David had not so much to thank You for as I have. What would David have said, had he known what You are going to give *to me?* Many kings and prophets have desired to see the things I see, and have not seen them, and to hear the things I hear, and have not heard them. Wait a little while, Lord, and I will pay You all. Yes, in a little while I will give You as much as You have ever given me—more than any favours You have ever bestowed upon me—more than the Heaven You are getting ready for me—I will give You Yourself.

Humility.—I think it ought to be very easy for me to be humble—for first I have nothing to be proud of—and next I have plenty to be ashamed of. My God, all that I have of good You have given me. I have nothing of my own, but my sins. And how many sins there have been. I have been so naughty, so careless, so ungrateful. St. Elizabeth was surprised that our Lady should come to see her. St. Peter cried out: "Depart from me, for I am a sinful man, O Lord." The pagan centurion said, "Lord, I am not worthy."

Sursum Corda!

And I too wonder that the God of Heaven and earth should come to me. I will not say, "Depart from me," but I do say with all my heart: "Lord, I am not worthy that Thou shouldst come under my roof."

"O God, be merciful to me a sinner."

Contrition.—My sins have made me most unworthy. But I am sorry for them—very sorry for them. I am sorry, because of all the harm they have done to my soul—more still because they have cost You so much, dear Lord—because they hurt You so much in Your Passion—they tortured Your Heart in the Garden of Olives—they stung You in the scourges —they pricked You in the thorns—they drove the nails into Your Hands and Feet. I am sorry for my sins, because they crucified You, my Saviour. And most of all I am sorry, because they have offended You, Who are so good in Yourself, so infinitely good.

Desire.—I am poor and weak and unworthy to come to You, dear Lord—and yet I do so want to come. Do not think the desire is all on Your side—for I do indeed love and long for You. You know all things. You know, Lord, that I love You. David said: "As the hart panteth after the water-brooks, so panteth my soul after Thee, O God." I wish I could long for You like that. Your loving words and ways make me desire You. And You like to come to those who desire You. Because Zacheus wanted so much to see You, You gave him more than he hoped for, not only one glance at Your beautiful Face as You passed him under the sycamore-tree, but the sound of Your voice, and Your

Blessed Presence in his house, with all the change in him that Presence wrought.

And how You liked to go to Bethany, to the two sisters there, who were always looking forward to Your coming. I wish I could receive You and make You welcome as they did. Martha spared no trouble in getting ready for You. She made the house clean and tidy and bright with flowers, and prepared all she could think of to show You honour. Help me to be like her—not cold now nor careless—but loving and diligent. And Mary sat at Your Feet and heard Your words. So let me listen to You when You come to me now—and in all the Communions of my life. You will speak to my heart, if only I will listen: "Speak, Lord, for Thy servant heareth."

If any time remains, you can say the Communion Beads, page 68 or the Litany, page 65.

At the Beginning of Mass

There in the Tabernacle is the Sacred Host in which our Lord is present *for me*. *My Host*, in which He knew from all eternity He would give Himself to me To-Day. He is there not for others, but *for me*. He is there as truly as He was in the manger and on Mary's lap. "*My* Lord and *my* God!"

At the Confiteor

How I wish I could say now, "My heart is ready, O God, my heart is ready." Indeed it ought to be ready after so many instructions and so many graces. And yet I dare not say my heart is ready—but I bow down my head and strike my breast—and own that it is through my fault that I am not better prepared for His visit. "Lord, I am not worthy that Thou shouldst enter under my roof, but say only the word and my soul shall be healed." There is yet time, my God, to do great things for me—I unite myself to the Sacred Heart of Jesus all through this Mass—desiring to do all that He does in union with Him. I adore You with Him—I praise and thank You with Him—I love You with all the burning love of His Sacred Heart—I desire to satisfy Your Divine Majesty through Him for all my sins. May His infinite praise supply for my weakness and poverty—and draw down upon me all the graces I need.

St. Peter, pray for me; St. Paul, pray for me.

St. Mary Magdalen, pray for me.

AT THE KYRIE ELEISON.

My God, I am Your little creature. I own that all I have and all I am belongs to You. I have it only because You have given it to me.

Have mercy on me, O God my Father—Who thought of me from eternity—Who created me to Your own image and likeness—Who sent Your only Son into the world to save me—Who made me Your child by Holy Baptism, and Who have been always so good—so careful—so kind a Father to me—so patient with me, forgiving me so many times. O my Father, I am sorry for having been such a heedless—such a wilful—such an ungrateful child. I throw myself into Your Arms. My Father, have mercy on me!

Have mercy on me, O God my Saviour—redeeming me in Your mercy—washing me from my sins in Your great mercy—coming to me in mercy and in love To-Day.

Have mercy on me, O God, my Sanctifier—Whom I have grieved so often by my sins and by my negligence. Prepare my heart as You prepared the Heart of Mary—overshadow me as You overshadowed her—that I may be ready for Jesus when He comes.

AT THE GLORIA.

Glory be to God on high—and on earth peace to men of good-will. We praise Thee—we bless Thee—we adore Thee—we glorify Thee. We give Thee thanks for Thy great glory—O Lord God, Heavenly King, God the Father Almighty. O Lord Jesus Christ, the only-begotten Son: O Lord God, Lamb of God, Son of the Father, Who takest away the sins of the world—have mercy on us. Thou Who takest away the sins of the world, receive our prayers: Thou Who sittest at the right hand of the Father, have mercy on us. For Thou only art holy—Thou only art the Lord—Thou only, O Jesus Christ, with the Holy Ghost, art most high in the glory of God the Father. Amen.

AT THE COLLECTS.

How many prayers are going up for me now! My parents and my friends are all praying for me, and my good Angel is carrying up their petitions to the Throne of God. In Heaven, too, they are thinking of me—my holy Patrons, my dear Mother Mary, all are interceding for me. My God, listen to all these holy prayers. Purify my soul more and more from every stain of sin, that I may worthily receive You. Amen.

St. John the Evangelist, pray for me.

AT THE EPISTLE.

The Saints and Prophets of the Old Law desired to see the things I see, and did not see them, and to hear the things I hear, and never heard them. How ardently Abraham and Moses, and David and Daniel, and Elias desired the coming of this Redeemer. They saw the types and figures—I see the reality. Moses saw the Manna and the Paschal Lamb—I see the Bread from Heaven and the Lamb of God Who takes away the sins of the world. The heart of David panted for You, my God, as the hart for the water-brooks—and Daniel was called "a man of desires." Oh, that I could desire You as they did! What a shame it would be if their desires were more fervent than my thanksgiving. I offer You all their desires—and with David I cry out, "What have I in Heaven but Thee—and besides Thee, what do I desire upon earth. Thou art the God of my heart, and my portion for ever."

Holy Abraham and Moses, David and Daniel and Elias, pray for me.

AT THE GOSPEL.

I stand up, dear Lord, to show that I am Your disciple—ready to do as You tell me—ready to follow You in keeping Your commandments—and in carrying my cross. And ready to listen to Your words. Your tenderest words were for the little children whom You loved and blessed. You thought of me when You said, "Behold the birds of the air, for they neither sow nor do they reap, nor gather into barns, and your Heavenly Father feedeth them." I, too, have neither sown nor laboured—I have been like the little birds of the air—without thought or care for myself—and my Heavenly Father has thought of me. Each day He has given me my daily bread—and now on this the Greatest Day of my life—He is going to give me His only Son to be the Food of my soul.

AT THE OFFERTORY.

My God, I know that You deserve infinite honour and worship. I have nothing of my own that is worth offering to Your Divine Majesty. But I offer You, in union with the priest, the bread and wine which are soon to be changed into the Body and Blood of Your Son. Soon will be offered up the Immaculate Host—which will give You infinite honour and glory, and infinite thanksgiving for all You have done for us—which will obtain pardon for our sins—and all the graces and blessings we need.

My God, I am delighted to think of the honour Your Divine Majesty receives from this Holy Sacrifice. What Jesus does here, I desire to do. O my Saviour, work in me a miracle like that which You are going to work upon the bread and wine—let me too be changed into You—so that I may say in truth—"I live, now not I, but Christ liveth in me."

AT THE LAVABO.

You are going, O dear Redeemer, to renew here for me the Sacrifice of the Cross. This altar is like a new Calvary, I come and lay my heart down here at Your Feet, as at the foot of the Cross—that it may be washed from all its stains in Your Precious Blood.

AT THE PREFACE.

To prepare the entry of an Eastern King into a city of his dominions was in olden times a work of toil and trouble. He was not expected to ascend the heights nor go down into the depths of a hilly country. Mountains were brought down; valleys were filled up; crooked ways made straight and rough ways smooth, to form a level and direct road and make his journey easy and pleasant. So was to be the entry of the King of Kings into the world. His Forerunner, St. John the Baptist, was sent before Him to prepare His way. He was to go before Him as heralds in the East run on before to announce the coming of a King, and with trumpet and loud voice bid all make clear the thoroughfares—"Prepare ye the way of the Lord, make straight His paths. Every valley shall be filled; and every mountain and hill shall be brought low; the crooked shall be made straight and the rough ways plain; and all flesh shall see the salvation of God."

Yes, surely, His road must be made ready; it must be made ready now. If such trouble was taken for one journey of an earthly King, what pains ought I to take to prepare my soul for You, O King of Kings! Prepare it Yourself—let there be no heights of pride between You and me—no crooked ways, little deceitful doings with You and with others—no rough ways, rudeness, unkindness, towards those You love. But make me straightforward, dear Lord, with You and with every one, and meek and humble of heart like Yourself.

St. John the Baptist, Precursor of Jesus, pray for me.

AT THE CANON.

"God so loved the world—as to give it His only-begotten Son"—God so loves *me*—that in a few moments He will give His only Son—to *me*.

I believe that He Who comes to me is the same Divine Babe Who lay beneath the cold bright sky on the first Christmas night—Who was worshipped by the Kings on Mary's lap—Who was passed about from her arms to St. Joseph's as they fled with Him across the desert-sands. I believe It is the same little Child that played, and slept, and prayed at Mary's side in the Holy House of Nazareth. I believe it is the same Jesus of Nazareth Who worked as a carpenter—Who called the Twelve—Who went about doing good to all—Who founded His Church *for me*—Who died *for me*—Who rose again and ascended into Heaven *for me*—Who is getting ready my place there—Who is coming to me now in tenderness and in love, hidden under the appearances of Bread—and Who will come again in glory and majesty to judge me—and to ask an account of all the graces He has given me—particularly of His visits to me in Holy Communion.

Sursum Corda!

Oh, give me grace, my Saviour, to receive You so fervently at Your coming now, that I may be able to meet You without fear at Your second coming to judge the living and the dead.

St. Paul says You love the Church, dear Lord, and delivered Yourself for it. And so You like me to pray for it. I ask You to guard and prosper it throughout the world—to bless our Holy Father the Pope, and all the Bishops and Priests. Bless my parents, my brothers and sisters—my companions—all those who have been good to me—and all who have taught me to know and love You. Have mercy on our dear country—on all poor sinners—and on all who are to die to-day.

AT THE CONSECRATION.

Our Lord is coming down on the altar. Bow yourself down and wait for His coming with all the Angels, who are descending in troops from Heaven to adore their God at the moment when the priest pronounces the words of Consecration. When the bell rings, adore Him with them, and beg Him by His Precious Blood here really present to cleanse your soul from every stain and prepare it to receive Him.

O Sacrament most holy, O Sacrament Divine,
All praise and all thanksgiving be every moment Thine.

AFTER THE CONSECRATION.

Eternal Father, look upon the Face of Your Christ. He is on the altar now—He is ours now—You have sent Him to us—given Him to us. I offer Him to You again. I offer You as my adoration of Your Divine Majesty—as my thanksgiving for all You have given me—the Precious Body, and Blood, and Soul, and Divinity of Jesus, now really present on the altar—the holy, pure, unspotted Host which is lying there—a Victim for our sins—to obtain for us forgiveness of them all—and every good gift we can need or desire. I offer You not only this Mass—but all the Masses that are being said in every part of the world to-day—from the rising of the sun—to the going down thereof.

I am so glad, my God, to be able to give You something You really care for—something worthy of You—something which is worth as much and more than all You have ever given me. And I am glad most of all—that what I have to offer You—is Yourself—only Yourself. I should not like there to be anything worthy of You except Yourself.

My God, have pity on the poor souls in Purgatory who are longing to get to You—longing more to see Your Face than to be freed from the fierce flames in which Your Justice is obliged to keep them till their debt is paid. I offer You the Precious Blood of Jesus, I offer You the Sacred Heart of Jesus to pay their debt.

AT THE PATER NOSTER.

Our Father Who art in Heaven—hallowed be Thy Name—Thy Kingdom come—Thy Will be done on earth as it is in Heaven. Give us this day our daily Bread—and forgive us our trespasses as we forgive them that trespass against us—and lead us not into temptation—but deliver us from evil. Amen.

Sursum Corda!

AT THE AGNUS DEI.

Lamb of God, Who takest away the sins of the world—have mercy on us.

Lamb of God, Who takest away the sins of the world—have mercy on us.

Lamb of God, Who takest away the sins of the world—come to me. Come to me, O pure, and holy, and gentle Lamb of God—I am very poor, very little, very unworthy to draw near to You—be kind and merciful to me, O Lamb of God.

My holy Patrons, pray for me.

My dear Mother Mary, pray for me.

My good Angel, pray for me and take me to Jesus.

AT THE DOMINE NON SUM DIGNUS.

Say from your heart with the good centurion:

"Lord, I am not worthy that Thou shouldst enter under my roof—say but the word—and my soul shall be healed."

Repeat the Confiteor *with the server, or make an act of contrition with all your heart. The absolution which follows the Confiteor is a sacramental, and can get you the forgiveness of all your venial sins if you are sorry for them.*

And now our Lord says to you: "Arise, my love, and come." *Go up to the altar. He is waiting for you. He holds out His Arms to you. Open your heart to Him and receive Him with deepest reverence and with tenderest love.*

AFTER COMMUNION.

Should you want any help, you may use the following acts:

1. Adoration.—*"Profoundly I adore Thee, O hidden God."*
"Down in adoration falling, Lo! the Sacred Host we hail."
"My Lord and my God."
"Thou art Christ the Son of the Living God."
"My God and my all."
"Sweet Sacrament we Thee adore, Oh, make us love Thee more and more."

"Adore Him all ye His Angels." Blessed Angels—my own Angel—and all you Saints of Heaven—adore my God for me.

Dear Mother Mary, adore Him for me—you see Him face to face Whom I see beneath the veils. Dear Lord, accept all this adoration as my offering to You. But it is not enough:

O Heart of Jesus—adore for me the Three Divine Persons—Father, Son, and Holy Ghost, here really present. O Sacred Heart, my very own now—let me offer Your adorations as my very own to the Ever Blessed Trinity.

2. Thanksgiving.—*Deo Gratias! Deo Gratias!* Oh, thanks be to God a thousand times!

"We praise Thee—we bless Thee—we glorify Thee. We give Thee thanks for Thy great glory!"

"My soul doth magnify the Lord—for He that is mighty hath done great things for me—and holy is His Name."

"Glory be to the Father and to the Son and to the Holy Ghost. As it was in the beginning, is now and ever shall be, world without end. Amen."

"Let us bless the Father and the Son with the Holy Ghost—let us praise and glorify Him forever."

"Blessed be Jesus, Who has come to me in Holy Communion!"

"Bless the Lord, all ye His Angels. Praise Him, all His Saints."

Dear Mother Mary, thank your Son for coming to me.

O Sacred Heart, be my thanksgiving to the Three Divine Persons now dwelling within me.

O Blessed Trinity, Father, Son, and Holy Ghost, I offer You the Heart of Jesus as my thanksgiving for all You have done for me.

3. Love.—*"It is the Lord, it is the Lord!"* "Rabboni, Master!"

"I have found Him Whom my soul loveth—I hold Him and will not let Him go."

"My Beloved is all mine and I am all His."

Now I have all I want, for I have Jesus.

Jesus, Jesus, be to me Jesus, and save me.

"O good Jesus, hear me—within Thy Wounds hide me—never let me be separated from Thee."

Jesus, I am Thine, save me.

"Give me only Thy love and Thy grace, and this is enough for me."

O my God and my Saviour, all this way for me! All through the long years from the Promise in Paradise till Your coming into the world—all through the long years of Your life on earth and the long years of Your Sacramental Life—and now from the Tabernacle into my heart!

O happy Angels and Saints who see Him face to face, love my God for me.

Love Him for me, O Blessed Mother. The Lord Who was with thee and is with thee always, is with me now.

O Sacred Heart, love for me the Blessed Trinity, Father, Son, and Holy Ghost, as They deserve to be loved.

4. Contrition.—*"Father, I have sinned, . . . I am not worthy to be called Thy child."*

My God, I am so sorry for having ever offended You. It is easy to make an act of contrition now that You are in my heart helping me to be sorry. I am sorry for all my sins—most for those that have grieved You most. You bear with me, dear Lord, because You love me. It must take a great deal of patience to bear with me. I thank You for all Your patience, but help me to give You less to bear.

Take all I have and keep it for me—that I may not sin again by using badly any of the things You have given me.

5. Petition.—*Give me Thy love and Thy grace.* Help me to love You with all my heart—with all my soul—with all my mind—with all my strength. And help me to show You my love in every way You want—not so much by words as by

Sursum Corda!

deeds—by doing what You like, not what I like—by hating all sin, even the least. O my God, keep me from sin—keep me all my life from mortal sin. I would rather die now after my First Communion than ever come to offend You mortally. O pure Lamb of God, You Who feed among the lilies, keep my heart pure for Yourself always. Help me in my temptations—and if I fall into any sin, make me come back to You without being discouraged. Help me to overcome those faults into which I fall the oftenest—which You most want me to correct. Help me to love You daily more and more—to love all that You love—and to be kind to all for Your sake.

My God, what can I give You in return for all You have given to me? I give You my heart—I give You my love—I give You my body with all its senses—my soul with all its powers. I give You all I have and am—now and always—in time and eternity. I bring to You all that I love—all my treasures—and give them all to You—my father and mother—my brothers and sisters and friends.

"Take, O Lord, and receive all my liberty, my memory, my understanding, and all my will, all that I have and possess. Thou hast given it to me; to Thee, O Lord, I restore it—all is Thine, dispose of it all according to Thy Will. Give me Thy love and Thy grace, for this is enough for me."

Have mercy, dear Lord, on the poor suffering souls in Purgatory, especially on those for whom I ought chiefly to pray, and help me now to gain this Indulgence for them.

Say the Prayer before the Crucifix, and five Paters and Aves.

I am going to leave You now, dear Lord; but stay with me spiritually all day. Give me Your blessing before I go—I will not let You go until You bless me. Remind me to keep close to You by often raising up my heart to You during the day. I will come back and visit You in the afternoon.

In your afternoon visit you may say the Litany (below), or go back upon the acts you have just made in your thanksgiving,

LITANY FOR HOLY COMMUNION
(before or after)

Lord have mercy on us.
Christ have mercy on us.
Lord have mercy on us.
Christ hear us.
Christ graciously hear us.

God the Father of Heaven,
God the Son, Redeemer of the world,
God the Holy Ghost,
Holy Trinity one God,
Jesus, Living Bread Which came down from Heaven,
Jesus, Bread from Heaven giving life to the world,
Hidden God and Saviour,
My Lord and my God,
Who hast loved us with an everlasting love,
Whose delights are to be with the children of men,
Who hast given Thy Flesh for the life of the world.
Who dost invite all to come to Thee,
Who dost promise eternal life to those who receive Thee,
Who with desire dost desire to eat this Pasch with us,
Who art ever ready to receive and welcome us,

Have mercy on us.

Sursum Corda!

Who dost stand at our door knocking,
Who hast said that if we will open to Thee the door,
   Thou wilt come in and sup with us,
Who dost receive us into Thy Arms and bless us with
   the little children,
Who dost suffer us to sit at Thy Feet with Magdalen,
Who dost invite us to lean on Thy Bosom with the
   Beloved Disciple,
Who hast not left us orphans,
Most dear Sacrament,
Sacrament of Love,
Sacrament of Sweetness,
Life-giving Sacrament,
Sacrament of Strength,
My God and my All,

} *Have mercy on us.*

That our hearts may pant after Thee as the hart after
   the fountains of water,
That Thou wouldst manifest Thyself to us as to the
   two disciples in the breaking of bread,
That we may know Thy Voice like Magdalen,
That with a lively faith we may confess with the Beloved
   Disciple—"It is the Lord,"
That Thou wouldst bless us who have not seen and have
   believed,
That we may love Thee in the Blessed Sacrament with our
   whole heart, with our whole soul, with all our mind, and
   with all our strength,
That the fruit of each Communion may be fresh love,

} *We beseech Thee hear us.*

That our one desire may be to love Thee and to do Thy Will,
That we may ever remain in Thy love,
That Thou wouldst teach us how to receive and welcome Thee,
That Thou wouldst teach us to pray and Thyself pray within us,
That with Thee every virtue may come into our souls,
That through this day Thou wouldst keep us closely united to Thee,
That Thou wouldst give us grace to persevere to the end,
That Thou wouldst then be our support and Viaticum,
   That with Thee and leaning on Thee we may safely pass through all dangers,
That our last act may be one of perfect love, and our last breath a long deep sigh to be in our Father's House,
That Thy sweet Face may smile upon us when we appear before Thee,
That our banishment from Thee, dearest Lord, may not be very long,
That when the time is come, we may fly up from our prison to Thee and in Thy Sacred Heart find our rest for ever,

We beseech Thee hear us.

Lamb of God, Who takest away the sins of the world,
                                      Spare us, O Lord.
Lamb of God, Who takest away the sins of the world,
                                      Graciously hear us.
Lamb of God, Who takest away the sins of the world,
                                      Have mercy on us.

  V. Stay with us, Lord, because it is towards evening.
  R. And the day is now far spent.

Sursum Corda!

Let us pray.

We come to Thee, dear Lord, with the Apostles, saying, "Increase our faith." Give us a strong and lively faith in the mystery of Thy Real Presence in the midst of us. Give us the splendid faith of the Centurion, which drew from Thee such praise. Give us the faith of the Beloved Disciple to know Thee in the dark and say, "It is the Lord!" Give us the faith of Peter to confess, "Thou art Christ the Son of the Living God." Give us the faith of Magdalen to fall at Thy Feet crying, "*Rabboni,* Master." Give us the faith of all Thy Saints, to whom the Blessed Sacrament has been Heaven begun on earth. In every Communion increase our faith; for with faith—love and humility, and reverence and all good, will come into our souls.

Dearest Lord, *increase our faith.*

COMMUNION BEADS

On the cross, say the Prayer of St Ignatius:

ANIMA CHRISTI.

Soul of Christ, sanctify me;
Body of Christ, save me;
Blood of Christ, inebriate me;
Water out of the Side of Christ, wash me;
Passion of Christ, strengthen me.

O good Jesus, hear me,
Within Thy Wounds hide me;
Never let me be separated from Thee;
From the malignant enemy defend me.
At the hour of my death call me
And bid me come to Thee,
That with Thy Saints I may praise Thee
For all eternity.

(300 DAYS' INDULGENCE.)

On the large beads, say the Our Father.
On the small beads, say:

Hail, Mary, full of grace, the Lord is with thee, blessed art thou amongst women, and blessed is the fruit of thy womb, Jesus, Whom thou didst receive so worthily. Holy Mary, Mother of God, pray for us sinners that we may receive Him worthily, now and at the hour of our death. Amen.

Recite three decades in this way.

Let us pray.

O God, Who in this wonderful Sacrament hast left us a memorial of Thy Passion, grant us, we beseech Thee, so to reverence the Sacred Mysteries of Thy Body and Blood that we may ever find in ourselves the fruit of Thy Redemption. Who livest and reignest with Thee, in the unity of the Holy Spirit, one God, forever and ever. Amen.

A SIMPLE CONFESSION BOOK

INTRODUCTION

In early 1900, having recently finished her works on Baptism *(The Child of God)* and Confirmation *(The Soldier of Christ)*, Mother Loyola turned her pen toward writing a manual of instruction for the Sacrament of Penance. This soon became not one, but two books: one intended to prepare young children for their First Confession, and another "maintenance manual" for those who had already made it, which she called *Forgive us our Trespasses*.

However, as these books were being published by the Catholic Truth Society, which sought wherever possible to present Catholic Doctrine in condensed and affordable versions, she was persuaded to simplify these books even further and create onepenny pamphlet versions of both books.

We have not included in this anthology the first of these, called *A First Confession Book for the Little Ones*, as the content of its brief 20 pages could largely be found in the 44 pages of the *Simple Confession Book*, which here follows.

Contents

Preparation for Confession

I.	Prayer for Grace	76
II.	Examination of Conscience	79
	1. Duties to God	79
	2. Duties to my Neighbour	80
	3. Duties to Myself	82
III.	Contrition	83
	1. Hell	86
	2. Purgatory	90
	3. Heaven	91
	4. The Sacred Passion	94
	The Scourging	95
	The Crowning with Thorns	96
	Calvary	98
	5. The Goodness of God	101
IV.	Purpose of Amendment	103

Confession

After Confession 107

A SIMPLE CONFESSION BOOK

PREPARATION FOR CONFESSION

We are going to confession. We have offended God by breaking His Commandments, and by so doing we have hurt our own souls. But thanks to His goodness and pity for our weakness, He is ready to forgive us and to make us well and strong again, no matter what we have done to hurt ourselves. "Come to Me, child," He says to us tenderly, "and I will put you right again." He promises. He does not say "perhaps." And so we do not *hope*, but *know for certain* that we shall be put right *if we do our part*. For the sacraments always give grace to those who receive them worthily. We come to Him, then, joyfully, asking Him to do His part, and promising to do ours, which we know consists of four things:

I. We must heartily pray for grace to make a good confession.
II. We must carefully examine our conscience.
III. We must take time and care to make a good act of contrition.
IV. We must resolve by the help of God to renounce our sins and to begin a new life for the future.

Sursum Corda!

I. We must pray for grace to make a good confession.

Because this is an important work and we can do no good work without the help of God's grace. Because it is sometimes difficult to tell our sins. And because prayer is the means fixed by God for getting His help. "Ask," He says, "and you shall receive." You may say one of the hymns to the Holy Spirit,

or

> I believe that there, behind the tabernacle door, is the Judge of the living and the dead, before whom I shall have to appear when I die, to give an exact account of my whole life. I believe that He will have to judge me then with strict justice, that there will be no time for confession and contrition then. O my Judge and my Saviour, now while I have time, help me to find out my sins and to confess them with true sorrow, that I may stand without fear before You in the terrible hour of judgement.
>
> Holy Mary, Mother of God, pray for me a sinner *now* and at the hour of my death.

II. We must carefully examine our conscience.

If you go to confession frequently, and always examine your conscience at your night prayers, preparation for the Sacrament of Penance becomes very easy. You come to it with the work half done. Set to work briskly the minute you get into church, not looking about and wasting time in distractions, but beginning at once with the first of the four points. Follow some order in the arrangement of what you have to say—the ten commandments of God; the six precepts of the Church; the seven deadly sins; or—to cover the same ground in another way—your duties (1) to God; (2) to your neighbour; (3) to yourself. Your sins will thus remain in your memory, and when your examination is finished you will be able to leave them quietly and turn to your next point. Without an orderly arrangement, examination of conscience becomes difficult and wearisome, and even when it is finished, you will be running after your sins instead of thinking how to get rid of them. Your sins have been called to mind in the examination of conscience which, of course, you make every night, and a very short time will bring them before you now. For a month's confession, eight or ten minutes, given in a businesslike way, to examination of conscience, is enough. Give the rest of the time, another ten minutes, to your contrition.

When we have not been to confession for some time, and even in our preparation for our weekly confession, we may sometimes find it useful to recall the places we have been in, and the persons we have met. This helps us to remember our sins. Any circumstance that changes the kind of sin and makes it much worse, *e.g.*, striking a parent, stealing anything belonging to a church, must be mentioned; and as far as we can, we should say the number of times a sin has been committed. After reasonable care has been given to examination of conscience, a sin forgotten is forgiven. Only, if a mortal sin were to come to mind later, we should have to confess it in our next confession, because every mortal sin must be confessed once.

Mortal means deadly. Three things are required to make a mortal sin: (1) grave matter; (2) full knowledge; (3) full consent.

(1) Grave matter: the sin must be a grievous sin—that is, the thought, word, action, or omission, must be something of very great importance, *e.g.*, going to Communion after breaking the fast; stealing a large sum, or a small sum from a person extremely poor.

(2) Full knowledge: not done by mistake or before we knew clearly what we were about. The mind must think of the act and of its sinfulness at the time the act is done.

(3) Full consent: the will must deliberately agree to the temptation, whether of thought, word, or deed.

If there was not full knowledge, or full consent, but hesitation in rejecting the temptation, or only half consent, the sin is venial, not mortal—the soul is injured but not killed.

Venial means pardonable. This sin is so called because it is more easily pardoned than mortal sin. A lie of excuse, a small injury to our neighbour, do not turn the soul away from God like mortal sin, and therefore do not take away sanctifying grace. Nevertheless venial sin is a great evil and should be repented of sincerely. It displeases God, deprives the soul of many graces, weakens it by taking away its fear of offending God, and in this way often leads to mortal sin. No one ever comes to mortal, except through carelessness about venial sin. Each venial sin deserves its own temporal punishment, and will prolong our purgatory.

The law of God is that every mortal sin is to be confessed and absolved once. But it would not be safe to confess those sins only which we know for certain were mortal, because we are so apt to deceive ourselves. The only safe practice is to confess whatever is on our conscience and gives us trouble—certain things as certain, doubtful things as doubtful. Those who keep things back, who have secrets about their sins, or try to settle their doubts themselves, are very unhappy. They find confession a torture, they lose their peace and their confidence in God, and perhaps give up His service altogether.

We are not bound to confess our venial sins, but it is well to do so. A good practice is to pick out two or three of the chief and try to be sorry for them. This is better than spending much time in trying to remember them all.

EXAMINATION OF CONSCIENCE

1. Duties to God

Confession. How long is it since my last? Did I do the four things by way of preparation? Did I leave out anything I ought to have told? Did I take time and care to make a good act of contrition? What was my purpose of amendment like? Did I say my penance carefully?

Communion. Did I make the usual acts before and after? And how?

Prayers. When I kneel down to pray do I remember that I am going to speak to God, and make at least a good start?

Sursum Corda!

Do I say my prayers in a hurry, or looking about all the time? Have I said my morning and night prayers, and without willful distractions? Have I examined my conscience at night and made a real act of sorrow for my sins? Have I laughed or talked in church, or shown any irreverence during Mass or Benediction? Have I done anything to distract others at prayer? How do I listen to sermons or catechism? Have I said grace before and after meals as I ought?

Have I done or read anything likely to injure my faith?

Have I spoken with disrespect of God, or of holy things? Have I said bad words?

Have I stayed away from Mass on any Sunday or Holiday of Obligation? Have I been late on these days, or inattentive?

2. Duties to my Neighbour

Have I disobeyed parents, or any one else in authority over me? Have I provoked them, or shown disrespect in word or manner? Have I caused them great sorrow, or not helped them when they were poor, or old, or sick? Have I done what I was told at once, or been angry, or answered back? Have I been obstinate, sulky, or impertinent when told of my faults? Have I deceived my parents or those who are over me?

Have I been in a passion? or kept up bad temper for a long time? Have I struck any one or quarrelled? Have I called people names, or in other ways provoked them? Have I wished harm to any one? Have I refused to forgive? Have I given bad example to any one by word or conduct? Or shared in any sin by proposing it, by defending it, by silence, or in any other way? Have I done anything to spite my parents, teachers, or companions?

Have I prevented others from studying, or working, or in any way doing their duty? Have I ridiculed others for doing good?

Have I given unnecessary trouble to parents or superiors?

Have I stolen anything, or kept what did not belong to me, without trying to find the owner? Have I cheated in buying or selling? Have I destroyed, wasted, or willfully damaged things, or in any other way been unjust in my dealings with my neighbour? Have I paid back anything I owed?

Have I told lies, or got others to tell them? (A lie of excuse that does not harm another is a venial sin.) Have I told any lie that I knew would be the cause of harm to another? (This is calumny, and *may* be a mortal sin.) Have I made known any one's secret faults? (This is detraction.) Have I injured my neighbour's character by speaking ill of him, or listened *willingly* to uncharitable conversation? Have I judged anyone rashly—that is, thought ill of him without sufficient cause? Have I made others quarrel, or made mischief by tale-bearing?

> Note.—If I have sinned by calumny, detraction, or theft, I must repair as well as I can the harm I have done, and ask my confessor's advice how to do it.

3. Duties to Myself

Have I done anything wrong, by thought, word, or deed, against purity or modesty? Have I got others to do wrong? Have I gone with bad companions? or to dangerous amusements? Have I read bad books, or given them to others?

> Note 1.—A bad thought which is not willful is no sin, but not to try to put away the bad thought, to take pleasure in it, to consent to it—this is a sin.

> Note 2.—Tale-telling to make mischief, or out of spite, is wrong. But if you know of any immodest conduct or conversation carried on, you must at once make it known to your parents, or those in authority, and not fear to be called "telltale." If you neglect to do this, you may become answerable for such sins by concealment.

Have I been vain of my abilities, my person, or my dress? Have I despised others? Have I been jealous of others, or vexed when my companions were praised?

Have I committed sin by eating or drinking too much? Have I, without leave, eaten meat on Friday, or on any day when it is forbidden? Have I kept the fasts of the Church unless lawfully dispensed?

Do I rise promptly in the morning, or am I lazy?

Have I been idle at my lessons? Have I stayed away from school or kept others away?

Have I, through curiosity, read letters or anything I ought not to have read? What about the duties and occupations of my daily life—how have they been done—conscientiously, or carelessly? Have I wasted time in overmuch novel-reading, recreation, or in other ways?

What is my chief fault, from which most of the others come—pride, anger, sloth, or what? Am I trying to conquer it?

Is there anything else I ought to confess, or as to which I want advice?

For parents and those in authority.—Do I see that all under my charge are properly cared for as to soul and body? That they are sufficiently instructed, and have time for the discharge of their religious duties? Do I watch over their companions, amusements, and reading, and keep them as far as possible from idleness and occasions of sin? Do I set them a good example? Have I been excessive in reprehending them, or neglected to give them just reproof?

For those who are in service.—Have I been disrespectful to my employers? Have I wasted or willfully damaged their goods? or allowed others to do so? Have I stolen from them or given away their things without leave? Have I been idle or careless at my work? or not done what I was told to do?

Think now of some sin of your past life for which you are specially sorry and which you intend to confess again. Make an act of contrition for it.

> My God, I am sorry for all the sins since my last confession, most of all for this one (name it) and for this sin of my past life (name it).

III. We must take time and care to make a good act of contrition.

This is the chief part of our preparation, without which all the rest is worse than useless. Have we gathered together every sin we have committed?—not one will be forgiven without contrition. And on the other hand, should any sin, even a grievous one, be forgotten after sufficient care, our act of contrition, which would include that and every other grievous sin if we remembered it, would blot it out.

The contrition we must have is "a hearty sorrow for our sins, because by them we have offended so good a God, together with a firm purpose of amendment." We get this sorrow by thinking of the motives or reasons our faith puts before us for being sorry. Be sure, then, to give yourself time, after your examination of conscience, to think quietly over the motives for contrition.

The best motive for sorrow is God Himself—to be sorry for God's sake, because He is infinitely good and deserving of all love, and because by sin we have displeased and disappointed Him whom we love. This perfect contrition is so pleasing to God, that it gets forgiveness at once for all guilt, mortal or venial, even before confession and absolution. If sufficiently intense, it remits all punishment too, eternal and temporal. It remits more or less, according to our dispositions. Imperfect contrition, called also attrition, is supernatural sorrow, but chiefly for our own sake, because we have lost heaven, or deserved hell or purgatory. Though less perfect than the other, it is good and put into our hearts by the Holy Ghost. It will forgive venial sin and remit a part of the temporal punishment, and is sufficient when joined with confession and absolution for the forgiveness of mortal sin.

Our sorrow must include every mortal sin of which we have been guilty. God cannot forgive some mortal sins and leave others unforgiven. If we confess venial sins only, we must be sorry for at least one. For all, if we want them to be forgiven by the sacrament.

God cannot forgive any sin, mortal or venial, without contrition. It is part of the matter of the sacrament, and we are bound to take it with us whenever we go to confession. To make sure of our contrition, it is well to tell some sin of our past life for which we are truly sorry and have *renewed our act of contrition.* We tell it, not to get it forgiven, that was done long ago, but simply because of the obligation to have sorrow for at least one sin that we confess. Hence, to tell it merely through habit and without having renewed our sorrow for it, is of no use whatever.

We are to get contrition by earnestly asking for it, and by making use of such considerations as may lead us to it. "Ask," says our Lord, "and you shall receive; seek and you shall find." We will ask for it with all our heart, and we will seek for it by thinking over some of the things which will move us to it. Thinking—not scampering over, not merely reading, but letting our mind and heart go with the words we read. This is our part; if we do it, God will come in and do His.

> My God, give me true sorrow for having offended You. I must come to You for it. I cannot get it by myself. But I know You want to give it to me more than I want to have it. I know there is nothing You are so pleased to give. You tell me to ask and I shall receive, to seek and I shall find, to knock and it shall be opened to me. I am asking, seeking, knocking now. Give me what I want—perfect contrition for all my sins, sorrow for them because they have offended You who are so good. Give me what I ask, through Jesus Christ our Lord.

If we want to be sorry for our sins, we must think quietly of the motives or reasons why we should be sorry; we must try to find out how bad sin is. It takes some trouble to do this—well, we must take the trouble. Surely the great God of heaven and earth, who, if He liked, might refuse to forgive us our sins, no matter how much trouble we took, or how sorry we were, does not ask too much when He bids us take ten minutes to find out the harm we have done ourselves and Him, and to be sorry for that harm.

Any thought that leads us to supernatural sorrow will serve our purpose, and if one is enough we need not use more.

You may think how dreadful a thing sin is in itself; of the dismal effects of mortal sin. How it kills the soul and deserves hell. How it takes away the merit of our past good works—that is, it makes us lose the eternal reward gained by all the good works we have done in a state of grace. How it prevents any good work we may do whilst in a state of mortal sin from meriting any eternal reward. Should not these thoughts make us fear and hate sin above all other evils?

Or take any thoughts about hell, purgatory, heaven, the sufferings of Christ, the goodness of God. You need not use all, some will help you at one time, some at another.

1. Hell

"Eye hath not seen, nor ear heard, neither hath it entered into the heart of man what things God hath prepared for those that love Him." (1 Cor. 2:9.) Yes, and on the other hand—eye hath not seen, nor ear heard, nor can we have any idea of what is prepared after death for those who have not loved Him, who die His enemies by mortal sin. The Judgement is swiftly over, and before the friends on earth know that the soul has left the body, it has gone to its place in hell, and begun its eternity of misery. The exact nature of its pain we do not know, but this we know: that our Lord always speaks of the punishment of that fearful place as *fire*. "*The wicked shall be cast into the furnace of fire.*" (Matt. 13.) "*Depart from Me, you cursed, into everlasting fire.*" (Matt. 25.)

Our Lord wants to frighten us about hell-fire *now* when the fear will do us good, that we may not come to fear it when fear will be too late. And so there are no words more fearful than the words about hell that fell from His gentle lips. "I am tormented *in this flame,*" He makes the rich man say. "Every one shall be *salted with fire.*" "*And the fire is not extinguished.*" "If thy hand scandalize thee, cut it off; it is better for thee to enter into life, maimed, than having two hands to go into hell *into unquenchable fire.*" (Mark 9.) Fire—how He repeats again and again that dreadful word! He wants to show us that we must wrench ourselves free from books, amusements, companions—things near and dear to us as hand or foot, rather than do anything to deserve the awful punishment of the life to come.

And who are these that He wants to warn? Bad people only who have no fear of mortal sin? No, but those too who are getting careless about venial sin, who say, "Oh, it is only a venial sin." He showed St. Teresa the place in hell prepared for her if she had not corrected a certain fault. The greatest saints must be afraid of hell. "I say to you, my friends, fear Him who has power to cast into hell." St. Paul was afraid, St. Philip Neri was afraid. The catechism says hell is one of the Four Last Things to be ever remembered. Why? That we may all be afraid.

"The *place of torments.*" Pain of every kind there. Pain most awful in its severity. Pain never ceasing; always at a pitch of unbearable intensity; never a little less bad; never soothed by hearing a kind word; never relieved by the least comfort, the least change. Pain without merit; of no good to the wretched soul; not getting rid of its guilt; not bringing it any nearer to the end of its punishment. Pain such as this, unbearable from the first moment, to go on—*forever!*

The pain of which our dear Lord speaks, whatever its nature may be, reaches the *soul*. How, we do not know. But we know that the pain it causes is more terrible by far than any pain of fire the body can suffer. And even this pain is nothing compared with that which makes hell what it is— the pain of loss. Until we know who God is, as He is known by all in the next world, we cannot understand in the very least what the soul feels that has lost Him.

He is the life of all. The good have gained everything in gaining Him. In losing Him, the wicked have lost *all*. "My God and my all!" the saints exclaim in transports of joy. "Let me get to God," the damned cry out in their suffocating agony, "I must, I will have Him." They leap up each moment to reach Him, and each moment fall back into the fire, wailing in their despair: "O God, whom I might have loved—*my God* once, *my God* still—I have lost You, I have lost You for ever, I have lost all—and by my own fault!"

One moment—God's beloved child,
    Heir to a throne,
Saints, Angels, Mary, God Himself,
    By right, mine own.

Another moment—mine by right,
    A felon's cell,
Companionship of demons, and
    The doom of hell.

One of the most unbearable thoughts in hell, that place of bitter thoughts, is: *"It is all my own fault!* I need not have given way to temptation. I should not have given way if I had prayed. I am lost, and for what? How long did the pleasure of a mortal sin last? I am lost for so little, lost when I might so easily have been saved! And now it is too late!" This thought those miserable souls have always before them—*It is too late!* What did the bad thief think of the choice he had made, when he found himself in hell, and knew that his companion of a few moments ago was in paradise with Jesus!

Is it not a fearful thought that I—I may be lost and go to hell! Must I not hate and keep away from mortal sin, and be afraid of venial sin?

Act of Contrition

My God, because of the dreadful punishments which sin deserves, I am heartily sorry for all my sins. Give me more and more sorrow, and keep me from sin in the time to come.

2. Purgatory

Many people are more helped by the thought of purgatory than by that of hell. They find purgatory teaches them more about the malice of sin and makes them fear and hate it more. Let us see why.

The souls suffering in hell are the enemies of God. The holy souls in purgatory are His friends and dear children. They love Him with all their strength, and He loves them more tenderly than the fondest mother ever loved her child. Yet see how He is obliged to treat them, because, though their sins are forgiven, a debt of temporal punishment remains.

The consequences of our sins do not end, as some of us seem to think, with the confession of them. Sin and punishment go together like a burn and pain. The first sacrament we receive takes away the pain with the sin, but the Sacrament of Penance leaves a punishment behind. We must try to bring home to ourselves the pain of the punishment of sin in purgatory.

Purgatory is a dark close prison. The exact nature of the sufferings there we do not know, but Holy Scripture says some "shall be saved yet so as by fire" (1 Cor. 3), and the greatest saints tell us that the least pain there is worse than anything that can be suffered in this world. No words can tell what the poor prisoners endure. They have nothing to do but to suffer intense and unceasing pain, without being able to help themselves in the least. What would violent toothache be for a week together! The pains of purgatory have to be borne for months, years, perhaps centuries. Should not this thought make us tremble! If I am careless about venial sin, how long I may have to be there!

From their terrible prison-house these souls cry to God, "Open to us, O Lord, open to us!" Oh, how they hate now the venial sins of which they thought so little once. The irreverence in church; the willful distractions in prayer; the unkindness to others in thought, and word, and deed; the impatience when things were not to their liking; the disobedience and disrespect to parents; the bad example to companions. "Oh, how foolish we were," they will cry," not to believe what we were told—that venial sin is not a little evil, but the greatest in the world after mortal sin—that each venial sin has its distinct debt of punishment to be paid either on earth or in purgatory!"

To come now to myself. What venial sins this past week will have to be punished by the grievous pains of purgatory, unless I do a little willing penance for them here? What venial sins must I avoid in future, to prevent my debt of punishment from growing heavier? Once inside those gates my sorrow and good resolutions will be too late.

Our Lord will say to me: "The night has come, in which no man can work. I tell thee thou canst not go hence till thou hast paid the last farthing."

Say heartily the Act of Contrition, p. 89.

3. Our Heavenly Home

Oh the pleasant sights and sounds that come up before us when we say the word "Home!"—the favourite nooks, the delightful rambles, the dear fireside, the faces of brothers

Sursum Corda!

and sisters, the familiar voices, the freedom, the fun, the laughter. And, before and above all, all in two words—father and mother!

"What is home?" a teacher asked.

"Where mother is," answered a little child.

And our Heavenly Home, what is that? Is it, as many seem to imagine, mere freedom from pain, and sickness, and sorrow, and death—a life without strife or care, without a moment's weariness or disquiet—and that for ever? It is this, but much more than this.

It is the possession of every joy that our wildest dreams can picture, joys which God Himself can only speak of as, "The good things of the Lord in the land of the living." (Ps. 26.)

It is to live in close and loving familiarity with angels and saints, our brothers and sisters in the Kingdom of God.

It is to kneel at Mary's feet; to look up into her face; to hear her words of love; to feel the touch of her motherly hand.

It is to be for ever in the company of Jesus, among His dear and chosen friends; seeing Him always; hearing His voice; receiving the marks of His love, and loving Him ourselves with every power of heart and soul.

It is to behold the unveiled Face of God; to know and love and praise with unspeakable delight, the Father, Son, and Holy Ghost, who created, redeemed, and sanctified us, and made us for heaven and for Himself. This is the joy that eye hath not seen, nor ear heard, nor heart conceived; the joy in which is all other joys; the joy that will satisfy to the full every desire of the heart, and that for eternity. Home is where our Father is, and therefore Heaven is Home.

This joy is the birthright of every baptized soul. It is my right. A place in my Father's house has been prepared for me. It is known there as mine, my name is written over it in letters of light.

> O Paradise, O Paradise,
>   I greatly long to see
> The special place my dearest Lord
>   Is furnishing for me.
>
> (*Faber.*)

But if ever I have committed a mortal sin, what have I done? Thrown away my title-deeds to that place; despised it; consented never to see it. "I cannot have it and the passing pleasure of this mortal sin," I have said. "Well, let it go. God may give it to another for all I care. I will exchange it for a place in the outer darkness, where there is weeping and gnashing of teeth."

Angels and saints heard me and trembled. What if God should take me at my word? And why not? Why should my place in heaven be kept for me? "*Thou hast lifted thyself up against the Lord of heaven, the God that hath thy breath in his hand.*" (Dan. 5.) They trembled; they waited. But why were not their swords unsheathed against me? Why was not their eager zeal for God's glory let loose to sweep me from off the earth into the place I had chosen? Why were they thus patient with me? Because they always see the Face of my Father who is in heaven. And they saw pity there. The Lord of heaven is my Father—and He had patience. He would not take me at my word. He would wait and call me back to Him, and give me grace, and restore to me all I had lost, if only I would be sorry, and let the Blood of Jesus flowing in the Sacrament of Penance make good my losses and win back for me my place at Home.

Say heartily the Act of Contrition, p. 89.

4. The Sacred Passion

It is good and useful to turn to hell and purgatory and heaven to find what we want—sorrow for our sins.

But the Sacred Passion is more to us than all the universe beside. There, if anywhere, we shall learn what sin is, by what sin has done. There, if all other founts fail us, we shall draw the sorrow we are seeking. But not all at once. It needs patient study before it gives out its treasures. Above all, it needs the love that dwells on detail. The reason why we can look at our crucifix unmoved and unhelped, is the carelessness of our glance. If we would pass slowly from wound to wound, we should find what we want before we had gone far.

And so with the other scenes of the Passion. We look upon them carelessly, as a whole. We try to grasp too much. If we would force ourselves now and then to stay before one single circumstance of our Lord's many pains, we should begin to understand something of what He suffered for us, and to grieve for the sins which cost Him so much to expiate.

Let us go to two or three of these scenes now, remembering that when we have found what we want, we are *to stay there,* leaving the remaining stores to be explored another day. Remembering, too, that it is not enough to read, *we must see; we must feel.*

The Scourging

See, then, at the foot of the marble steps leading from the balcony of the governor's hall, a large court paved with reddish stones. At one end a low pillar, not more than two feet and a half in height, with an iron ring in the top. To this ring our Lord is fastened by His wrists, so that His Sacred Body is painfully bent.

See those long lashes tipped with spikes of iron. They are the scourges. Handle them, and think how they will rend and bruise and tear to pieces when wielded by the strong arms of soldiers. Watch these cruel men as they gather round their victim, who stands, as we should, trembling and terrified, awaiting the first stroke.

Look at the scene in the courtyard as the scourgers begin their cruel work. See how pitilessly, on back, and shoulders, and arms, their furious blows are dealt. The delicate skin becomes red and swollen, the Blood begins to trickle and flow down. Then the iron points falling thick and fast tear the flesh, until the sacred Body is one great wound. And still they go on striking—striking on the open wounds. The scourges and the ground are covered with fragments of His sacred flesh; the Blood streams down upon the pavement.

A whole hour of torture such as this! Five thousand stripes! No pity, no thought for Him, as the tired soldiers relieve one another. "From the sole of the foot to the top of the head, there is no soundness in Him—wounds, and bruises, and swelling sores." (Isaias 1:6.)

And all for me! Do I thoroughly understand this? I believe it, but have I ever tried to make it real to myself? If I had, I should surely hate my sins which have been so cruel. I should love Him who has loved me so much as to bear this willingly for me.

Act of Contrition

> O my Lord and my Saviour, I do indeed hate my cruel sins which have brought Thee to this. How much it has cost Thee to undo the harm that I have done. Give me true sorrow for my sins and true love of Thee. And keep me from sin in the time to come.

The Crowning with Thorns

The scourging over, our Lord is loosed from the pillar. See Him staggering feebly to find His clothes which the soldiers have thrown here and there. See Him trying with weak and trembling hands to lift the seamless robe over His head, and how the woollen tunic adheres to the raw wounds on every side. No pity, no help, no word of comfort from any. "I looked for one that would grieve together with me, but there was none, and for one that would comfort me, and I found none." (Ps. 68.)

Not only did He find none to pity Him, but a fresh torment, one especially invented for Him, was at hand. From the court of the scourging He is dragged into the barrack-yard.

Jesus had been called the King of the Jews. The soldiers can get some sport out of this. They throw an old scarlet cloak on His shoulders, seat Him on a stone bench, and put His crown upon His Head. Look at that crown. Feel it. A long spiny branch of brier, roughly plaited into a wreath—only roughly, for the soldiers must take care not to hurt their hands with the thorns, which in Palestine are longer, sharper, and much stronger than any we have over here.

They take this crown, put it on His Head, and, lest it should fall off, beat it down with their sticks. The thorns pierce His Head on every side. Through His hair the blood trickles down in many streams over His forehead, and with the rush of tears caused by the awful pain, fills His eyes and blinds them. See His noble brow covered with blood. His beautiful Face on which the angels desire to look, all spoilt and disfigured. His eyes not knowing where to turn in their intolerable agony. Think how He fixes them on you and asks you if you are not sorry for your share in bringing Him to this.

It was for our evil thoughts He suffered in His Head. For our vanity that His beautiful Face was disfigured, and His eyes were filled with blood.

Say heartily the Act of Contrition, p. 89

See how in one mystery we may pass from pain to pain to feed our loving sorrow. This third among the sorrowful mysteries seems to be a favourite with children. Ask them to which of the scenes in the Passion they go by preference

Sursum Corda!

to gather sorrow for their sins, and you will hear again and again: "Oh, to the crowning with thorns."

Calvary

And now let us climb Mount Calvary and stand beneath the cross as we might have stood that Friday afternoon long ago. The darkness and stillness of night is all around. Roman soldiers, Jewish priests, the scoffing Pharisees, the rabble, have been frightened into silence. Look at Him as He hangs there, so white against the blackness, so still in His awful agony. Look at Him, and see how "from the sole of the foot to the top of the head there is no soundness in Him, wounds and bruises and swelling sores." (Isaias 1:6.) The bleeding hands and feet arrest our attention, and rightly so. Yet we must not forget that in this, the last scene of torture, the pains of every other are renewed, and grow worse instead of lessening as the hours drag on.

Look at His Head. For four hours it has borne its cruel crown, a crown so often snatched off and put on again, so knocked about when He fell, that the wounds it has made now number many hundreds. He has nowhere to rest this aching Head. If He leans it against the cross, the thorns are forced in deeper; if He lets it hang forward upon His breast, the strain upon His hands becomes more intolerable.

See that pale, disfigured Face; the bruised, sunken cheeks; the parched lips; the eyes growing glazed and dim. "There is no beauty in Him, nor comeliness,...no sightliness that we should be desirous of Him." (Isaias 53.) And He was the most beautiful of the children of men!

Each moment the nails driven into those delicate hands and feet tear wider and wider the rent they have made. The wounds of the scourging are smarting in the cold wind. The whole frame is quivering in its unbearable agony. At ease on a soft bed, we cannot remain long without turning. What was it to be stretched for three hours, raw and bleeding as He was, on the hard, knotty wood of the cross! We shudder at the thought of a limb out of joint. What must it have been to hang for three hours on those disjointed arms! We count it a hardship to be thirsty on a hot day. What was the fierceness of the thirst which broke the silence of those uncomplaining lips!

And the sufferings of His Soul? Pitied by none in that immense crowd. Only words of mockery and hatred rising before His cross. Only gall and vinegar lifted to His lips. Only four or five friends true to Him, out of all the hundreds He had healed and helped. And those few faithful ones, so far from being able to comfort Him, sorely needed comfort themselves.

All He possesses on earth, His few poor clothes, are taken from Him and divided among the soldiers. He has nothing left to Him in the world. He lifts His eyes above the world. He seeks the Father's Face—the Father whose Will He has done so perfectly, so perseveringly—to whom He has been obedient from His first breath in the manger to this death of the cross. And that Face is turned away from

Him. He is treated as a sinner—as the chief among sinners, for all the sins of the world are laid upon Him now. O sacred, suffering Soul of Christ, who shall tell the anguish of Its desolation upon Calvary! See Him as He drinks to the dregs this bitterest drop of His bitter chalice. Hear the cry of His breaking Heart: "My God, My God, why hast Thou forsaken Me!"

The lightest pain suffered by Him who was God as well as man, the least shedding of His most Precious Blood, was enough to redeem a thousand worlds. But He would pour it out to the last drop, that I might know how bad, how terrible a thing is sin.

Because I must be clothed with the best of everything—He must hang naked on the cross!

Because I am proud and desire to be thought better than I am—He is treated as a sinner and a fool!

For my greediness, His tongue is tormented with vinegar and gall, His throat is parched with thirst!

Because I like to be comfortable in everything and hate the least little pain or inconvenience—His shoulders are furrowed with stripes, His hands and feet are bored with nails!

Because I can suffer nothing at all in satisfaction for my sins—He must be tortured from head to foot!

Because I have deserved to be abandoned by God—He is forsaken by His Father in His hour of direst need!

All this *for me!* Oh, if I had seen Him on Calvary, and known His pain was all for my sake, could I have found it in my heart to go away and sin against Him! Could I be as careless as I am? Was it worth His while to show me so much love, for the little bit of love I have given him in return?

He need not have suffered all this. He was not obliged to bear all this for me. He might have left me to perish. His Heart would not let Him. From the height of His cross He saw all the ages to come, all the men, women, and children that were to look to him to save them from sin and hell. He saw *me*. He knew me just as I am. Did that sight comfort Him? Or did His eyes fill with tears as He thought how little I should care for Him after all, how little I mind wounding His Heart by my sins?

But He saw me preparing for confession now. He saw I should want now to be sorry for my sins. He was comforted by seeing me kneeling here to-day.

Say heartily the Act of Contrition, p. 89.

5. God infinitely good in Himself

From seeing how good God has been *to us*, we pass on easily to think how good He must be *in Himself.*

God has given me all that I have—my body, my soul, my health, my senses. He has given me my father and mother, my home, my friends, my education. How many children I see—children who have to save their souls as I have—yet who have fewer helps by far than God has given me—no one to love and care for them; to teach, and to warn them;

to help them to get to heaven. What should I be now, were I in their place?

God watches over me as the most loving of fathers, providing plants, animals—all I need for food and clothing; books, games—all I need for my mind; the Sacraments, Mass, Benediction, Holy Communion, holy inspirations and instructions—all I need for my soul. All the beauty I see in the sunshine and the flowers; all that delights me in scent or in song; all that makes me happy in the goodness and kindness of others, is God's gift to me, *to me*, as if He had no one else to think of. In everything He has made, He had me in view; for me He has been contriving and planning as though I were alone in the world. Oh, what a good, good God our God must be!

For notice this—If He can be so good to little weak creatures that can never be of any use to Him; if He wants to have them all round and about Him in a happy eternity that He may delight in their joy—how good He must be *in Himself!* Is it hard to be sorry for having offended Him *because He is so good?* Is not perfect contrition the easiest as well as the best?

Should any one of these thoughts about hell, heaven, the sufferings of our Lord, move you to sorrow for your sins, stay upon it. You need not go on to others, for you have found what you were seeking. Many considerations are offered, not that you may scamper through all, but that there may be a variety to suit different tastes and moods. It is because we hurry from one thought to another, that we are moved by none. The less we take to think about, the more fruit we often find. But—the rule applies here as everywhere—nothing is to be found without trouble. We must be willing to take pains.

Remember, then, when you want to rouse yourself to contrition, that it is not the number of motives you take, but the thoughtful pondering of one or two that will help you to wish you had never had anything to do with sin, wish to tear yourself free of it, to hate its bad work in yourself or others.

You will have noticed that these motives for sorrow mount like the rungs of a ladder. All are useful and help us up to God. We should use all, but not all at once. The highest is perfect contrition. Ask God to put into your heart this best sorrow—sorrow for having offended Him *because He is so good.*

Act of Contrition

> My God, if there were no hell or purgatory, no pain of any kind to punish sin, I would be sorry for my sins because they have offended Thee who art so good. Give me more and more of this perfect sorrow, and keep me from sin in the time to come.

IV. We must resolve by the grace of God to renounce our sins and to begin a new life for the future.

There can be no real sorrow for what we are going to take no pains to avoid. If you are really sorry for having offended

God by such and such a fault, you will take reasonable pains not to offend Him by repeating that fault.

Remember we have to make a *purpose* of amendment. Now a purpose is not a mere passing wish, it is a strong intention or determination, it is the *making up of our mind* about something. Clearly then it needs time and thought. This purpose, as has been said, is really part of our act of contrition, for there can be no true sorrow for the wrong we have done unless we intend not to do it again. Indeed, one of the ways of testing the reality of our contrition is to see if we are going to take any pains to do better for the time to come. The purpose of amendment we are bound to have is a firm determination to avoid all mortal sin and the proximate occasions of mortal sin.

Any circumstance leading to sin is called an occasion of sin. It may be proximate or remote. A *proximate* occasion is one which usually leads us into sin. A *remote* occasion is one in which we sometimes, though seldom, commit sin. Persons, places, and things may all become occasions of sin, some to one person, some to another. Certain things, such as bad companions, improper conversations, bad books, are always proximate occasions of sin. Each one of us is strictly bound to avoid what is a proximate occasion of mortal sin to him. Sometimes by means of prayer, a more frequent use of the sacraments, and other precautions, a proximate occasion may be made remote. But should there be any person, place, or thing which, no matter what we do, always leads us into mortal sin, we are bound to keep away from it at any cost. Our Lord says, "If thy hand or thy foot scandalize thee,"—that is, if something you care for as much as hand or foot, leads you to commit sin—"cut it off and cast it from thee. It is better for thee to go into life maimed or lame, than having two hands or two feet to be cast into everlasting fire." (Matt. 18.)

We should, of course, resolve to avoid venial sins too, and if we have these only to confess, we should pick out one at least and make a firm resolve about that. If you cannot make up your mind what to choose, think what our Lord would advise, and you will make a good choice.

To be of any use, a resolution must be sensible. Here is one that is not sensible: "I am never going to commit a sin again. I am going to be bad in nothing and good in everything." The devil laughs at a resolution like that. But if instead of this I say—"I will avoid that dangerous occasion—I will say this aspiration when I am tempted—I will watch over myself at such a time, or when talking to such a person, so as to avoid *that fault*—I will try to lessen the number of times I fall; and when I do fall I will come back to God *at once* with an act of sorrow or love, and try again as if nothing had happened"—oh, the devil does not laugh at this. He cannot afford to laugh. For this means dead loss to him, the overthrow of all his plans. Anyone keeping resolutions such as these will come

Sursum Corda!

safely out of all his temptations and march over him up to a high place in heaven.

Remember lastly, we are to resolve *by the grace of God* to renounce our sins. We cannot do it of ourselves, by our own strength. But God has promised to help us always if we ask Him, and the weakest of us may say with David, "In the strength of my God, I shall go over a wall." (Ps. 17.) And with St. Paul, "I can do all things in Him who strengtheneth me." (Phil. 4.)

It need hardly be said that if our sorrow and purpose of amendment are sincere, we shall be ready to do what is necessary to get our sins forgiven and to amend our life. To refuse to forgive one who has offended us, to give back ill-gotten goods, to restore as far as we can a good name when we have taken it away by calumny or detraction, would prove that we are not really sorry for our sins, and therefore not in fit dispositions to receive the Sacrament of Penance.

Just before going into the confessional, make another hearty act of sorrow for all the sins you are going to confess, and for some sin of your past life for which you are truly sorry. This confession of a past sin is a most excellent practice, if we remember it is *done for the sake of arousing contrition*. But nothing can be more useless— to say the least—than to confess it merely by routine. Hence it is well in our act of contrition to distinctly include this sin.

CONFESSION

Remember once more that you are going to confess your sins to our Blessed Saviour, who is waiting to hear you, to help you, to absolve you. Think of Him; tell it all to Him. This will take away any feeling of fear as to what the priest may think or say. Never hide anything in your conscience that makes it troubled or uncomfortable. If you have any difficulty in telling any sin, or do not know how to say it, begin with that sin, asking the priest to help you. Do not leave it to the end. The priest will never be angry with you. And as for a little pain or shame, we must willingly go through it to get the sin forgiven. Else we shall have the shame of hearing that sin told before the whole world at the Last Day. One prayer to Our Lady for help, one brave effort, and you will be rewarded immediately by a flood of peace and happiness. Make each confession as if it were to be your last. Leave nothing to be said at some future time—when you feel better able to say it—when you come to die. Clear up everything now, so that whenever you leave the confessional you can say to yourself: "If this should be the last time I ever receive the sacrament, I think I could be content to meet our Lord at Judgement as I am now."

1. Kneeling down in the confessional, make the sign of the cross:
   > In the name of the Father, and of the Son, and of the Holy Ghost. Amen.

2. Ask a blessing:
> Pray, Father, give me your blessing for I have sinned.

3. Say the first part of the *Confiteor*:
> I confess to Almighty God, to Blessed Mary ever a Virgin, to Blessed Michael the Archangel, to Blessed John the Baptist, to the holy Apostles, Peter and Paul, to all the Saints, and to you, Father, that I have sinned exceedingly, in thought, word, and deed, through my fault, through my fault, through my most grievous fault.
>
> Since my last confession which was (so many weeks, or months ago,) I accuse myself of... I also accuse myself of the sins of my past life, especially of....
>
> For these and all my other sins which I cannot at present call to my remembrance, I am heartily sorry, purpose amendment for the future, and most humbly ask pardon of God and penance and absolution of you, my ghostly father.
>
> Therefore I beseech the Blessed Mary ever a Virgin, Blessed Michael the Archangel, Blessed John the Baptist, the holy Apostles, Peter and Paul, all the Saints, and you, Father, to pray to the Lord our God for me. Amen.

4. After confessing your sins, *leave them.* Do not begin to think if you have told all. Whatever you have forgotten is forgiven. Listen attentively to the advice of your confessor. Then, while he gives you absolution, renew your act of sorrow as if you were kneeling at the feet of Jesus and He Himself was absolving you.

If you have restitution to make, whether of good name or of anything else, and do not know how to do it, or if on any other point you want to know what you ought to do, ask your confessor's advice about it.

Returning to your place, thank God very heartily for the Precious Blood that has been applied to your soul and has cleansed it from all its stains. Say some psalm or hymn or prayer in thanksgiving.

> Hail, Jesus, hail! who for my sake
> Sweet Blood from Mary's veins didst take
>   And shed it all for me;
> Oh, blessed be my Saviour's Blood,
> My life, my light, my only good,
>   To all eternity.
>
> To endless ages let us praise
> The Precious Blood, whose price could raise
>   The world from wrath and sin;
> Whose streams our inward thirst appease,
> And heal the sinner's worst disease,
>   If he but bathe therein.
>
> O sweetest Blood, that can implore
> Pardon of God, and heaven restore,
>   The heaven which sin had lost:
> While Abel's blood for vengeance pleads
> What Jesus shed still intercedes
>   For those who wrong Him most.
>
> Oh, to be sprinkled from the wells
> Of Christ's own Sacred Blood excels
>   Earth's best and highest bliss:
> The ministers of wrath divine
> Hurt not the happy hearts that shine
>   With those red drops of His!

Sursum Corda!

> Ah! there is joy amid the saints
> And hell's despairing courage faints
>   When this sweet song we raise:
> Oh, louder then, and louder still,
> Earth with one mighty chorus fill,
>   The Precious Blood to praise!
>
> —*Faber* (100 days' Indulgence.)

or

Give praise to our God, all ye His servants; and you that fear Him, little and great. (Apoc. 19.)

O give thanks to the Lord, because He is good: because His mercy endureth for ever and ever. (Daniel 3.)

Let them say so that have been redeemed by the Lord, whom He hath redeemed from the hand of the enemy. (Ps. 106.)

Bless the Lord, O my soul, and let all that is within me bless His holy Name. (Ps. 102.)

Bless the Lord, O my soul, and never forget all that He hath done for thee. (Ps. 102.)

What shall I render to the Lord, for all that He hath rendered to me? (Ps. 115.)

My soul doth magnify the Lord, and my spirit hath rejoiced in God, my Saviour. (Luke 1.)

For He that is mighty hath done great things to me; and holy is His name. (Luke 1.)

Blessed be the Lord, for He hath shown His wonderful mercy to me. (Ps. 30.)

Blessed be the Lord for evermore. So be it, so be it. (Psalm 88.)

or

My God, I give You thanks with all my heart for forgiving me my sins once more. Oh, keep me from sin in the time to come! Give me grace to hate mortal sin more than death itself, and to avoid all occasions that would lead me into it. Once more I repent of all the sins of my past life. I renew my promises made in Baptism. I beg Your blessing on my resolutions.

> O good Jesus hear me,
> Within Thy wounds hide me,
> Never let me be separated from Thee,
> In the hour of my death call me
> And bid me come to Thee,
> That with Thy saints I may praise Thee,
>   For all eternity.

You were told just now to leave your sins after confessing them; because anything forgotten was forgiven. Should anything grave have been forgotten and come to your mind later, you are not obliged to confess it before going to Holy Communion; mention it in your next confession.

Say your penance, if possible, before you leave the church. Say it humbly and gratefully. Though so short, it has more power of satisfaction than any other act of penance, because it acts sacramentally and has the merits of Christ's Precious Blood upon it. It therefore remits much of the punishment due to our sins, and *may* remit *all* if our dispositions and state before God permit it.

Think of what your confessor told you to do or to avoid. Should you have any restitution to make, whether of good name or anything else, see how soon you can do it.

Sursum Corda!

If you wish, you can make a visit to Our Lady's altar to offer your resolutions to her and give them into her keeping. And do not forget to ask your good angel's help too. Those resolutions interest him very much indeed.

Remember these two things about every confession of your life:

1. Never go in a hurry. Do not put off the preparation to the last moment, but see that you have sufficient time to prepare.

2. Never go into the confessional till your act of contrition is made. If you scramble over it, or make it a mere matter of routine, you will endanger the most important part of the sacrament and prepare for yourself great trouble of mind hereafter. Whatever else you forget when you come to our Lord's feet, whatever you risk, be sure to secure one thing—your act of sorrow.

Learn from your confessor how often you are to go to confession, and keep regularly to the appointed times. If you foresee you will be prevented from going on the usual day, go before rather than after. Never put off if you can possibly help it. The longer you defer, the more it will cost you to go. You will lose your peace, your strength, your joy in the service of God. Worst of all, you will accustom yourself to make light of the reproaches of conscience and to think little, first of small, then of great sins. In this way has begun the loss of multitudes of souls.

A SIMPLE CONFIRMATION BOOK

INTRODUCTION

In the years immediately following the success that convinced her (with the publication of *The Child of God* in 1899) to add her name to her published works, Mother Loyola seems to have been writing constantly, with one manuscript in process, another being looked over by her editor, Rev. Herbert Thurston, S.J., and yet another in the process of being printed. In fact, in a single letter to Father Thurston from June of 1900, she mentions the recently printed *Mass for First Communion*, the four books on Confession then in the works, the collecting of material for the future *Little Children's Prayer Book*, and German translations of the books *First Communion* and *Confession and Communion*—while just two weeks later she mentions printers proofs for *Coram Sanctissimo* and a recent review of *The Soldier of Christ*.

Yet amidst all this, without a single mention, she also managed to create more onepenny pamphlets for the Catholic Truth Society in the vein of her *Simple Confession Book*. The first of these, on Confirmation, is not a condensing of the material in *The Soldier of Christ*, but instead a brief look at the matter and form of the Sacrament, its purpose in the lives of the faithful, and a nine-day novena in preparation for the reception of Confirmation, involving the seven gifts of the Holy Spirit.

Contents

A Simple Confirmation Book

I.	A Parting Promise	117
II.	The Promise Kept	120
III.	The Comforter	122
IV.	The Sacrament of Confirmation	128
V.	The Seven Gifts	132
	1. The Gift of Wisdom	133
	2. The Gift of Understanding	134
	3. The Gift of Knowledge	135
	4. The Gift of Counsel	137
	5. The Gift of Fortitude	138
	6. The Gift of Piety	141
	7. The Gift of the Fear of the Lord	143
VI.	A New Friend	144
VII.	Come, Holy Spirit!	147
VIII.	Before Confirmation	148
IX.	The Rite of Confirmation	149
X.	After Confirmation	152
	Questions	155

A SIMPLE CONFIRMATION BOOK

I

A PARTING PROMISE

Had we stood on Mount Olivet with our Lord's disciples and watched Him ascend slowly till the cloud received Him out of our sight, we might surely have thought that His work for us was done.

He had taken our nature. He had lived a human life amongst us for three and thirty years. He had taught us with the words of His blessed lips. He had healed the diseases of soul and body of all who came to Him for cure. He had fed the famishing crowds that followed Him, and promised them a food for the soul which should preserve to eternal life those who should eat it. He had given His Mother to be the Mother of us all. He had founded His Church to carry on His teaching, to offer His unending Sacrifice, to feed, and heal, and guide, and comfort, and strengthen our souls in His name. He Himself was to remain in our midst to the end of the world, ready in every tabernacle to welcome and help all the heavy-laden who should come to Him. He was ascending now to the Father to prepare a place for us and to be forever

Sursum Corda!

our Advocate in heaven. What more could He do for us? What more could even His inventive love find to do?

Was there anything left to give us? Yes. He had a Gift not yet bestowed, a Gift that remained even after the Eucharist had given us the Body and Blood, the Soul and Divinity of the Eternal Son. It was the Third Divine Person, who proceeds from the Father and the Son. It was He who is called by excellence *the Gift of God*.

His disciples were filled with bitter sorrow when He gently broke to them at the Last Supper that He was going away. In vain He told them that it was expedient for them that He should go, that He would come again and take them to Himself, and that where He was going, they, too, should be. What were they to do in the meantime? Had He not said: "Without Me you can do nothing?" With Him to turn to in every trouble, to provide for them, to defend them against their enemies, they had known no fear. But what would become of them when He was gone?

Our Lord looked round with pity on His forlorn little flock. He knew they had left all they had in the world for His sake. He knew how they loved Him and leaned on Him, how terrible would be the void in their hearts when He was gone. His own heart was wrung with anguish at the parting. He said to them tenderly: "I will not leave you orphans. I will ask the Father, and He shall give you another Paraclete,"—that is, Comforter—"that He may abide with you forever." All in vain. They looked at Him piteously. They looked at one another. "What is this that He saith to us? We know not what He speaketh." They only knew that in losing Him they were losing all. Who could ever be to them what He had been! They did not understand the doctrine of the Blessed Trinity as clearly as we understand it, and they marvelled to hear their Master speak of One able and willing to take His place. They noticed that when He spoke of Him who was to come it was with the reverent love and awe with which He uttered His Father's Name. They felt His heart was full of this Holy Spirit to whose guidance He was leaving them. And it was the same after the Resurrection. "Receive ye the Holy Ghost" was the first glad greeting to them on Easter Day. Before ascending to His Father He gave them the charge: "Going, teach ye all nations, baptizing them in the name of the Father, and of the Son, and of the Holy Ghost." His last command to them was not to depart from Jerusalem but to wait for the promise of the Father, for "you shall be baptized with the Holy Ghost," He said, "not many days hence."

They did not understand His words, but they trusted Him. He knew all things. He was able to help them. At the Last Supper He had kept His promise to give them His body and blood for the food of their souls. They confided in Him for the fulfillment of this new promise, and waited in patience and in hope for Him who was to be sent.

II

THE PROMISE KEPT

The Apostles having seen their Master ascend into heaven, came slowly down the slope of Olivet and re-entered Jerusalem. They were full of joy because He had reached the end of His sufferings and was seated at the right hand of His Father, where no malice of His enemies could hurt Him. But when their thoughts turned from Him to themselves, could they rejoice? "Go ye into the whole world and preach the Gospel to every creature," were His parting words. How was this vast task to be accomplished? They could not even guess. All they knew was that some marvellous Presence was to come amongst them and make them ready for all things. This was enough to fill their hearts with joyful expectation. They went up into the chamber on Mount Sion and began to prepare for His coming. We are told expressly that our Lady was with them and that they prepared in her company. "All these continued with one accord in prayer, with the women, and Mary, the Mother of Jesus."

On the tenth day, about nine in the morning, "there came a sound from heaven as of a mighty wind coming, and it filled the whole house where they were sitting. And there appeared to them parted tongues as it were of fire, and it sat upon every one of them. And they were all filled with the Holy Ghost; and they began to speak with divers tongues according as the Holy Ghost gave them to speak." The

Comforter had come. Their patient prayer and perseverance were rewarded. The promise of their Master was fulfilled, their expectation satisfied beyond anything they could have hoped. For each one felt that a wonderful change had taken place within him. He was another man. The impatience, envy, ambition, selfishness in a thousand forms, with which he had been struggling, had suddenly given way, like a glacier that, coming in contact with a warm current in the sea, melts, falls, and disappears.

Think how surprised they must have been. They scarcely knew themselves. For not only had the bad disappeared, but the good in them was strengthened and perfected. James and John, whose hasty temper our Lord had had to reprove, whose desire to be first betrayed them into faults despite their good resolutions, found themselves changed. The ardor and their eagerness remained, but for their Master's service, not to feed selfishness. Peter, who was inclined to put himself forward and to trust to his own strength, was henceforth so humble that he took rebuke meekly even from his own subjects. And so with the rest. The Holy Ghost corrected what was faulty in each, strengthened what was weak, ripened and perfected all that was good. They had been very ignorant of divine things, notwithstanding the three years spent with our Lord, and all the instructions they had heard from His divine lips. They had shown themselves dull and forgetful, ready to promise but slow to perform, so afraid of suffering and persecution, that when our Lord came to them after the Resurrection He found

Sursum Corda!

the doors closed and barred "for fear of the Jews." All this was altered now. The Holy Ghost had filled them with courage. They went forth boldly to preach the Gospel to every creature, and when they were brought before rulers, and threatened and scourged, they went away rejoicing "that they were accounted worthy to suffer reproach for the name of Jesus."

Had not our Lord more than fulfilled His promise? How full of thankfulness they must have been! They understood now what our Lord meant when He said that it was expedient for them that He should go, for if He went not, the Paraclete would not come to them.

Holy Spirit, do for me what thou didst for the Twelve at Pentecost!

III

THE COMFORTER

Our Lord says that from the abundance of the heart the mouth speaks. No wonder, then, that the writings of the Apostles are full of the praises of the Holy Ghost, to whom they owed so much. No wonder that they were eager to pass on this gift to others by the Sacrament of Confirmation. When the people of Samaria had been converted by the preaching of St. Philip, St. Peter and St. John went to them and prayed for them that they might receive the Holy Ghost. "For he was not as yet come upon any of them.... Then they laid their hands upon them, and they received the Holy

Ghost." A fierce persecution was raging against the Church, and all converts had to be ready to lay down their lives for their faith. Therefore the Apostles made haste to strengthen the new Christians by giving them that Holy Spirit whose power they knew so well by their own experience.

Our Lord promised Him to all His followers. "We have the first fruits of the spirit," says St. Paul to his converts in Rome. The later fruits are for us, in proportion to our desires and preparation to receive them.

Think how well off we should be if this Divine Guest were to come to us with graces in any degree like those He gave to the Apostles. Not striking external gifts, such as speaking all languages, reading the secrets of hearts, prophecy, miracles. These were bestowed for the sake of others, and were necessary for their work of converting the world. What we want and ask are graces to work a change within our own hearts—the power to conquer ourselves; to bear bravely any pain, any loss, rather than offend God by sin; to love all men for His sake; to be kind, forgiving, patient, unselfish; the grace to persevere in prayer when it is hard and God does not seem to hear us; a love of our Lord so strong and generous that it leads us to imitate Him, and to give up our own will for His whenever He asks this of us.

O Holy Spirit, that Thou wouldst work a change like this in me!

The Holy Ghost is glad to come to us, but, like other guests, He expects to be invited. The more pressing our invitation, the more gladly He comes and the richer are the gifts He brings. The two disciples with whom our Lord walked to Emmaus on Easter Day would not let Him go when they reached the little inn at the end of their journey. "Stay with us," they-cried, as He took leave of them, pretending He was going further; "stay with us, for it is toward evening." And they constrained Him, St. Luke tells us. They would take no refusal. He was obliged to satisfy them, to go in with them, to become their guest. The Holy Ghost, too, loves to be constrained.

But you will say: "Of course the disciples were eager to keep our Lord, whom they knew and loved. We do not know the Holy Spirit like this. How, then, can we long for His coming?" There is some truth in this, and happily He knows it and makes allowance for us. But we can do something to help ourselves. We can bring our hearts to desire Him by considering the work He comes to do in us and for us. Let us try to understand it.

Those who have practised drawing from life or from plaster models know how the eye and hand have to be trained to study and to reproduce the objects set before them. A model is placed within the reach of us all, and life is given for this end alone—that we may copy it. It is a perfect model. It is our Blessed Lord, true God and true man. God has determined that all who enter heaven shall be like our Lord. He says to each one of us as we come to the use of reason: "See, child, look and do according to this pattern. Make yourself like Him. Correct what you find amiss in yourself. Copy into your heart what you find in His. Do not waste time. Work hard. I will help you, and you shall have your holiday bye-and-bye."

"Work hard," He says. Is it difficult, then, to imitate our Lord?

Had we no evil inclinations, no self-will which wants to go its own way whether right or wrong, this imitation would be very sweet and easy. But being what we are, we cannot make ourselves like Him without taking trouble and going against our own humors, inclinations, and passions. It is to help us in this struggle with self at the time when it is at once most important and most difficult, that the Holy Ghost comes to us in Confirmation.

How do we transfer to our paper the beautiful lines, the light and shade of the model we are copying? We look at it long and thoughtfully. We try to understand and appreciate it, and thus mind and heart guide the hand and teach it to reproduce what the eye sees. For a long time our attempts are clumsy, but perseverance is rewarded at last. By constantly comparing our work with our model, we see where we have failed. The eye becomes trained, the hand gains skill, and at length our work becomes, not creditable only, but delightful.

In much the same way we study our Blessed Lord. We know how He acted in circumstances somewhat similar to ours, or from our knowledge of Him we know how He would have acted had He been in our place. He has shown us how to behave as children, and when we are grown up; at home, amid daily duties and little trials; towards parents, equals, friends, enemies; how we are to pray, to overcome temptation, to suffer, and to die. We compare our thoughts with His, our words, our way of treating others, with His. Is our behavior at prayer an imitation of His reverence? Are

Sursum Corda!

we diligent at our work, patient when disappointed, humble and gentle when blamed, like Him? If we find that in any one of these points we are unlike our model, we must try quietly and patiently to correct what is faulty in our character or in our habits. Perhaps we are lazy in rising in the morning, lazy at prayer and at work. Or we are irritable, upset by every little trouble, unbearable to ourselves and to others when things fall out contrary to our desires. What we like is our sole concern;, the wishes and feelings of those around us are of no consequence. All this is very different from our model, and, you will say, very hopeless. Different, certainly. But hopeless, not at all. Let us try to see exactly where the difference lies; this will help us to the remedy.

If we examine these faults or any others, we shall find one root to them all: selfishness. It is this that makes us so unlike our Master. It was said of Him that "He pleased not Himself." Perhaps our study from morning till night is to please ourselves. Call to mind the faults found in your daily examination of conscience, those you take to confession every week or month, and see if there is one that does not come from selfishness. You do wrong because you will not give up some pleasure or bear some pain. You will not go against yourself. Self, then—that is, the wrong love of ourselves—is the enemy to our happiness in this world and the next. It is the enemy our Leader calls us to fight when He makes us His soldiers at Confirmation.

And because the struggle is hard, the Holy Spirit comes to help us. He is called the Comforter, which means the Strengthener. He comes to confirm—that is, to invigorate and brace us. He is the Almighty God; what enemy will be too strong for us? He is the Spirit of Jesus; what more do we need? If we have with us, have within us, the Spirit of Jesus, shall we not think and speak like Jesus, be gentle and kind like Jesus, brave and patient like Jesus, ready to deny ourselves, to think less of pleasing ourselves, more of pleasing others and of pleasing God, like Jesus!

We must not, then, be disheartened when we see how much there is to overcome. It is a great matter to see our foe. In these days of smokeless powder, the poor soldiers are shot before they know the enemy is near. The devil tries to hide our faults from us, to shut our eyes to what is plain to every one except our poor silly selves. But if we are honest and truthful enough to own to the ugliness and badness that is in our hearts, he suddenly changes his tactics. Not being able to deceive, he tries now to overthrow us by discouragement. "There is so much to mend," he says, "and the work will be so hard that you will never manage it, and will only lead a miserable life for nothing." If he cannot prevent us from putting our hand to the work, he pounces upon our failures. We shall fail, we shall break our resolutions hundreds of times. But what of that? Are we to believe him when he tells us our efforts are no use? Our faults are not worse because we see them better. On the contrary, to see them is a great grace and a sign of better things. Our Heavenly Father never discourages us. He is very gentle, very patient with us, even when we fail. We must be patient with ourselves. We must not expect to correct our faults all at once. Even if it is a life's work, it is the work for which life is given. We shall have all eternity for our holidays. And we must remember this. We cannot conquer one fault without conquering many, for, like virtues, they are closely linked; they come and go together. We overcome anger, let us say, by passing over unnoticed a provoking word. Here is an act of patience. But it is also an act of self-denial, of humility, of meekness and charity, of love of God for whose sake we kept back the angry word, and love of our neighbor, whom our impatience would have provoked. We shall get on fast, then, if only we make use of our daily opportunities. The quickest and easiest way to advance is to set our Lord before us and to imitate Him through love. To help us to bring out in our souls that likeness to Him which we must have to be admitted into heaven, the Holy Spirit comes to us in Confirmation.

IV

THE SACRAMENT OF CONFIRMATION

Confirmation is a Sacrament by which, through the imposition of the Bishop's hands, by anointing, and by prayer, those already baptized receive the Holy Ghost to enable them steadfastly to profess their faith and faithfully to live up to it.

From Scripture and from the teaching of the Church we know that Confirmation is one of the seven Sacraments. The time of its institution however, is not known. It was probably after our Lord's Resurrection. It is not, like Baptism, absolutely necessary for salvation. But all Catholics who have come to the use of reason ought to receive it if they have the opportunity, for without its strengthening grace it is all but impossible to overcome temptation and avoid mortal sin.

All baptized persons may receive the Sacrament validly—that is, may be actually confirmed. Until the twelfth century infants were confirmed after baptism. The present custom is to defer Confirmation to the age of discretion, that children may be better prepared. To receive the Sacrament worthily the state of grace is required. Anyone presenting himself knowingly in the state of mortal sin would forfeit the effects of the Sacrament till the sin was removed, and would commit a sacrilege. Those about to be confirmed must be sufficiently instructed in the truths necessary for salvation, and as to the nature of the Sacrament they are about to receive. When possible they should have a knowledge of the Christian doctrine as contained in the Catechism. It is not now necessary to receive Continuation fasting.

The *matter* of the Sacrament, holy chrism, is composed of oil of olives and balsam, a precious plant of Eastern lands. The chrism with which the Sacrament of Confirmation is administered is solemnly consecrated by the bishop on Maundy Thursday, and is used in the consecration of such things only as are in a particular manner set apart for the service of God. With this holy ointment are consecrated bishops, churches, altars, and chalices. Whatever is thus anointed is dedicated to God in such a way that it would be no less a crime than sacrilege to turn it to profane uses. The properties of chrism signify the effects of the Sacrament. Oil which is used for light, food, healing, consecration, and for giving strength and suppleness to the body, fitly represents the similar effects of the Holy Spirit on our souls. Balsam sends forth a sweet smell and preserves from corruption. It indicates the power of this Sacrament to preserve the soul from sin and to enable it by a good life to shed abroad the sweet fragrance of virtue.

The *form* of the Sacrament consists of the words: "I sign thee with the sign of the Cross, I confirm thee with the chrism of salvation, in the name of the Father, and of the Son, and of the Holy Ghost. Amen."

At the beginning of the rite the Bishop stretches his hands over those to be confirmed, praying the Holy Ghost to come down upon them with His seven Gifts. He then anoints each on the forehead in the form of a cross, saying: "I sign thee with the sign of the Cross," etc. This anointing on the forehead is to show that a Catholic must never be ashamed of his faith, but profess it boldly and openly, and live as a disciple of Christ crucified. The Bishop gives a little blow on the cheek, saying, *"Pax tecum,"* that is, "Peace be with thee." This is to remind the soldier of Christ that he must be ready to bear, not patiently only, but with cheerfulness and courage, the hard things that may come to him in the service of his Master, and that no injuries, persecution, or troubles of any kind should rob him of inward peace.

The rite of Confirmation is short, but the whole of it is of obligation. Those to be confirmed must be present for the general imposition of hands at the beginning, and must remain for the final blessing.

The Christian name and the name of the Patron Saint chosen at Confirmation should be clearly written and handed to the Bishop's assistant, as the person to be confirmed kneels to receive the Sacrament. No one must leave the altar or touch his forehead till the chrism has been wiped off by the assistant.

"Confirmation makes us strong and perfect Christians and soldiers of Jesus Christ."

The special grace given by the Sacrament is strength to believe firmly all the Church teaches, to profess our faith courageously, to lead a life worthy of it, and to suffer for it if needful.

This brave profession of our faith as soldiers of Christ is signified by the signing of the Cross on the forehead, the most open part of the countenance. The persecuted Catholics of England of days gone by had such trust in the grace of fortitude given by Confirmation, that when no Bishop remained in the land, and for forty years the Sacrament was not administered, they besought the Pope in touching words to remember their need and send them a Bishop, that they might not, by wanting this grace, be tried beyond their strength.

The Sacrament gives us a title to receive, as needs arise, all the actual graces we require. It also imparts a *character*, or spiritual mark, on the soul that can never be effaced, but will be for its glory or for its shame to all eternity.

Sponsors in Confirmation, like those in Baptism, undertake to see that the child is brought up in the Catholic faith and in the practice of its religion if the parents die or neglect this duty. One only is required, a godfather for boys, a godmother for girls. They must be different from the baptismal sponsors, must be Catholics, of good character, of age to fulfill their duties as sponsors, and must have been confirmed. They contract the same spiritual relationship and impediment to marriage as in baptism. At the Confirmation they lay their hand on the right shoulder of the person to be confirmed.

V

THE SEVEN GIFTS

We must now see the means by which the Holy Ghost brings out in our souls that likeness to our Lord in which holiness consists. Isaias the Prophet says of Christ: "The Spirit of the Lord shall rest upon Him, the Spirit of Wisdom and of Understanding, the Spirit of Counsel and of Fortitude, the Spirit of Knowledge and of Godliness. And He shall be filled with the Spirit of the Fear of the Lord." The same Spirit is coming to rest upon us that the members may be made like their Divine Head. These seven Gifts, so rich and grand that they were conferred on the sacred Soul of our Blessed Lord Himself, are to be bestowed also on us. They are given to every soul to which the Holy Ghost comes in Confirmation, in greater measures or less according to its dispositions. They help it in a marvellous way, making that easy and pleasant which seemed a hopeless task.

We were speaking just now of the long and laborious work of copying from a cast. But put the model before a camera and let the sun be the artist, and in an instant there is a perfect likeness. This may help us to understand what the Holy Spirit does in the soul by his seven Gifts and His twelve Fruits. He accomplishes quickly what we could never have achieved by our own toil. Yet notice. Though the sun does so much it does not do all. Its work has to be developed by our industry. So the Gifts and Fruits of the Holy Spirit bestowed on us in Confirmation do not dispense us from labor. But they make the labor lighter, pleasanter, and richer in its results.

Suppose we consider one of the Gifts on each of the nine days of preparation for our Confirmation, reading slowly and thoughtfully what we find about it, and earnestly praying the Holy Ghost to bestow this Gift in full measure on our soul. If we like we may say the *Veni Creator* or the *Veni Sancte Spiriitus* for this intention. We will take first the four Gifts that enlighten the mind, then the three that strengthen the will.

1. The Gift of Wisdom
(First Day)

The Gift of Wisdom teaches us to love God above all things; to value what He prizes; to hate what He hates. It leads us to think often of the life that is to come; to compare time with eternity, heaven with earth; to care little for joys that are passing away, or at least to care much more for those that will last forever. It makes us so prize our immortal soul, that not for the sake of any gain in this world, and not to escape any pain here, would we so much as think of risking our salvation by a mortal, or even by a deliberate venial sin.

This Gift of Wisdom gives us a relish of God and of heavenly things. It makes us love prayer, the lives of the Saints, the services of the Church. It was the Gift of Wisdom that made the martyrs suffer torments and death rather than commit a mortal sin. It leads hundreds in these days to give up home and the love of those who are dearest to them in order to follow God's call to the one true Church. By its help boys and girls who hate to be laughed at, brave the titter of Protestant acquaintances or of careless Catholics when they are seen keeping the abstinence of the Church on Fridays. It makes them careful of the books they read, of the companions they go with. "What is this for eternity?" they ask themselves. The answer decides their course.

> Holy Spirit, give me the Wisdom Thou hast given to the Saints. Let my chief desire be to know Thee, love Thee, and serve Thee in this world, and to be happy with Thee forever in the next; to lay up treasure for heaven, and so to use the good things of time as not to lose those of eternity.

2. The Gift of Understanding

(Second Day)

How hopeless work looks till we begin to see our way through it! The child's pitiful complaint when his sums come out wrong is that he does not understand what he is about. But a day comes when light breaks in upon the darkness. That is clear, interesting, and delightful which was so dull a while ago. Thus it is with the truths our faith teaches us. We may learn about them for years and yet be ignorant, as we may hunt long in the dark for a thing our hand has all but touched a score of times. The Gift of Understanding opens the eyes of our soul to these truths. Now we not only believe, we know, we appreciate them. They become realities to us. What a difference this will make to our prayers!

> I can never fully comprehend what my faith teaches me. But I can understand a great deal. Holy Spirit, make the truths I believe—the joys of heaven, the pains of hell, the presence of our Lord in the Blessed Sacrament—as real to me by the Gift of Understanding as if I had had a glimpse of these things. And teach me, Holy Spirit, how to pray.

3. The Gift of Knowledge
(Third Day)

The Gift of Knowledge is something like the Gift of Wisdom. The two together remind us of Jacob's ladder by which the Angels came down from God to earthly things and ascended from these things to God. By the Gift of Wisdom we start from God and come down to the things of this world, His light helping us to judge of them aright. By the Gift of Knowledge we use creatures as steps for mounting up to God. They show us His greatness, His beauty, His power, His love. Creatures are all the things we see around us, all things that happen to us and bring us joy or pain. All are meant to help us to God, to remind us of Him. They cry out to us like the policeman in the crowded thoroughfare. "Pass on, please;

pass on." The sun high in the heavens at mid-day, the lily of the valley that attracts you by its delicate beauty, the kind word that makes your heart glow with joy and gratitude, all cry out to you: "Pass on. Let me help you to know and praise Him who is all sweetness and loving-kindness. I am only a little thing, sent to speak to you of your God." The Saints let all these things and all events, sorrowful and joyful, lift them up to God. St. Paul of the Cross would gently tap the flowers with his stick as he walked through a country field. "Be quiet, be quiet," he said to the buttercups and the cowslips; "I understand; you need not speak so loud. You tell me to love my God. I do indeed love and praise Him who made you." And his eyes filled with happy tears.

You will say, perhaps, that the beautiful things in the world and the pleasant things that happen do lift up your heart to Cod in praise, but disagreeable things turn your heart away from Him? This must be because you have not yet received the Gift of Knowledge as God wants you to have it. His dear servants, Job, and Abraham, and St. Joseph, and our Lady, the martyrs, yes, and every one of the Saints, were raised to God by the things they did not like, by trials and losses, and the death of those they loved, by sharp pains of body and soul. Ask them all now, and they will tell you that these troubles were the steep steps that helped them up quickest to God and to their thrones in heaven.

> O Holy Spirit, I wish I could be like the saints in this. I wish I knew how to make pleasure and pain, everything that happens, all Thou dost send for my good, remind me of Thee. I should thank Thee then for the

things of life, which I often forget to do; and it would not be hard to bear the things I dislike if I could remember that they, too, come to me from Thee. Give me the Gift of Knowledge, and teach me to make everything a ladder by which I may climb up to Thee.

4. The Gift of Counsel

(Fourth Day)

The Holy Ghost tells us that a faithful friend is a strong defence, and he that hath found him hath found a treasure—that nothing can be compared to a faithful friend who will continue steadfast in the day of distress, and advise us wisely in our doubts that we may choose the best. All life long we are choosing. We have to take this step or that. A wrong choice may do us much harm. In some cases it may bring us misery in this world and in the next. We must not, then, act hurriedly, on the whim of the moment, without taking time to reflect, without asking advice. Whose advice will be always safe, always what is most for our good, will secure us against mistakes for which we should be grievously sorry later? What Friend can never lead us astray, because He can never be mistaken? Only our God. And see! Just as we reach the age when our choices are most important, He comes forward and offers Himself to be our Friend all through life, to bring us safely through all its dangers, to lead us along that path which is to bring us to a happy eternity. Can we thank Him enough for His goodness and His love?

Sursum Corda!

My God, I am young and very ignorant. I do not even know the dangers that surround me. My enmy, the devil, bad example, my evil inclinations, are cleer and cunning. They are sure to lead me wrong if I follow them. Holy Spirit, be my Guide. Before I act in any important matter make me pause to ask, not: *What do I want?* but: *What does God want of me here?* Would He like me to choose such a one for a friend? To make this promise? To go to this place of amusement? Would He tell me to speak to my father or mother or confessor about this? Shall I read this book of which I know nothing, but about which I have my doubts? Holy Spirit, counsel me always and I shall not go astray. Counsel me above all when the time comes for me to choose my path in life. "Make the way known to me wherein I should walk. Teach me to do Thy will, for Thou art my God."

5. The Gift of Fortitude

(Fifth Day)

The Gift of Fortitude is the special Gift of the soldier of Christ. What is he if he is not brave? Brave in the fight, brave in defeat, brave on the march. He is brave in the fight if he meets temptation promptly and vigorously, taking up at once the shield of prayer: "O Lord, make haste to help me!" and then without hesitation resists the attack; if he quietly but with determination puts away an evil thought, and again and again if it returns; if he goes against the inclination to be disobedient, impertinent, deceitful, to read a dangerous book or newspaper, to injure a neighbor by speaking ill of him.

If he has met with defeat, the true soldier does not waste time in discouragement, but quickly repairs his loss and resolves to do better another time. Do what we will, we shall fail a thousand times. But we must never be discouraged. "Try again," our Leader says to us. "I am at hand ready to help you." Of all good resolutions we can make none better than this: Whenever I fall into a fault, no matter what, I will make a good act of sorrow, and try again as if nothing had happened. Do this however often you fall, and you will be brave indeed.

The soldier is brave on the march if he bears patiently the little troubles every day brings—disagreeable work, weariness, bodily pain, disappointment, a word that hurts. Pain of some sort we must meet on every day's march. But there are different ways of meeting it. We may be impatient and grumble, and so increase our trouble here and our purgatory hereafter. Or we may take it submissively from the hand of our Heavenly Father, believing He will bring our greater good out of it, that by it we are to be made more like our Master and model, and deserve a place nearer to Him and a brighter crown for all eternity. We are not asked *to like* our troubles—our Lord Himself did not do that—but to take them as we take medicine, sensibly and bravely, knowing it will do us good.

Going against self is hard. There is no use pretending it is anything else. If anyone imagines it to be easy, it is because he knows nothing about it and has never put his hand to the work. Some of us seem to think we have nothing to do

Sursum Corda!

but to saunter along the road to heaven, and glide smoothly through the narrow gate into glory. We think all this talk about the enemies of the soul is a way of speaking that does not mean much, at least not to us. But life is not a sauntering or a gliding; it is a fight. Else why does the Holy Spirit speak of helmet, and shield, and breastplate for defence, of sword for the combat, of shoes for the weary march? We have to fight our way on, remembering that often enough the bravest part of fighting is bearing—bearing above all with ourselves.

We read of martyrs who were sewn up in a sack with a dog and a serpent and cast into the sea. It is a figure of our life-long martyrdom. Here we are, tossed about on the sea of this world with disagreeable companions that continually disturb our peace. Sometimes we feel within us the sting of envy. Sometimes we hear the sullen growl of anger or resentment. What can we do but, like the poor martyrs, have patience and bear our tormentors as well as we can—till the end!

> Give me, O Holy Spirit, Thy Gift of Fortitude. It is strength that I need. Often enough I know what I ought to do. But I am too weak to go against myself. Make me strong to resist temptation; to bear up against trouble; to have patience with myself when I break my resolutions. Help me to rise quickly and try again however often I fall. Give me strength to persevere like this to the end.

6. The Gift of Piety

(Sixth Day)

The Gift of Piety makes us love God because He is our Father. Our Lord taught us to think of God as the kindest and most loving of fathers, always watching over us to keep us from harm, providing us with all that is needful and good for us. If He does not give us all we should like to have now, it is not because He grudges us anything, but because many things would hurt, not help us. When we have prayed long and earnestly for a thing and it does not come, this is the reason. But He has promised that if He does not give us the very thing we ask, He will give us something better. And when He has us safe in heaven, where nothing can harm us, then He will give us the very things we want and the moment we want them. He will never for all eternity let anything come near us that would overcloud our happiness for an instant. Who would not love a Father so wise, so kind!

Children have a natural affection for their father. They get ready presents to please him. They long for the holidays that they may be with him. They feel safe when he is near. They cannot bear to hear a disrespectful word said of him, to see him hurt or sad. Am I like this? Do I ever do anything simple to please my Father who is in heaven? Do I long to be with Him there? Am I glad to speak to Him in prayer? Am I at least reverent in His presence? Do I talk to Him of my joys and my troubles? Do I run to Him when temptation comes? Am I pained when I hear of sins by which He has been offended and injured? Am I grieved for my own sins? Think of a child saying: "I would not give my father a mortal wound. I would not do anything for which he would turn me out of doors. But as for hurting his feelings, for distressing him in little things, I do not mind doing this." Do I ever seem to say this by my venial sins?

It was because the Saints had the Gift of Piety that they were able to pray so long and so fervently. It was a pleasure to them to speak with their Heavenly Father. It was this gift that gave them their filial confidence. Difficulties and troubles did not cast them down. They knew their Father was watching over them; that nothing could touch them except by His will; that He would comfort and help them in His own time. They trusted Him. Whatever He allowed to happen to them they were sure would turn out for the best. This was the secret of their peaceful hearts and their happy faces.

> Holy Spirit, fill my heart with tender childlike love for my Father who is in heaven. Make me dread above all other evils the loss of His friendship, and make me afraid of little sins that might lead to this loss. Let me be eager to please Him for the sake of reward. But much more because I love Him for Himself.

7. The Gift of the Fear of the Lord

(Seventh Day)

This fear is of two kinds. We may fear God on account of His dreadful punishments, and this is a great grace. In strong temptation the remembrance of these punishments is necessary to keep us from sin. If I have not this fear in my heart, I must ask for it. Without it I shall not be safe from mortal sin. But there is a better, filial fear which makes us afraid of all sin, of anything that would grieve the Holy Spirit and disappoint our Father who is in heaven. It is not so much the fear of harming ourselves, as of saddening Him whom we love. This fear makes us listen to the whispers of conscience, which check us when we are going to do wrong. It will make us remember that little sins lead to great sins, and that one great sin is enough to deprive us forever of our Father's face, to shut us out from His presence with whom we hope to pass our eternity.

We must not think that the first kind of fear is for those only who are God's enemies by mortal sin. It was to His dear Apostles our Lord said: "I say to my My friends: Fear Him who after He hath killed hath power to cast into hell. Yea, I say to you, fear Him." Of the four Last Things to be ever remembered by us all, three are meant to keep up this holy fear in our souls.

> Holy Spirit, give me the fear of God which all the Saints have had. Make me afraid above all things of grieving, of losing Him whom I love. Make me so live that I may be safe with the Saints on the last tremendous day.

Any one of these seven Gifts would make us rich. And the Holy Ghost is bringing them all. And as if these were not enough, He comes with twelve beautiful virtues called Fruits—sweet, pleasant, refreshing, grateful to the soul as the fruits of earth are to the body. Like the Gifts, they were poured out on the Soul of our Blessed Lord. Even to name them is to bring Him before us: Charity, Joy, Peace, Patience, Kindness, Goodness—what was He but all these, as He went about among friends and enemies, the sick, the suffering, poor sinners, little children. Think of the very same Fruits being brought to our souls by the Holy Spirit. Shall we not desire them, pray for them, open our hearts wide to make room for them? They will make us like our Lord and Master—"other Christs."

VI

A NEW FRIEND

(Eighth Day)

Our Lord says of those blessed servants whom at His coming He shall find watching, "Amen, I say to you, that He will gird Himself, and make them sit down to meat, and passing will minister to them." Like one waiting on honored guests, He will go round and serve them, giving them all the desires of their hearts. But He does not wait for that hour. From the moment we open our eyes in this world we find God ready to serve us, and pressing all He has into our service. God the Father, the Creator, the Preserver of all things, gives His creatures to us that they may supply our wants and gladden our hearts. It is His sun that lights up this beautiful world and keeps alive the plants and beasts that exist only for the service of man. It is His air we breathe, His fire that warms us, His earth that brings forth all we need for clothing and for food.

And if God thus serves us as to the body, much more is He at the service of the soul. The moment the waters of Baptism flow over our forehead, the Blessed Trinity comes into our soul to take up His abode there and provide for all its needs. Every morning, upon every altar where Mass is said, the Second Person of the Holy Trinity descends from heaven into the hands of the priest, to be given as the life and food of their souls to all who desire to receive Him. And at the age when the soul's dangers begin to be greatest, and its enemies have most hope of seeing it destroyed by mortal sin, the Third Divine Person comes with His Gifts and Fruits to strengthen it against all their wicked plots for its ruin. Is there anything more He could do for us, anything more we should like to ask for?

Something more He has thought of. It is true He, our Father and our God, is at our service. But we might like to have as helpmates others too, those who are nearer to us, His intelligent creatures as ourselves. His Blessed Mother He has made over to us. But there is still His Angels and Saints. Would it help us to have a servant out of their glorious ranks, over and above the patron we have at Baptism?

Sursum Corda!

Suppose He were to say to us: "Shall I give you an Angel or a Saint for your special guardian and friend in heaven?" we might be at a loss which to choose. An Angel might understand better the wiles of one who, like himself, is a spirit. It might be safer to choose him. But then a Saint, one who has had to struggle like ourselves against bad passions, and evil habits, and self-will, who has had his weakness, his discouragement, his weariness, his fears, his falls—does he not seem nearer to us than the bright spotless Angel? Would he not have more sympathy, perhaps, with one weak and changing as we are? "Lord," we say, "I do not know which to ask for: both seem best for me." And His answer is: "You shall have both, My child." He leads us up and down among the bright ranks of His Saints, and bids us take for our special patron and helper that one to whom we feel most attracted, either because his life, his character, or his circumstances, bear some resemblance to our own, and on this account we think he will serve us for a model, or because we have already experienced the effects of his patronage, and desire to knit ourselves in closer alliance with him. The Saints look lovingly upon us. Any one of them, however high in glory, will gladly begin a friendship with us. We ponder. We make our choice. We go away delighted, thinking what treasures we have got—an Angel for our guardian, a Saint for our particular friend. And from that hour—we scarcely give a thought to either! Are we not trying? Have not God and His Angels and Saints need to be patient with us?

The Saint of our choice looks upon us as his special charge, and is ready to prove himself a devoted friend. But friendship, we must remember, cannot be all on one side. If he protects us, intercedes for us, offers us the example of his life as an encouragement, we on our side should invoke him with confidence, study his life, try to imitate his virtues. Unless we do this, what will it avail us to add Joseph or Agnes to our name?

VII

COME, HOLY SPIRIT!

(Ninth Day)

Before receiving Confirmation we should cleanse our souls by a good Confession. The greater their purity the more willingly will He come to us who "feeds among the lilies."

The rest of our preparation may consist of invitation. Our Lady says in her canticle that God fills the hungry with good things. We must hunger if we are to receive in abundance His Gifts and His Fruits. Therefore we cannot better spend the last day of our novena than by opening our hearts wide to Him by loving desire. "Come, Holy Spirit, come!"

> O Blessed Lord, who didst promise to send down on Thine Apostles the Spirit of truth to teach them all truth, send Him also to me to teach me.
>
> Spirit of Jesus, purify my soul and prepare it for Thyself, that it may be filled with Thy Presence and be consecrated as Thy temple forever. Come, Holy Spirit, fill the hearts of Thy faithful. Come, fill my heart and kindle in it the fire of Thy love. Thou who at Pentecost didst change the Apostles into new men,

come and work a change in me. I am the child of God by Baptism; make me a brave soldier by Confirmation. So strengthen me with this power from on high that I may persevere until death in the practice of my faith, and show myself a true child of God and of Holy Church.

Holy Mary, Mother of God and my Mother, by the fervor with which thou didst prepare to receive the Holy Ghost at Pentecost, pray Him to prepare my heart for His coming now.

Holy Apostles, who received in abundance the Gifts and Fruits of the Holy Spirit, all you blessed Saints who have been sanctified by this same Spirit, obtain for me that my heart may be purified from its stains, and become a temple pleasing to Him who is coming to dwell therein.

VIII

BEFORE CONFIRMATION

Take care to be in the church in good time, and instead of looking about whilst you are waiting, say one of the hymns to the Holy Ghost, or the above prayer for the Seven Gifts, praying the Holy Spirit to bring these Gifts with Him into your soul.

When the Bishop stretches his hands over those to be confirmed, say:

Holy Spirit, be my Light, showing me what I ought to do; my Strength, helping me to do what I know to be right; my Physician, healing the wounds sin has made in my soul.

When you kneel before the Bishop, raise your head, cast down your eyes, and join your hands. Say with all the earnestness of your heart:

"Come, Holy Spirit!"

Take care not to touch your forehead till the chrism has been wiped off by the assistant.

IX

THE RITE OF CONFIRMATION

The Bishop, wearing over his rochet an amice, stole, and cope of a white color, and having a mitre on his head, proceeds to the faldstool, before the altar, and sits with his back to the altar, and his face towards the people, holding his pastoral staff in his left hand. He washes his hands, still sitting; then, being without his mitre, he rises, and, standing with his face towards the persons to be confirmed, who are kneeling before him, he says:

May the Holy Ghost come down upon you, and may the power of the Most High preserve you from sins.

R. Amen.

Then making the sign of the Cross, he says:

V. Our help is in the name of the Lord.

R. Who hath made heaven and earth.

V. O Lord, hear my prayer.

R. And let my cry come unto Thee.

V. The Lord be with you.

R. And with thy spirit.

Sursum Corda!

> *Then with his hands extended towards
> the persons to be confirmed, he says:*

Let us pray:

Almighty, everlasting God, who hast vouchsafed to regenerate these Thy servants by water and the Holy Ghost, and hast given unto them the remission of all their sins, send forth upon them Thy sevenfold Spirit, the Holy Paraclete, from heaven.

R. Amen.
V. The Spirit of Wisdom and of Understanding.
R. Amen.
V. The Spirit of Counsel and of Fortitude.
R. Amen.
V. The Spirit of Knowledge and of Godliness.
R. Amen.

Replenish them with the spirit of Thy fear, and sign them with the sign of the Cross ✠ of Christ, in Thy mercy, unto life eternal. Through the same Thy Son, Jesus Christ our Lord, who liveth the sacrament of confirmation and reigneth with Thee in the unity of the same Holy Spirit, God, world without end.

R. Amen.

> *The Bishop, sitting on the faldstool, or, if the number of persons to be confirmed requires it, standing, with his mitre on his head, confirms them, arranged in rows and kneeling in order. He enquires separately the name of each person to be confirmed, who is presented to him by the*

Godfather or Godmother. Having dipped the end of the thumb of his right hand in the holy chrism, he says:

N, I sign thee with the sign of the Cross ✠.

Whilst saying these words he makes the sign of the Cross with his thumb, on the forehead of the person to be confirmed, and then says:

And I confirm thee with the chrism of salvation. In the name of the Fa✠ther, and of the Son ✠, and of the Holy ✠ Ghost.

R. Amen.

Then he strikes him gently on the cheek, saying:

Peace be with thee.

When all have been confirmed, the Bishop washes his hands. In the meantime the following Antiphon is sung or said:

Confirm, O Lord, that which Thou hast wrought in us, from Thy holy temple which is in Jerusalem.

R. Glory be to the Father, etc.

Then the Antiphon, Confirm, *etc., is repeated, after which the Bishop, standing turned towards the altar, says:*

V. Show us Thy mercy, O Lord.

R. And grant us Thy salvation.

V. O Lord, hear my prayer.

R. And let my cry come unto Thee.

V. The Lord be with you.

R. And with thy spirit.

Then, with his hands joined before his breast, and all the persons confirmed devoutly kneeling, he says:

Sursum Corda!

Let us pray:

O God, who didst give to Thine Apostles the Holy Spirit, and didst ordain that by them and their successors He should be delivered to the rest of the faithful, look mercifully on the service of our humility; and grant that the hearts of those whose foreheads we have anointed with the sacred chrism, and signed with the sign of the holy Cross, may, by the same Holy Spirit descending upon them, and vouchsafing to dwell therein, be made the temples of His glory. Who with the Father and the same Holy Spirit, livest and reignest, God, world without end.

R. Amen.

Then he says:

Behold, thus shall every man be blessed that feareth the Lord.

*And, turning to the persons confirmed,
he makes over them the sign of the Cross, saying:*

May the Lord bless you out of Sion, that you may see the good things of Jerusalem all the days of your life, and have life everlasting.

R. Amen.

X

AFTER CONFIRMATION

Returning to your place, say:

Holy Spirit, Gift of the Most High God, I bow myself down before Thee. I adore Thee as well as I am able. I cannot understand what Thou hast done for me in giving me Thyself. I cannot thank Thee as I ought for this unspeakable Gift. Accept as my thanksgiving the praises of Angels and Saints, and above all the love and praise of most holy Mary. Thou hast given Thyself to me; I give myself to Thee with all the love I have. I offer Thee my mind, that Thou mayest enlighten it, my heart, that Thou mayest inflame it with Thy love. I offer myself to Thee body and soul with all I have and am. I give Thee thanks with all my heart for having come to me anad taken up Thy abode in my soul. Let me die rather than ever drive Thee hence by mortal sin. Glory be to the Father, and to the Son, and to the Holy Ghost, as it was in the beginning, is now, and ever shall be, world without end. Amen.

Forgive me, Holy Spirit, for having so often saddened Thee by refusing to listen to Thy voice. Help me to be more docile and more faithful now. Spirit of Jesus, make me a perfect Christian and a true soldier of Christ. Give me strength to confess my faith, if need be at the peril of my life. Let me never be ashamed of the Cross of Christ, with which I have been signed and sealed. Let me show myself His true soldier. I shall have to fight against myself, to conquer my bad habits. My enemies are powerful, and I am very weak. But I can do all things in Him who strengthens me. I will fear no evil if Thou, my God, art with me. I will trust in the Sacrament of Strength which I have received. I know that Thou art faithful, that I shall never be tried above that which I am able. I know that laid up for me in this Sacrament is every help I shall need, grace to overcome every temptation however strong that, without fault of mine, will come in my way, grace to persevere to the end.

Sursum Corda!

✠ Remember that perseverance does not mean never falling, but rising promptly after every fall and, without discouragement, going on.

✠ Remember that temptations, trials, hardships of many kinds, must come. The little blow on the cheek which has meant so much to many will mean something to you. You have not come into Christ's army to suffer nothing, but as a brave soldier to follow your Leader through pain and conflict, to victory and glory. You must not be beaten back by difficulties, nor turned aside by dangerous pleasures.

✠ Remember that by your Confirmation you are entitled to receive every grace you need, at the hour you need it. Trust, then, and fear nothing. When tempted, listen to your Good Angel or your Patron Saint whispering to you: "Grieve not the Holy Spirit of God whereby you are sealed."

✠ Remember that the character which now marks you as a soldier of Christ, will be your glory or your shame to all eternity.

✠ Remember to say each day a short prayer to your Angel Guardian and Patron Saint, even if it be only "My good Angel and holy Patron, pray for me and watch over me today."

One of our Bishops always recommends those he is about to confirm to make three resolutions on the day of their Confirmation:

(1) Never to miss Mass on Sunday.

(2) Never to neglect the abstinence on Friday.

(3) Never to omit morning and night prayer, however short.

Striking examples of fidelity in the service of God in face of great difficulties have proved the value of this counsel, and he is accustomed to say he will answer for the perseverance of all who are faithful to it.

QUESTIONS

I. A Parting Promise *(pp. 117-119)*

1. Why were the Apostles in such bitter grief when our Lord told them He must go away?
2. What did He say to comfort them?

II. The Promise Kept *(pp. 120-122)*

1. What mixed feelings filled their hearts as they came down from Olivet?
2. On reaching Jerusalem, what did they do?
3. Who were together in the upper chamber, and how did they spend their time in preparation?
4. On the morning of the tenth day what happened?
5. What change did the Holy Spirit work in the hearts of the Apostles?

III. The Comforter *(pp. 122-128)*

1. Is there any mention in the Bible of Confirmation having been given to the first Christians?
2. Why were the Apostles so anxious to confirm their converts?
3. What wonderful external gifts came to the Apostles with the Holy Ghost?
4. For whose sake are such external gifts bestowed?

5. What are the internal gifts we want and ask?
6. If the Holy Ghost desires so much to come to us, why are we told to invite Him earnestly?
7. How can we bring ourselves to desire Him earnestly so as to be pressing in our invitations?
8. What makes our life's task of imitating our Lord a difficult one?
9. Why is it just at this time in our lives that the Holy Ghost comes to us in Confirmation?
10. Show how the study of our Lord is like the study of of a model we are copying with our pencil or our brush.
11. What does the word "Comforter" mean? Why is the Holy Ghost called by this name?
12. Is it a bad sign to see our faults? If not, why not?
13. If the devil cannot hide them from us, what use does he try to make of them?
14. Why must we never be discouraged when we commit faults?
15. What thoughts will encourage us in the work of correcting them?
16. What is the quickest and easiest way to correct them?

IV. The Sacrament of Confirmation *(pp. 128-132)*

1. What is Confirmation?
2. How do we know Confirmation to be one of the Seven Sacraments?
3. When was it instituted?
4. Is it necessary for salvation?
5. What is necessary to receive the Sacrament *validly* and *worthily?*
6. At what age used Christians to be confirmed?
7. What is the present custom to defer its administration till later?
8. What instruction is necessary?
9. Must this Sacrament be received fasting?
10. What would happen should a person present himself to receive Confirmation knowing himself to be in a state of mortal sin?

11. Three things are necessary to make a sacrament:
    (1) The Outward Sign, i.e., Matter and Form;
    (2) The Inward Grace;
    (3) The Institution of Christ.
    What is the *Matter* in Confirmation?
12. What is Chrism?
13. How do the properties of Chrism signify the effects of the Sacrament?
14. What is the Form of the Sacrament?
15. What does the Bishop do at the beginning of the rite?
16. What does the anointing on the forehead signify?
17. And the little blow on the cheek?
18. The rite of Confirmation is short, but the whole is of obligation—what does this mean?
19. What do we hand to the Bishop's assistant as we kneel to receive the Sacrament?
20. And what must we be careful about as regards the Holy Chrism?
21. What is the *effect*, that is, the special grace of this Sacrament?
22. What part of the rite signifies the brave profession of our faith?
23. How did our persecuted Catholic forefathers show their trust in the grace of Confirmation?
24. The Sacrament gives a title to the actual graces we shall require—what does this mean?
25. What duties do sponsors in Confirmation undertake?
26. What is required as to these sponsors? What spiritual relationship and impediment to marriage do they contract?

V. The Seven Gifts *(pp. 132-144)*

1. How does the Holy Spirit bring out in our souls that likeness to Christ in which holiness consists?
2. Are His Seven Gifts given in the same measure to all?
3. What do these grand Gifts do for us?
4. Do they do all, leave nothing to be done on our part?

Sursum Corda!

NOVENA OF PREPARATION
1. THE GIFT OF WISDOM
(First Day)
1. What does this Gift make us prize, and hate, and relish?
2. What did it make the Martyrs do?
3. What is it leading hundreds in these days to do?
4. What kind of things will it make children careful about?

2. THE GIFT OF UNDERSTANDING
(Second Day)
1. What will the Gift of Understanding do for us?
2. How will it make Prayer easier for us?
3. Tell us some of the truths of faith that it will help to make real to us?

3. THE GIFT OF KNOWLEDGE
(Third Day)
1. How is this Gift like, and unlike, the Gift of Wisdom?
2. How do beautiful and pleasant things help us to lift our minds to God?
3. And how do disagreeable things help?

4. THE GIFT OF COUNSEL
(Fourth Day)
1. What does the Gift of Counsel do for us?
2. Why do we need this Gift very much just at this time of our lives?
3. What are some of the questions it will make me ask myself?

5. THE GIFT OF FORTITUDE
(Fifth Day)
1. In what three ways must the soldier of Christ show himself brave?
2. What is it to be brave in the fight?
3. And to be brave in defeat?
4. And brave on the march?

5. Why is it a good thing to find going against self hard, and a bad thing to suppose it is easy?
6. Is there any bravery in bearing with ourselves? Why?
7. Why are some of us like the martyrs who were sewn up in a sack with a dog and a serpent?

6. The Gift of Piety
(Sixth Day)
1. What does this Gift make us do?
2. Find five ways in which our Heavenly Father shows Himself the most loving of Fathers.
3. Find five or six ways in which we should show ourselves His loving, obedient children.
4. How was it the Saints were able to pray so long and so fervently?
5. Why had they such peaceful hearts and such happy faces?

7. The Gift of the Fear of the Lord
(Seventh Day)
1. How many kinds of the fear of the Lord are there?
2. Is the first kind good, and even necessary? Why?
3. Suppose we have not got it, what must we do?
4. Why must we never think that this kind of fear is for those only who are the enemies of God by mortal sin?
5. Why is the second kind of fear better?

VI. A New Friend *(pp. 144-147)*
(Eighth Day)
1. Why does God give us in Confirmation a Saint for our special Patron and Friend?
2. Which of all His glorious servants are we going to choose for our special Patron? And why?
3. What will the Saint of our choice be ready to do for us?
4. And what are we to do in return?

Sursum Corda!

VII. Come, Holy Spirit! *(pp. 147-148)*
(Ninth Day)

1. Before Confirmation we have to cleanse our soul by a good Confession. What are the four things we have to do to prepare for Confession?
2. Is examination of conscience the chief part of our preparation? If not, why not?
3. Why is contrition so important?
4. How are we to get contrition?
5. Is it enough to ask for it?
6. Show from the words of the Catechism that we have to take some pains to secure it.
7. What is meant by "motives" for contrition?
8. Will any kind of motive do; for example, that we have lost some pleasure, or deserved some disgrace or pain?
9. Suppose the pleasure were Heaven, and the disgrace or pain Hell or Purgatory, would this motive do?
10. Which are the chief motives for contrition? What is the best?
11. What is perfect contrition? What does it do for us?
12. Is it necessary to have perfect contrition when we go to Confession?
13. Is it ever necessary; that is, would a person's salvation ever depend on a real act of perfect contrition?
14. In a railway accident or fire, would an act of perfect contrition be likely to come readily to one who had no habit of making such acts?
15. What, then would be a wise resolution to make?
16. There are two times when it is well always to accustom ourselves to make a good act of perfect contrition; what times do you think?
17. Make an act of perfect contrition now.
18. Make an act of contrition with the sufferings of our Blessed Lord as the motive, with the thought of Purgatory.
19. Can we make a hearty act of sorrow if we do not *feel* very sorry?
20. Why should we often invite the Holy Spirit on the eve of our Confirmation?

VIII. and IX. Before Confirmation *(pp. 148-152)*

1. How should we spend our time in church whilst we are waiting for the Bishop?
2. How are we to kneel before him and what prayer should be in our heart?
3. What must we have ready for the Bishop's assistant?
4. And what must we take care not to do till the assistant has wiped off the Holy Chrism?

X. After Confirmation *(pp. 152-155)*

1. What five things should those remember who have been confirmed?
2. What three resolutions does one of our Bishops strongly recommend to be made on the day of Confirmation?

A SIMPLE COMMUNION BOOK

INTRODUCTION

There exist now no details of the history behind the writing of *A Simple Communion Book*. These onepenny pamphlets printed by the Catholic Truth Society often did not include any copyright notice, so our best clue as to when it was first produced comes from a comprehensive list of Mother Mary Loyola's works in the brief biography published in *The Mariale* (mentioned earlier in this volume, in the introduction to *How to Help the Sick and Dying*). This list places *A Simple Communion Book* in 1903, nestled between *Hail! Full of Grace* in 1902 and *Welcome! Holy Communion Before and After* in 1904.

Could its loose resemblance to the latter of the two give us a small clue? Could it be that she set out to write another little manual, this time on the Sacrament of the Altar, to match the *Simple Confession* and *Simple Confirmation Books*...and then decided to expand greatly on that material to make a full-sized volume? Or perhaps the larger of the two was written first, while this briefer derivative, being smaller and easier to produce, went to print first?

Whichever version she penned first, there certainly are marked similarities between the meditations for before and after Communion in this little book, and those in *Welcome*—and yet the two are not so much alike as the different iterations of her books on Confession. Thus this pocket gem serves to augment the sum total of her work, rather than being simply a repackaging, in smaller format, of an identical text.

CONTENTS

Come to Me, All!

I. Jesus, Our Physician	175
Before Communion	175
After Communion	180
Prayer Before a Crucifix	185
II. Jesus, The Bread of Life	186
Before Communion	186
After Communion	193
III. Jesus, Our Friend	195
Before Communion	195
After Communion	199
IV. My Only One	200
Before Communion	200
After Communion	203

A SIMPLE COMMUNION BOOK
COME TO ME, ALL!

"Come to Me, all you who labour and are heavy burdened, and I will refresh you!"

Who amongst us does not labour? Who is without a burden? Therefore our Lord's invitation is to every one of us: "Come to Me, all."

We might have thought that those who believe in His real Presence amongst us would not need invitation. Without being invited, the crowds pressed upon Him during His life on earth. The lame struggled to His feet; the blind lifted to Him their sightless eyes; the lepers and the fever-stricken waited eagerly His healing touch. "Great multitudes stood about Him so that they trod one upon another." "There was no room; no, not even at the door." It is true these needy ones knew Him and saw Him, heard the sound of His voice, felt the attraction of His Presence and the touch of His hand, went away with the signs of His power upon them. It is not so with us. We have only faith to trust to, and it cannot be expected, some will say, that without seeing, hearing, or feeling, we shall show the eagerness of the Jewish crowds.

Sursum Corda!

Perhaps not. Yet the very loss of what we miss so much is meant by our Lord to turn to our good. He has rich blessings in store for those who believe. After Thomas had seen the wounds in hands and feet and side, after he had heard the tones of the voice he knew so well, after he had learned by experience that his thoughts were known to Him who stood before him, he cast himself in ecstasy at those sacred feet and cried: "My Lord and my God!" How did our Lord receive this act of faith? With the gentle reproof: "Because thou hast seen Me, Thomas, thou hast believed: blessed are they that have not seen and have believed."

"Seeing is believing," we say. But incorrectly, for seeing is not believing. The merit of faith is to hold, on the word of God, what as yet we do not see. He prizes so much this trust in His word, that He has promised to reward it hereafter with the unveiled sight for ever of the beauty and the glory which are hidden from us now.

Meantime, we have all that is good for us in His sacred Presence. Like the people of Judea and Galilee we may come to Him and lay open to Him all our needs. If He does not now cure the sickness of the body, it is because this is not the work for which He came into this world, for which He is in the tabernacle and comes into our hearts. He has something more important to do. There are wounds worse by far than the sores of lepers: the wounds of sin. There is the blindness which makes us unable to see the needs of our soul. There is the fever of rebellion or impatience when things fall out contrary to our desires.

There is the deafness which prevents us from hearing the voice of God in our conscience—warning, reproving, inviting us. There is the dumbness which hinders us from telling our sins in confession or speaking to God in prayer. All these maladies our Lord is on the altar to heal. His great desire is to bring His healing touch within our reach. We notice in the Gospels that He used to lay His hands on those who came to Him for cure. He willed that, as for us men He took flesh and dwelt amongst us, His sacred flesh should be the means of bringing us all spiritual life and strength.

Therefore He invites us to Him: "Come to Me, all! Come, that I may lay My hands on your wounds. However inflamed, however longstanding they may be, My touch shall heal them, if not at once, yet surely at last."

Why do we not listen to Him and go to Him? Chiefly for two reasons. We who are so much alive to anything that is amiss with our poor bodies, take little heed to the state of our souls. Some of us live almost as if we had no souls— as if all our thought, labour, and anxiety were to be spent in procuring comforts for the body. Our soul is perishing for want of proper care. It needs food, medicine, warmth, shelter—and we turn a deaf ear to its cry. We have too much to do to think of the one thing necessary. We say our daily work requires all our attention, and we have no time for long prayers. Meanwhile life is going fast; the sands are running out. Soon—sooner maybe than we think—the life that was lent us will be called for again. Whilst we are thinking only of bettering our position here, of providing the body with conveniences and pleasure in the present, and ease for days to come, a voice perhaps is saying: "Thou fool, this night do they require thy soul of thee, and whose shall those things be which thou hast provided?"

Our Lord's earnest counsel to us is: "Be ready. Watch! For at what hour you think not, the Son of Man will come." He bids us work out our salvation whilst we have time, in the day of this life: "the night cometh in which no man can work." He knows quite well that the needs of the body have to be cared for; that our families have to be provided for; that our duties to our fellow-men must not be neglected. He is willing to allow that we have not much time to give to the affairs of our souls, if by this we mean long prayers on our knees. And it is just for this reason that He invites us to come to Him in Holy Communion. We know what a help it is, when our hands are full of work, to be able to make over some of it to a trusty friend, to say: "Look to that for me," and to feel that in the safe keeping of one who cares for our interests as if they were his own, all will go well—better than if we had seen to it ourselves.

Our dear Lord wants to be this friend. "Trust your affairs to Me," He says, "I will see to them. Let Me come to you and help you. Let Me hear about your troubles, and anxieties, and plans. I will advise you and make things turn out for your good. And let Me hear about those affairs of your soul in which you are less interested and less expert, but which for all that are the chief business of life. I know exactly how they stand, what is wanting, where danger threatens. I know when you will be called to your account.

"You will come to Me then and I shall have to be Judge. All the good and all the bad will be brought to me for judgement, and there will be no time to amend then. Time, opportunity, grace—there will be no more of these for you. No sorrow for the past will bring it back or blot out the harm it has done. As I find you I shall judge you. Make use of Me now whilst I am with you as your Friend. Invite Me often to come to you. Put your soul and all that concerns it into My hands. I will keep it safe. Have Me often as your Guest during life, and when death opens to you the gates of eternity you shall be My guest for ever and ever."

One reason why we do not listen to our Lord's invitation we have seen. It is because we are indifferent—that is, stupidly careless in the affairs of our soul. Because we cannot see it, we forget it, and let the poor miserable body that is going fast to corruption take up all our thoughts.

But with some of us there is another reason. It is not thoughtlessness that keeps us from Him, but fear. We are afraid of Him in the Sacrament of His love. We know that He who is there is truly God. We know we could never be worthy to receive Him even once. And so we think it safer to keep at a distance, to make our Communions few and far between. We are afraid to accept His invitation: "Come to Me, all." But not afraid to be like those for whom a great supper was prepared and who refused to go, saying: "I pray thee hold me excused." Not afraid of being, like them, rejected by Him who calls us: "I say unto you that none of those men that were invited shall taste of my supper."

Our Lord has done all He can to take away this unreasonable fear from our hearts. When He came to His disciples on the stormy sea or in the upper room on the night of the Resurrection, His first care was to see that they were not afraid of Him: "Be of good heart; it is I, fear ye not." "Peace be to you; it is I, fear not."

So He says to us now: "It is I, be not afraid." He wants to see us often at His table. In the early days of the Church it was customary for all His followers to communicate daily. To hear Mass and to receive Him at the close meant one and the same thing. But by degrees the first fervour cooled, and at length men became so ungrateful for this Bread of life, so cruel to their own souls, that to prevent these being starved outright the Church had to command them, under the severest penalty, to receive It at least once a year.

But her wish, now as in the early days of Christianity, is that her children should communicate frequently—daily if possible. Dangers are not less than they were. We do not indeed hold our lives in our hands like the first Christians and our persecuted Catholic forefathers in this land, who never knew, as they rose from the altar rails, whether they had received their Lord for the last time and would need His help to carry them safely through torture and death. Our foes are more hidden, and for that very reason perhaps more to be feared. Catholics are not openly persecuted for their faith, but they are tempted to be ashamed of it; to go with the stream; to forget the next world that they may get on in this; to live as if this life were to last for ever; or as if Death, Judgement, Hell, Heaven, in no way concerned them.

Our Lord knows all the dangers that beset us. He knows what will bring us safely through them. It was His frequent Sacramental Presence that guarded and strengthened His servants in the past; the same blessed Presence must protect us. Hence He has made it so easy for us to receive Him in Holy Communion. Provided we are not actually His enemies by mortal sin, we may go to Him and be sure of a welcome. The first Christians had, like us, their homes to attend to, and their daily toil. They were not all saints by any means. But they remembered our Lord's tender words: "They that are whole need not the physician, but they that are sick." They listened to His invitation: "Come to Me, all." They noticed that it is just the heavy-burdened and the toilers that He calls. And so they went to Him with their burdens—husbands and wives, labourers, servants, tillers of the soil, and workers in busy cities; went each day for the needs of each day. They received daily the daily Bread that would support and cheer them, and hallow all their toil and all their pain. Why should not we be like them?

Seeing that our Lord requires so little of us, and for that little makes us so rich a return; that He invites us so lovingly to His table, and makes us so welcome there; that our need of Him is so great, and that left to ourselves we are so weak—how is it that we stay away from Him as we

Sursum Corda!

do? What if we were to make a change; to listen to His invitation at last; to find room for Him in our hearts a little oftener! Life would be easier, happier, holier; Death safer; Heaven gladder for all eternity.

Our chief concern in preparing for Holy Communion should be to increase our faith. If our faith is firm and lively, all good dispositions will flow from it. The fervour and fruit of every Communion depends on our faith. For this reason a consideration on an event of our Lord's life is given in each of the preparations for Holy Communion in this little book. We must strive to bring home to ourselves that the very same tender Lord who invited Himself to the house of Zaccheus, who called Himself the Bread of life, who was the welcome Guest of Martha and Mary, is coming to us—just the same as He was then, wanting to be our Physician, our Food, our Friend, all He was to those who loved Him and received Him long ago.

If you read the Gospel story thoughtfully, and put yourself in the place of those who entertained our Lord during His life on earth, your heart will speak to Him freely and naturally as you go along. He will like this better than a set form of prayer. When your head is tired or your heart is dry, you can use the prayers you find here. But whenever you can speak easily to our Lord in your own words, stop reading and talk to Him as friend to Friend.

It is well to have a special intention in each Communion, as to get some grace for yourself or another, or some temporal favour if it be God's will. Commend this need to our Lord when you have Him in your heart. Make the intention, too, to gain what Indulgences you can. By saying the Prayer before a Crucifix, p. xx, with five times the Our Father and the Hail Mary for the Pope and the Church, you may gain a Plenary Indulgence each time you go to Communion. Sometimes, perhaps often, you will offer Indulgences for the poor souls in Purgatory always suffering, always looking for the help of our prayers.

I

JESUS OUR PHYSICIAN

Before Communion

As our Lord walked one day through Jericho, surrounded as usual by a crowd, a man named Zaccheus sought to see Him. This man was chief of the publicans, or tax-gatherers, a class of men hated and despised by the Jews by reason of their employment and for the injustice on which they grew rich. Zaccheus was short of stature, and the people so hemmed in the young Prophet of Nazareth that he could not get a glimpse of Him. Running on, therefore, before, he climbed into a sycamore tree that he might see Him as He passed. No thought of demeaning himself, no fear of ridicule; at any cost he must see Jesus. Our Lord drew nearer and nearer. There He is—and oh! worth waiting for, worth paying any price to see. Now He is beneath the tree. He is passing. But no. Suddenly he stops as if by appointment, looks up, and says: "Zaccheus, make haste and come down, for this day I must abide in thy house." Scarcely believing his good fortune, Zaccheus came down, hastened home, and "received Him with joy."

"And when all saw it, they murmured, saying that He was gone to be a guest with a man that was a sinner." Is not this strange? We know nothing of the previous life of Zaccheus, but even supposing him to have deserved this reproach, what cause was there for complaint? Because the Saviour was seeking a sinner, the Physician was visiting His patient, the Guest was going where He was desired?

See the fruit of that one reception of Christ. Zaccheus, standing, said to the Lord: "Behold, Lord, the half of my goods I give to the poor, and if I have wronged any man of anything, I restore him fourfold." Here was correspondence with grace. After the glad welcome, the thanksgiving and love such condescension called for, came a generous resolution. He must have been a single-hearted man in spite of his position and his wealth. Human respect could not prevent him from climbing into the sycamore; it did not check him now in an act of self-humiliation. He did not seek to justify himself when, all around, he heard himself called a sinner. But he turned to his Divine Guest, to Him whom men called the Friend of sinners, and showed Him His merciful visit had not been in vain.

It was then our Lord turned lovingly to him and said: "This day is salvation come to this house." We must correspond with His grace. We must listen to what He whispers when He comes, and carry out what He wants of us. We lay our dangerous symptoms before a doctor. He listens, he considers. Then the injunction comes: "You must give up this amusement. You must put yourself on this diet. That place is unhealthy, you must leave it." If we have faith in our adviser, we act on his counsel. The sick of our Lord's time carried out His prescriptions promptly, to the letter, even when He ordered what was unaccountable to them. "Go, wash in the pool of Siloe.... Go, show yourselves to the priests." "He went, therefore, and washed, and came seeing.... And as they went they were made clean."

Our spiritual cure will probably not be immediate. But this must not discourage us. The effect of our Lord's healing touch on the body was not instantaneous always. Laying his hands on the eyes of a blind man, "He asked him if he saw anything. And looking up, he said: I see men as it were trees walking. After that again He laid His hands upon his eyes and he began to see, and was restored, so that he saw all things clearly." Our Lord could work a sudden cure in our souls and set them free at once from every disease and every infirmity. But He sees that it is better for us to come to Him again and again that He may work a gradual cure. Often it is so gradual as to be almost imperceptible to ourselves. Yet, looking back—say, over a year—we find there has been a change. We see more clearly; we fall less frequently and less heavily; we rise more quickly. If you are able humbly to admit this improvement, "give thanks," says St. Bernard, "to the Body of the Lord, for Its virtue worketh in you."

Sursum Corda!

Sinners were not afraid of our Blessed Lord. They invited Him to their houses and were quite at home with Him. How could they be afraid? Was it not plain to all that He liked to have them about Him? Were not His tenderest words for them? "The Son of Man is come to seek and to save that which was lost," He said when all murmured that He was gone to be a guest with a man that was a sinner. Another publican He called to be His familiar friend and Apostle. "And it came to pass that as He sat at meat in the house of Matthew, many publicans and sinners sat down together with Jesus and His disciples. And the Scribes and Pharisees said to his disciples: Why doth your Master eat and drink with publicans and sinners? Jesus, hearing this, said: They that are in health need not a physician, but they that are ill.... I am not come to call the just, but sinners."

These are my examples and my encouragement in drawing near to Thee, O tender-hearted Lord. Thou wert easy of access to all, but most of all to sinners. The most degraded, the most despised met with no condemnation, no rebuke from Thee, but only: "Thy faith hath made thee safe, go in peace." "Go, and now sin no more." It was for the sinners of all time these words of mercy were spoken. All are welcome who turn to Thee in their humiliation and distress. For all without exception is the promise: "Him that cometh to Me I will in no wise cast out."

I come to Thee, O Saviour, Physician, Friend. I come to Thee who alone canst heal and comfort me. Like Zaccheus and Matthew I will receive Thee into my house, and receive Thee with joy. Thou art come not to call the just but sinners. They that are well need not the Physician, but they that are sick. I need Thee, then. I come to Thee, O Lord.

I believe, O Lord Jesus, in Thy Real Presence here for me. I believe in Thy love of me, in Thy desire to be with me, to help, console, and strengthen me. I believe that by the virtue of the Sacrament itself, by the very fact of Thy visit, I shall be made more pleasing to Thee, more fit for Thy company in heaven. And though I desire to do what lies in me to profit by Thy coming, yet I will take comfort in the thought that it is not my preparation or thanksgiving, but Thy blessed Presence itself, that works a change in my heart.

And believing this, how can I help hoping in Thee, O dearest Lord? Why hast Thou made it so easy to come to Thee, if not to take away all pretext for staying away out of fear, and to fill our hearts with joyful trust that Thou wilt do great things for us at Thy coming? In spite of all Thou hast done for us, of the miracles Thou dost work daily in order to come into our midst, of Thy sweet invitations and promises, how few there are who satisfy Thy love by coming to receive Thee. Wilt Thou not welcome those few, be pleased to see them, make much of them, fold them to Thy Heart, and send them away refreshed and comforted?

But, after all, I come to Thee, dear Lord, not so much for what Thou givest as for what Thou art. I come out of love, to satisfy Thy love, O Loving One, and to increase my love by uniting it with Thine, as if the flame of a rushlight should unite itself with a vast fire and be lost in it, and shine with its brightness, and consume with its ardour, and inflame with its heat. Take my desires to love and thank and praise Thee, not for what they are, but for what I wish them to be. Thou hast promised to measure our desires by our goodwill, not by the frailty of our poor distracted hearts. Whatever displeases Thee in my soul, whatever hinders Thy work therein, I am sorry for. Whatever would make me pleasing to Thee, I desire and crave for. Accept as mine what by the Communion of Saints is mine—all the fervent devotion of Thy Saints in approaching Thee in this Sacrament, all their devotedness in Thy service, all the heroism of their sacrifices, all their fidelity in the duties and trials of daily life, all their zeal for Thy honour and for the salvation of souls, all their union with Thee in prayer, all their disinterested love of Thee. I offer Thee all the joy Thou hast ever had and wilt ever have in the souls that love Thee, Thy joy in the great multitude that no man can number around Thy Throne in heaven, Thy joy in the myriads of spotless angels there; Thy joy in Mary; Thy joy in the Father and in the Holy Spirit, with whom Thou art one God blessed for ever.

After Communion

Jesus, my Physician and my Saviour, I bow myself down to adore Thee, here within my heart. Here beneath my folded hands is He who by His touch and by His word cured all diseases of soul and body. Thou hast said it, Thou hast the words of eternal life—I believe, I adore.

O ye Angels of the Lord, bless the Lord; praise and exalt Him above all for ever.

O ye servants of the Lord, bless the Lord; praise and exalt him above all for ever.

O ye spirits and souls of the just, bless the Lord; praise and exalt Him above all for ever.

Oh, magnify the Lord with me, and let us extol His name together.

Give glory to the Lord, for he is good: for his mercy endureth for ever.

For He hath satisfied the empty soul, and hath filled the hungry soul with good things.

Bless the Lord, O my soul, and never forget all He hath done for Thee.

What shall I render to the Lord for all that He hath rendered to me?

My soul doth magnify the Lord, and my spirit hath rejoiced in God, my Saviour. For He that is mighty hath done great things to me, and holy is His name.

Oh, how hast Thou magnified Thy mercy, O God! Let all Thy works praise Thee, and let all Thy Saints bless Thee.

What have I in heaven but Thee, and besides Thee what do I desire upon earth? Thou art the God of my heart, and the God that is my portion for ever.

Thanks be to God for His unspeakable Gift!

"I am not as bad as I look," an invalid will at times say to a visitor. Would, dear Lord, that I could say this when

Sursum Corda!

Thou comest to visit my sick soul. But, alas! I am worse by far than I seem, worse than anything which appears to others, worse than even I myself have any idea of. Thine eye sees all, but Thy Heart puts up with all. There is no shrinking, no disgust. Thou comest to me with the brightness of manner that befits the sick room, nothing of surprise, nothing discouraging in Thy words and ways. A little improvement yesterday brings Thy congratulations; a little falling off to-day calls for Thy sympathy. O patient Physician, who would not love and trust Thee, and lay open to Thee all the secret wounds that self-love seeks to hide even from oneself!

The sick of Galilee and Judea were eager to make known their miseries as soon as they found themselves at Thy feet: "Lord, if Thou wilt Thou canst make me clean." "Lord, that I may see." The great thing was to make use of their opportunity, to display their misery and move Thy Heart, so easily stirred to pity and to mercy. No one ever left Thee unhealed. Again and again a sufferer was cured unasked. At times the restoration to health was gradual. But Thou wert never known to refuse their cure to any. Yet it was not for this Thou didst come on earth. If it was Thy delight to heal the body, it was to show Thy readiness to heal the soul. Heal me, O kind Physician. Lord, if Thou wilt Thou canst make me clean, with a word Thou canst wash away my many stains. Lord, that I may see; see Thee in the mysteries of Thy blessed Life on earth, and understand better what Thou hast done for me; see Thy hand in all that befalls me, so as not to be overthrown or disturbed when trouble comes; see Thee in all around me and try to be kind to all and to help all for Thy sake. Thou art all powerful and all wise; Thou knowest me through and through. There is no uncertainty in Thy treatment of me. Thine eye goes straight to my danger, Thy finger touches my hidden wound. And Thy love for me is boundless. What, then, have I to do but to trust myself to Thy gentle handling, to leave Thee free to work, to abandon myself to Thee?

Work a change in me, O dearest Lord—a change of heart. Thou comest to me with all the eagerness of love, Thy hand full of gifts. I come to Thee cold and selfish, scarcely moved by all the marks of Thy tenderness. And where is the gift in my hand? Yet I do love Thee and I desire to love Thee daily more and more. Make my love stronger and more generous. Make me eager to give Thee proofs of my love. I give Thee now the resolution so often made at Thy feet, so often broken through my weakness, yet by Thy grace my resolution still. [*Name it.*] Bless it again, dear Lord. I trust it to Thy keeping. Let me be strong with Thy strength, and when Thou comest to me again, may there be a real improvement to gladden Thy Heart.

Grant me grace, my God, to be all my life a true and loyal child of Holy Church; to frequent her sacraments regularly and devoutly, to love her festivals and her services. By the faithful practice of my religious duties, by an industrious and useful life, by fidelity to all the duties of my state, above all by vigilant care of those entrusted to me, let me show

Sursum Corda!

myself a practical Catholic. I want to love and serve Thee with my whole heart, and to be ready to suffer anything rather than offend Thee by sin. Keep me from all mortal sin, and give me a fear of all deliberate venial sin. Give me grace to injure no one by word or example, and to be of use to many on their road to heaven, to those especially with whom I live. Help me to make my home pure, peaceful, and joyous—a home that Thou canst bless.

Save me, my God, from being too much taken up with the cares or the pleasures of this life, and give me grace so to pass through the good things of time as not to lose those of eternity. Let me love Thee so truly that it may be easy to think of Thee often; to do all my work for Thee; to come back to Thee promptly by an act of sorrow after a fall; to take from Thy hand all that happens to me, and to turn to Thee with an act of love or praise, of trust, or acceptance of Thy Will when trouble comes. Let me live not for myself, but for Thee, think like Thee, deal with others like Thee, be self-forgetting like Thee, humble and meek like Thee. I offer to Thee my mind to know Thee better, my heart to love Thee, my will to serve Thee, all the senses of my body, all my thoughts, words, actions, and sufferings to be united with those of Thy well-beloved Son, who did always the things that please Thee, and who has promised that those who receive Him in Communion shall live by Him.

I commend to Thee, my God, all for whom I ought to pray—our Holy Father the Pope, and all bishops and priests; all who are dear to me, especially *N.*; all who are entrusted to me and for whom I shall have to give an account. Have mercy on this country and on all Christian princes and people. Have mercy on the poor heathen, that they may come to know Thee, the only true God, and Jesus Christ whom Thou hast sent. O God, who willest that all men should be saved, have pity on all who are outside Thy One, Holy, Catholic Church. Have pity in particular on my relatives and friends, and bring them to the knowledge of Thy truth. Have mercy on all who within the Church lead lives unworthy of their faith. Have mercy on all poor sinners; on all who are under temptation; on all who are in their agony and to die to-day. Forgive us all our sins, grant us the grace of final perseverance and a happy death, and bring us to life everlasting. Amen.

Have mercy also on the poor souls in Purgatory, especially [*here mention any for whom you wish specially to pray*], and grant them eternal rest.

Say this Indulgenced Prayer:
Prayer Before a Crucifix

Behold, O kind and most sweet Jesus, I cast myself on my knees in Thy sight, and with the most fervent desire of my soul, I pray and beseech Thee that Thou wouldst impress upon my heart lively sentiments of faith, hope, and charity, with true repentance for my sins, and a firm desire of amendment, while with deep affection

Sursum Corda!

and grief of soul I ponder within myself and mentally contemplate Thy five most precious wounds; having before my eyes that which David spake in prophecy: "They pierced My hands and My feet; they have numbered all My bones."

*Say five times the Our Father and Hail Mary
for the Pope and the Church.*

II

JESUS THE BREAD OF LIFE

Before Communion

Our Lord stood one evening in a desert place. But it had been no desert that day. Crowds had "flocked thither on foot from all the cities." And now five thousand men, besides women and children, cover the grassy slopes and press around Him. No thought of food or shelter, or of the fast declining day; content, more than content, so they may see Him, hear Him, be with Him. The marvellous charm about His Person, His voice, His ways, captivate every heart. And not for a brief space only. Hour after hour they throng about Him, giving place to others, and coming back to refresh their souls anew by gazing on that beautiful Face, and listening to Him who speaks as never man spake before.

Teaching, healing, comforting, He has been the happiness of all, every hour of this bright day. And now the day is far spent, and the Apostles meaning to be kind, come to Him and say: "This is a desert place and the hour is now past;

send them away, that going into the next villages and towns they may buy themselves bread." And He answering, says to them: "They have no need to go; give you them to eat." He tells them to make all the people sit down by companies upon the green grass. And they sit down in ranks, by hundreds and by fifties. See Him standing in the midst on the rising ground; all those upturned faces fixed upon Him. The people watch His every movement. He takes the five loaves brought to him by a boy in the crowd, blesses, breaks, and gives them to the Twelve. The bread is borne up and down in every direction. It is here, in the hands of all around Him; over there among all those companies; out yonder carried to the outstretched hands on the farthest skirts of the crowd. Five thousand men, besides women and children! How hungry they all are after their long fast! How happy that this bread, so sweet, so satisfying, is His gift to them, His reward for their faith and trust!

Our Lord looks down upon them with love. He follows them with His eye as, rested and refreshed and blessed and dismissed by Him, they collect in groups and make their way home under the stars, their minds full of what they have seen and heard to-day. The Apostles at His bidding have gone down to the boat and are crossing the Lake. He is alone. The people are far away now. And still He stands in the fast gathering darkness on the scene of this day's miracle. He is thinking of another Bread that He is to give for the life of the world, a Bread that shall feed His own in every land and in every age, the Bread of which He is to speak for the first time on the morrow.

Sursum Corda!

The news of the marvel in the desert spread like wildfire, and our Lord was met next day by an eager throng who hoped to have a share in the favour granted to so many the day before.

He looked round upon the expectant faces and began to show the people that the soul too has its needs, its hunger and its thirst, which must be satisfied or it will droop and die. Their days were spent in toiling for the bread which supports the life of the body, a life that with all their care must soon fail. But they had a higher life that need never die, that must not be allowed to die or they would be for ever miserable. Their labour, then, must not be altogether for the meat that perisheth. They must take pains to secure a food that would bring them to everlasting life. This food He had ready for them. They did not understand Him, and thinking only of the wants of the body, wondered if He was going to give them the manna with which God had fed their fathers during forty years in the desert. "He gave them bread from heaven," they said. But our Lord told them the manna was not really bread from heaven. "The true Bread from heaven is the Bread of God which cometh down from heaven and giveth life to the world." Their expectation was now raised high. What bread could this be to which the manna was not worthy to be compared? They did not understand, but they felt it was a gift to be earnestly desired and prayed for, and with one voice they cried out to Him: "Lord, give us always this bread." Our Lord's first object was gained. His way is to bring us to desire and to ask for His best gifts, and then to grant them to our prayer. They had begged for this marvellous bread—He would tell them now what it was.

And Jesus said to them: "I am the Bread of life, the living Bread which came down from heaven. If any man eat of this Bread he shall live for ever: and the Bread that I will give is My flesh for the life of the world."

At once the Jews began to murmur: "How can this man give us His flesh to eat?" Then Jesus said to them: "Amen, amen, I say unto you, except you eat the flesh of the Son of Man and drink His blood, you shall not have life in you. He that eateth My flesh and drinketh My blood hath everlasting life, and I will raise him up in the last day."

When we come to consider any scene of our Lord's life on earth, we must remember that He had before Him, not only the Jewish crowd, to whom He was actually speaking, but the men and women of all races and of all ages even to the end of time. His words were spoken to each one of us as distinctly as if that one were the only soul He had in view. And therefore these words of His at Capharnaum were intended for me—as much for me as if I had been there bodily present before Him with my needs and my weaknesses; as if His one thought in the marvellous Gift He was promising was to provide for my soul, to prevent it from perishing by hunger, to keep it safe for its eternal life that is to come. Have I thought of this? Do I take His words as spoken affectionately and earnestly *to me?*

Sursum Corda!

"My child," He says, "do not labour only for the life that is passing away so fast, the life that means ease, and comfort, pleasure, the enjoyment of the good things of this world. You are bound to provide for the life of the body. But you are still more strictly bound to spare time and to take pains to preserve and strengthen that life of your soul on which the eternal happiness of both soul and body depends.

"Your soul needs food, a food suited to so noble a creature. You do not understand yet, you could not take in now the grandeur of that within you which is made to My image and likeness. I know it. I treasure it. I hang over it with an intensity of affection which all its weakness, all its sinfulness cannot alter. I search in My infinite stores for a food worthy of it—and I find none. Nothing is good enough for that which I have loved better than My life. I gave My life for it once, but that does not suffice. I will give My life, I will give Myself to it all through its pilgrimage on earth. I will be not only its God, its Saviour, Brother, Companion, Friend—but its Food, its daily Food if it will. Come to Me, then, that you may have life. You are sick and weak; come within reach of My healing touch. Your soul is very needy; let Me pour into it the treasures I have to give.

"All that food does for the body, I Myself as its Food am ready to do for your soul. Food repairs the daily waste of the body and wards off disease and death. I, as the Food of your soul, restore what sin and slothfulness have weakened, and fortify it against that most dreadful of deaths: mortal sin. This is the Bread which cometh down from heaven, that if any man eat of It he may not die.

"Food refreshes and invigorates. It makes you cheerful, active, ready for work. Come to Me, all you that labour and are heavy burdened, and I will refresh you. I will give you strength to bear cheerfully your daily cross. I will give you that joy in the service of God which will make you persevere to the end.

"It is by food that you grow. By feeding on the Bread that is Myself you grow up in My sight, you put away the things of a child—feebleness, ignorance, waywardness, and become like Me because you live by Me.

"The food of the body can but sustain its life for a little space: but he that eateth this Bread shall live for ever. Not only is It life everlasting to the soul, but in the body also It sows the seed of a blessed immortality. He that eateth My flesh and drinketh My blood hath everlasting life, and I will raise him up in the last day.

"You must not, then, stay away from Me! You must not excuse yourselves from My feast, saying: 'I have bought a farm, and I must needs go and see it; I have married a wife, and therefore I cannot come.' No pretext must keep you from Me; no worldly cares must make you forget the one thing necessary. I tell you the truth when I say: Except you eat the flesh of the Son of Man, you shall have no life in you.

"Come to Me and all I have shall be yours. You shall be weak, no more, for I will be your strength. You shall be poor and needy no more, for I will share with you My treasures. I will enlighten your mind, ease your conscience, gladden your heart. The virtues of My Heart shall pass into yours, for we will share and exchange all that we have. You shall bring to

Sursum Corda!

Me your plans, your troubles, your failings, your fears. And I will give you My sympathy, My help, My comfort, and My strength. I will make over My merits to you. I will pray with you and in you. Together we will meet all dangers and all trials. What wonder if little by little you come to be like Me! For he that eateth My flesh and drinketh My blood abideth in Me and I in him. As I live by the Father, so he that eateth Me, the same also shall live by Me."

O God, my Creator, who openest Thy hand and fillest with blessing every living creature, what a Food hast Thou provided for this dearest of Thy creatures, this soul of mine! I might have looked for some wonderful nourishment, seeing that for the perishing body Thou didst rain down bread from heaven. But who could have dreamed that the food of the soul would be—Thyself! Shall I say with the unbelieving Jews: "How can this be?" Or shall I cry out: "Lord, give me always this Bread!"

I believe most firmly that Thou who didst multiply bread in the desert hast made Thyself in the Sacrament of the altar the Food of my soul. O truly Blessed Sacrament, O Hidden God, I adore Thee. I love Thee, I put my trust in Thee, I desire to receive Thee into my heart. Make me hunger for Thee, O Bread of life. My soul was made for Thee, and nothing of this world can satisfy it. Give me this day my daily bread. Come, Lord Jesus!

(If you have time you may make the Acts of Faith, Hope, and Charity, p. 179: "I believe, etc.")

After Communion

Jesus, living Bread, true Bread from heaven, I adore Thee profoundly, here within my breast. Here beneath my folded hands is the God of heaven become my food. Thou hast said it. Thou hast the words of eternal life—I believe, I adore.

O ye Angels... (p. 181)

I need Thee, Lord, and so I have come to Thee. I dare not think of Thee as the Holy of Holies, as Judge, as "a consuming fire," and Thou wilt not have me so to think of Thee in this Sacrament of Thy love. But I am to come to Thee as my Food. Thou givest Thyself to me as bread, that I may draw near to Thee without fear. I have not the cleanness of heart becoming one who is to touch the Saint of saints. I have not the love that should be a return for Thine, O Lover of my soul. But what dispositions are required for my daily bread? Only that I be hungry. Or if even this is wanting, if I am too sick to feel this hunger—then not even so much, but only that weak, needy, out of sorts, I come, "take, and eat." So long as a spark of life remains in the body, food may profit it. So long as my soul is alive by Thy grace, this divine Food is sure to profit it: "Take, and eat."

This much, O loving Lord, O living Bread, I can do, and will do again and again. Without desire, without relish, I will still come. I will take and eat, not because I am worthy, or even hungry, but because I am frail and faint. I thank Thee, who hast humbled Thyself so low for me as to become my food. Let not such love be in vain. Let me come to

Sursum Corda!

Thee often that my soul may live by Thee, for so Thou hast promised: "He that eateth Me, the same also shall live by Me." My soul is weak, easily overcome by temptation, easily troubled by the cares and trials of daily life. Strengthen it, O Bread of the strong and of all who feed on Thee. Keep me safe from the dreadful death of mortal sin, and sustain me that I may not fall into deliberate venial sin. My soul is listless and weary, not without good purposes, but soon tired, for ever halting on the upward way. Refresh it as thou hast promised, for labouring and heavy-burdened it has come to Thee. All through life be its Viaticum, its Food by the way. And when the end has come, be its support on its last journey, that it may pass safely through the Valley of Death, and meet Thee unveiled, meet Thee with joy, sweet Lord, in the Land of the Living. Amen.

Grant me grace, etc.; and Prayer before a Crucifix, p. 185.

III

JESUS OUR FRIEND

Before Communion

"And it came to pass that He entered into a certain town, and a certain woman named Martha received Him into her house, and she had a sister called Mary, who sitting also at the Lord's feet heard His word."

Happy days for the little household of Bethany when our Lord was expected! He was a Friend, such as men had never seen before, had never even imagined. His friends knew Him, felt Him to be more than man, yet they were not afraid of Him. They carried on their ordinary work and talk, their little disputes even, in His presence, without fear of rebuke. Whatever happened to be in their minds came out, unchecked by the thought that He might think it irreverent or foolish. "Lord, show us the Father." "Lord, bid me come to Thee upon the waters."

Martha and Mary acknowledged Him to be the Christ, the Son of the living God, yet they turned to Him trustfully for sympathy and help, not in great trials only, but in the small worries of daily life. "Lord, he whom Thou lovest is sick." "Lord, if Thou hadst been here my brother had not died." "Lord, come and see." And they led Him to the grave to weep with them over the friend He had loved and lost. They entertained Him each after her own fashion, Mary seated herself at His feet, to hear for herself alone the words of Him who spake as never man spake. Martha passed to and fro the while, preparing the meal He was to share with them. Full of her household cares, she thought it no irreverence to break in upon His conversation with Mary in order to draw His attention to them: "Lord, hast Thou no care that my sister has left me alone to serve? Speak to her therefore that she help me." There is no constraint. His friends are quite at their ease with him. They want help; He is there; what more natural than to turn to Him? He did chide at times. But what of that? Were they not all disciples under training, conscious of their failings, anxious to improve in His school? "Martha, Martha, thou art careful and art troubled about many things." Would Martha have missed that loving admonition for any praise the world could give? Oh, that we could be more like our Lord's disciples and friends—at home with Him, turning to Him in all our needs, treasuring all His whispered words to us, even words of blame!

What were the thoughts of Martha and Mary when, as evening drew on and His thankless work in Jerusalem was over, He was seen on the white dusty road? As He crossed their threshold and His tired face lit up at their words of welcome? It was God who came to them footsore and weary; God whom their roof sheltered and their love cheered; God who as their Guest stood indebted to them, and held Himself bound to repay their hospitality by His gratitude and His gifts. It was God at whose feet they poured out their hearts, who trusted to them the secrets of His own.

The Beloved Disciple spoke from experience when, with the thought of his Master in his mind, he told us that God is love. So all our Lord's friends would have described Him. All that was gracious, winning, sympathizing, all that could attract and satisfy love—this was Jesus Christ. What a Friend He must have been, never preoccupied, absolutely self-forgetting, welcoming every confidence, eager in every need to comfort and to help! He is our Friend no less than theirs. And unchanged from the days when the Twelve followed Him about in Galilee, and Martha and Mary welcomed Him to their home. He does so want to persuade us of this—that He is "Jesus Christ, yesterday, and to-day, and the same for ever." His friends of to-day may treat Him with the same loving familiarity as His friends of long ago, confide to Him their secrets, count upon His interest and help in all their trials. No detail of home life is beneath His notice, no trouble too insignificant to call forth His compassion. He not merely suffers our presence in the Sacrament of His love, but shows Himself desirous of our company and beholden to us for our entertainment of Him.

O dearest Lord Jesus, how is it that my heart is not drawn to Thee so as to be unable to keep away? The simple folk of Galilee had their trades and their household cares. Yet Thou hadst but to show Thy face and they flocked after Thee. There was the will to be with Thee, and they found the way. If duty kept at home any who called themselves Thy disciples, it was a hard necessity, and, duty satisfied, they flew to Thy feet. Where there were sick, nothing was left undone to bring them into Thy presence or to coax a visit from Thee.

Sursum Corda!

Ah, Lord, why is there nothing of this now? Why is eagerness to be with Thee, to harbour Thee, almost the exception among those who call themselves Thy friends? There is some excuse, perhaps, for us. The charm of Thy Person, the glance of Thine eye, the tones of Thy voice, the sweetness of Thy smile that drew the crowds after thee—these are wanting to us. But the Church tells us, and we sing continually: "*Sola fides sufficit*," Faith alone suffices. Not to satisfy, but to draw us to Thee. It should suffice as Thy will for us in the present, as the trial which is to win for us the reward of seeing Thee face to face for ever—and that before many years are past.

But there is another reason why Thy friends no longer besiege Thee, O Lord. Our churches would be thronged if the cure of the body was to be won from Thee. But because Thou art there as the Physician of the soul, few care to present themselves before Thee. O Lord, increase our faith. Increase mine. Give me the faith that will make me think more of my immortal soul than of the poor perishing body; that will be eager to come to Thee with the wants of my soul. Give me the faith that will make me not only worship Thee in this Sacrament as the Christ, the Son of the living God, but love Thee as the dearest of friends and desire to receive Thee under my roof, desire to make up to Thee by my love for the coldness and ingratitude of so many. I believe most firmly that Thou art coming to me who didst show Thyself the tender sympathizing Friend of all who came to Thee. I believe that Thou art glad to come; that as Thou didst enter willingly into the little humble homes of Galilee and Judea, waiting only for invitation, so at my invitation Thou wilt come joyfully to me. Come, Lord, and do not delay! Come, Lord Jesus!

(If you have time you may make the Acts of Faith, Hope, and Charity, p. 179)

After Communion.

I fall down before Thee and adore Thee, O Jesus, tenderest and truest of friends. Here beneath my folded hands is the Heart of Him who loved me even unto death. Lord, let me return Thee love for love. May all creatures love and praise Thee for me.

O ye Angels... (p. 181)

I am better off, dear Lord, than if I had lived during Thy life on earth. I might not have been among the few who out of the world's millions saw and heard Thee. Even had I been one of the chosen nation, heard Thy marvellous teaching, looked upon Thy face, seen Thy miracles, I might not have become thy disciple. Not all were drawn to Thee. Like the proud, self-satisfied Pharisee, I might have closed my heart against Thee; or followed Thee for a while and gone with the stream in the end, and died estranged from Thee, my Saviour. Even as one of Thy faithful disciples, should I have been really happier than I am now? I may come to Thee when I will. I may bring to Thee all my needs, and find Thee always ready to listen to me and to help me. I cannot see Thy face nor hear Thy voice, but in a little while I shall have this, my heart's desire. I have the promise: "Thine eyes shall see the King in His beauty." I am loved and blessed by Thee because, not seeing, I have believed. Increase my faith that I may learn to come to Thee, like Thy friends of long ago, with all my needs, all my joys, all my troubles. Increase my trust that like them I may fear no evil when Thou art with me. Increase my love that with my whole heart and soul and mind and strength I may cling to Thee, my Saviour and truest Friend.

Grant me grace, etc.; and Prayer before a Crucifix, p. 185.

IV

MY ONLY ONE

Before Communion

"And behold a man among the crowd, falling down on his knees before Him, cried out, saying: 'Master, I beseech Thee look upon my son because he is my only one.'"

Was it the imperfect faith of the father or the misery of the child, possessed by an evil spirit, that drew a weary sigh from our Lord: "O unbelieving and perverse generation, how long shall I be with you, how long shall I suffer you?" But the father's touching prayer had prevailed: "He is my only one." The Sacred Heart, never hard to move, was won. "Bring him to Me."... and the child was cured from that hour.

I, too, O Lord, bring to Thee my only one, the one treasure which is wholly mine—my precious, immortal soul.

Upon its fate in eternity all for me depends. If I lose it, all is lost. If I save it, all is safe. The body will follow its lead into heaven or into hell; in its company will be happy with the happiness of God Himself, or miserable beyond anything the mind can conceive—and this for ever! I call it "my only one," as if it were something belonging to me; but it is nearer to me, dearer to me than this. It is myself. I am my soul. Have mercy on me and heal my soul: have mercy on me, O Lord, according to Thy great mercy.

See how our Lord draws the father out; how He gets from him the story of the long and terrible trouble, thereby to increase his desire for deliverance and to improve his dispositions. "How long time is it since this hath happened unto him? But he said: From his infancy. And oftentimes hath he cast him into the fire and into waters to destroy him, but if Thou canst do anything, help us, having compassion on us." With what earnestness, despite his imperfect faith, the poor father pleads for his only one!

Our Lord seeks to draw us out in the same way and for the same purpose. "How long is it, child, since this temptation, this difficulty came upon you?" Of course He knows all about it, and much better than we know ourselves. But it is good for us to tell it. Let us be as ready as the poor father in the Gospel to pour out our trouble to Him. The answer may be: "From my infancy, O Lord. It is part of my nature, and because I have been slothful in fighting against it, because I have often yielded, I am now the slave of a habit which I cannot break through. Again and again my enemy

Sursum Corda!

tries to cast me into sin to destroy me. But Thou who canst do all things, help me, having compassion on me."

"Bring him to Me," our Lord said. "And as he was coming to Him, the spirit troubled him, and being thrown down upon the ground he rolled about foaming." Perhaps we never suffer more from the attacks of our enemy than when we are on our way to our Lord for cure. We must not be surprised; it is a good sign. "And Jesus said: Deaf and dumb spirit, I command thee, go out of him, and enter not any more into him; and crying out and greatly tearing him, he went out of him, and he became as dead. But Jesus, taking him by the hand, lifted him up and restored him to his father."

Lord, I will make my way to Thee in spite of all the efforts of the evil one to stop me. He knows that at Thy touch his power will be checked, that with one word Thou canst deliver me and save me. Free me from the deafness that prevents me from hearing Thy voice, or from pretending not to hear that I may not have to heed. Free me from the dumbness that would hinder me from telling my sins in confession, and that makes it hard to speak to Thee in prayer.

"I command Thee," Thou didst say to the spirit that for so long had tormented this poor boy. Speak thus in Thy power to all that holds my soul captive and keeps me back from Thee. Say but the word and I shall be healed.

(If you have time you may make the Acts of Faith, Hope, and Charity, p. 179)

After Communion

I bow myself down to adore Thee, Jesus, Son of God, to whom all power is given in heaven and on earth. With Thy angels and saints who see Thee face to face, I worship Thee, and bless Thee, and praise Thee. I give Thee thanks for Thy great glory. I give Thee thanks that Thou, O God of Glory, hast stooped to visit me.

O ye Angels... (p. 181)

My God, have pity on my soul because it is my only one. Make known to me that sin, or fault, or tendency on which Satan chiefly relies for my ruin. He has watched me with envious eyes from my infancy. He knows my evil inclinations; he knows my weakness. Matched with him, I have no chance alone. But with all his strength and cunning he is as an insignificant insect before Thee. It is he, then, who has no chance. O my God, give me wisdom to keep united with Thee. As I value my salvation, let me come often to Thee in the Sacrament of Thy love, that I may be one with Thee. Keep me in Thy love and in Thy grace. Teach me to know and fear myself, to know and trust Thee. Help me to battle with those inclinations which are my enemy's hope. Of myself I am weak, but I can do all things in Him who strengtheneth me. I may fall again and again, but only with Thy help to rise again. Up to the end my enemy will molest me, now with open attack, now with temptation to weariness and despondency. Up to the end I will resist him with

Sursum Corda!

the help of Thy grace, and Thou hast promised, my God, that he who perseveres to the end shall be saved.

Grant me grace, etc.; and Prayer before a Crucifix, p. 185.

CREDO: WHAT CATHOLICS BELIEVE

INTRODUCTION

The original title of this pamphlet when it was first printed by the Catholic Truth Society in 1905 was *Credo: A Simple Explanation of the Chief Points of Catholic Doctrine*. Ironically, what was intended as a "Simple Explanation" proved to be the most troublesome of all the short works Mother Loyola put her hand to.

Surely it was somewhat ambitious from the start, to try to encapsulate the basics of Catholic teaching into one short pamphlet without excluding any crucial points. But unexpected complications set in as the pamphlet became popular and versions were being printed in the US and elsewhere. This was due largely to the fact that, while the main tenets of the Church are Universal, some practices, like fasting and abstinence, can vary in their minor details from one diocese to the next. In addition, certain practices are modified from time to time, such as the requirements for valid marriage in the Church as laid out in the 1907 decree *Ne Temere*.

These variations and modifications ensured that as soon as one updated edition went to print, it was already in need of an insert to keep it up to date until the next print run. Mother Loyola mentions at least five major updates in her letters to Father Thurston: one previous to 1914 and another that year, and subsequent rewrites in 1918, 1921 and 1927.

During these intervening years, the title of the work eventually became *What Catholics Believe: A Simple Explanation of the Chief Points of Christian Doctrine.* It is the work under this title, published in 1925 by The Paulist Press in New York that we reprint here.

WHAT CATHOLICS BELIEVE

A Simple Explanation of the Chief Points of Christian Doctrine

❈ FAITH ❈

God

The Church teaches that there is but one God, the Creator of all things. He is supreme—that is, over all other beings—for He alone exists of Himself. He had no beginning; He will have no end. He is everywhere. He knows and sees all things, even our most secret thoughts. He can do all things; nothing can resist His will.

God is a Spirit. He has no form, and therefore we cannot see Him in this life. But He is a real Person, containing in Himself all that is good. All power, wisdom, holiness, beauty, goodness—everything that calls for adoration, for praise, for love and service, is found in Him. Because He is infinitely above us, He is incomprehensible. We cannot understand Him, and many of the things He does and permits are a puzzle to us now. But because of His infinite wisdom and goodness we know that all He does is right and good, and we adore what we cannot understand. The day will come when all men will see the reason of God's ways with His creatures, and will own that "He has done all things well."

In this one God there are three Persons, equal in all things: the Father, the Son, and the Holy Ghost. How these three Persons are all one and the same God is a mystery—that is, a truth above reason, but revealed by God. Many people nowadays refuse to believe what they cannot understand. This is foolish, for how many wonders there are around us and within us that our reason cannot grasp! The midnight skies, the flowery fields, the soul which checks and approves us by turns—all these things are full of mystery. To deny what they cannot comprehend is to act against the very reason freethinkers pretend to stand by. In all things relating to God we have to remember that He is a Being infinitely above us. He would not be God if we could understand Him. But in reward for our faith during this time of trial, we shall one day see far into the mysteries that perplex us now. The mystery of Three Persons in one God is called the mystery of the Blessed Trinity.

Jesus Christ

Jesus Christ, the Second Person of the Blessed Trinity, has two natures: the nature of God and the nature of man. He is truly God because He has one and the same nature with God the Father. He is truly man because He has the nature of man, having a body and a soul like ours. He was always God, born of the Father from all eternity. He has been man only from the time of His Incarnation, when He took to Himself the nature of man in the womb of Mary ever Virgin. He has a true human Mother and because He is God, His Mother is truly Mother of God. He had no father on earth; St. Joseph was only His guardian or foster father.

Jesus Christ became man to redeem us from sin and hell, and to show us the way to heaven. During thirty-three years He gave us for our imitation an example of every virtue. He preached His divine doctrine, trained His Apostles, and founded His Church; then He laid down His life on the Cross for our redemption. On the third day after His death He proved Himself to be God by rising from the dead by His own power. Forty days after His Resurrection He remained on earth, teaching the Apostles how they and their successors were to carry on His work to the end of time. On the fortieth day He ascended into heaven in their presence, and ten days later He sent down upon them His Holy Spirit, Who was to lead them into all truth and to abide with them for ever.

The Holy Ghost

The Holy Ghost is the Third Person of the Blessed Trinity. He proceeds from the Father and the Son, and is the same Lord and God as they are. He came down upon the Apostles on Pentecost to enable them to preach the Gospel and to plant the Church. He is the Lover and Sanctifier of our souls, cleansing, strengthening, comforting them, and helping them to deserve by good works the rewards of heaven.

Sursum Corda!

My Soul

God has loved each one of us from eternity. We had no claims on His love. He drew us out of nothing. He gave us all that we have and are—our body with all its senses, our soul with its three powers: memory, understanding and will. He made this soul to His own image and likeness. Like Him, it is a spirit and can never die. The body will soon be a little dust in the grave, but the soul will live on for ever, for it is made for eternity. At the Last Day it will be joined again to the very same body it had in life, and body and soul will begin a new life which will never end. What will this new life be like? To answer this question, we must ask another: *Why did God make us?*

God, Who is infinitely wise and good, must have a noble end in all His works, and the higher the work the nobler must be the end. Man is the highest of His visible works, therefore man must have the highest of all ends. God made me, not to live simply for myself, not for the service of those around me, not for any creature, however high, however dear, but for Himself. He has made this soul of mine to know, love, and serve Him, and to enjoy the same happiness He has Himself. Since this is its end, it can never be satisfied and at rest unless it is carrying out this end. As God's creatures, belonging completely to Him, we should be bound to serve Him without any reward, but He has promised us the grandest of rewards for serving Him during the short time we have to spend here on earth—no less than the possession of Himself, with all that He has; the satisfying of every desire of our soul; joys that eye has not seen, nor ear heard, nor heart of man conceived—and this for ever.

The chief thing, then, that I have to do in this world is to secure for myself the everlasting happiness of the world to come—to save my soul. But this word "to save" brings a solemn, even terrifying, truth before me. God is infinite in all His perfections—infinitely good and loving, and infinitely just. He cannot make a creature for an end, and give it every help to reach that end, and then leave it to itself without caring whether it reaches the end or not. He cannot command it to know, love, and serve Him, and not mind if it disobeys His command. He must either reward or punish. If I save my soul, my whole self, body and soul, are saved from utter and hopeless ruin. If I lose my soul, all is lost.

The Particular Judgment

In the moment of death our time of trial will be over, and we shall be called to give an account of the use we have made of it. Trembling and alone, our soul will be presented before the judgment seat of Jesus Christ to give an account of every thought, word, and deed of its life on earth. "It is appointed unto men once to die; and after this, the judgment."[1] The judgment is followed by the sentence which fixes the state of the soul for eternity. If it is found free from the least stain of sin, and with no debt of punishment owing to the Divine Justice, it passes at once to its place in heaven. If there is on it the guilt of even one grievous offence against God, it is

---
1 Heb. 9:27.

Sursum Corda!

banished from His presence for ever. Hell must be its abode for eternity, for only in this life are repentance and change possible. If it is free from grievous but stained with venial sin, or has a debt of punishment still due for forgiven sin, it will be saved, "yet so as by fire."[1] It will be sent to Purgatory, the place of suffering and expiation, where it must remain till it has paid the last farthing. The judgment immediately after death is called the Particular Judgment, because each soul appears singly before Christ our Lord, and alone with Him the life is examined and the sentence passed.

The General Judgment

But there is a General Judgment to come at the Last Day, that the sentence passed on each may be made known to all; that the Justice of God, which so often allows the good to suffer in this life whilst the wicked prosper, may be made known to all men; and chiefly, that Jesus Christ, so humbled and despised on earth, may be glorified in the sight of all mankind. At the sound of the Archangel's trumpet all men will rise from their graves with the same bodies they had in life, but very different from what they are now. The bodies of the just will be beautiful and glorious; those of the wicked hideous and loathsome. "Then shall appear the Sign of the Son of Man," (that is, the Cross) "in heaven, and they shall see the Son of Man coming in the clouds of heaven with great power and majesty; and all nations shall be gathered before Him." Then every thought, word, and deed shall be made

---

1 Matt. 16:27; Apoc. 21:27; 1 Cor. 3:15.

known, and the secrets of all hearts shall be revealed. Then will Christ say to the wicked, "Depart from Me, ye cursed, into everlasting fire"; and to the just, "Come, ye blessed of My Father, possess you the kingdom prepared for you from the foundation of the world." The Angels will separate the good from the bad, "and these shall go into everlasting punishment, but the just into life everlasting."

Life Everlasting

Life everlasting means the glory and happiness of heaven, where the good shall see, love, and enjoy God for ever. This happiness is so great that the Scripture says of it, "Eye hath not seen, nor ear heard, neither hath it entered into the heart of man to conceive what things God hath prepared for them that love Him."

There is another eternity which the Scripture calls "eternal death." It is the eternity of those whose names are not in the book of life; who have been too busy with the things of this world to attend to "the one thing necessary"; who have died the enemies of God. Men try to keep the awful fact of hell out of mind, as if this would prevent its being a reality. Or they try to believe it will not last for ever. Yet what can be plainer than Our Lord's words, repeated again and again: "Where the fire is not extinguished"; "Depart from Me, ye cursed, into everlasting fire." He bids even His friends think of that terrible eternity with fear. "Fear Him Who after He hath killed, hath power to cast into hell, yea, I say to you, fear Him." It is especially when temptation is strong that we need this check of holy fear. A saint used to pray, "My God, if ever Thy love should grow cold in my heart, at least let the thought of Thy punishments keep me from falling into sin."

The Catholic Church

How are men to escape the punishments of the life to come, and reach the eternal happiness prepared for them? Our Lord tells us. "Hear the Church," He says.[1] He knew that learning and study are not enough: He knew that most of His followers would be poor and simple, bound to work all day and every day for their daily bread, and unable to puzzle out hard questions. So He made an easy way to heaven for all men. He did not say "Read the Bible," but "Hear the Church." The Bible is the holiest of books, and of inestimable worth to the disciples of Christ. But because it is the word of God, it is too deep to be understood throughout by anyone, however spiritual, however learned; and Christ never meant it to take the place of the living voice of His Church. There must be an authority to tell us that the Bible is the word of God, and to decide important and difficult questions as they arise. A mother in the midst of her little children teaches by word of mouth. She may open a book before them and encourage them to read, but they read under her guidance and for the explanation of hard passages they turn to her. Catholics are encouraged to read the Scriptures: her priests and religious read them daily, but they read as children of the Church.

---

[1] Matt. 18:17.

The Marks of the Church

The Catholic Church is the union of all the faithful under one Head: Jesus Christ our Lord. She has four marks by which we may know her: she is *One;* she is *Holy;* she is *Catholic;* she is *Apostolic*. The Church is *One* because all her members agree in one Faith, have all the same sacrifice and Sacraments, and are all united under one Head. There is no difference among Catholics in matters of faith. In habits and tastes, in pious practices even, there is plenty of variety; but in questions of faith they are absolutely one. Catholics in Ireland and in Japan, in the university and in the factory, hold precisely the same doctrines—not because they seem reasonable, but because they are the teaching of the Church, which Christ has commanded them to hear. Catholics worship God everywhere by the offering of the same Sacrifice, the Holy Mass; they are all brought on their way to heaven by the same seven Sacraments, and all acknowledge as their supreme Head on earth the Vicar or representative of Christ, the Bishop of Rome.

The Church is *Holy* because she teaches a holy doctrine, offers to all the means of holiness, and is distinguished by the eminent holiness of so many thousands of her children. She leads all to the faithful observance of God's commandments, to an uninterrupted fight with the devil, the world, and their own corrupt inclinations and passions, to a hatred for sin, and to the practice of good works. She not only exhorts us to holiness, but by her Sacraments, her feasts, and her devotions she helps us to become holy. And she proves her right to the mark of holiness by the multitude of her saints. There are bad Catholics no doubt, as there was cockle among the wheat in Our Lord's parable, but they are bad because they disobey the Church and neglect the means of grace she offers them.

The Church is *Catholic* or Universal because she subsists in all ages, teaches all nations, and is the one Ark of Salvation for all. She is the only Church that can go back nineteen hundred years to the time of Jesus Christ; the only Church that has preached to all nations, and is found in every country of the world; and the only Church appointed by God to bring men to eternal salvation. This does not mean that none but Catholics get to heaven; many Protestants are saved and many Catholics are lost. But since Christ has appointed a Church as the great means for the salvation of men, it follows (1) that all men are bound to make use of this means, and to enter the Catholic Church as soon as they recognize her as the Church founded by Christ; and (2) that it is far easier to be saved within this Church than without, even though a man may be in good faith without.

The Church is *Apostolic* because she holds the doctrines and traditions of the Apostles, and because through the unbroken succession of her Pastors, she derives her orders and her mission from them. Scripture is the written, tradition the unwritten word of God. The Apostles taught chiefly by word of mouth, as they had themselves been taught by Our Lord. During the forty days after the Resurrection He told them many things concerning "the

Kingdom of God" which are not contained in Scripture, but which have come down to us in various ways—by the teaching of the Church everywhere and always, in creeds or professions of faith, in holy rites and ceremonies, in the prayers of public worship, and in the writings of the holy Fathers and Doctors, for tradition is written as well as unwritten. This teaching of tradition has the Holy Ghost for its guardian, and is as inspired and binding as the written words of Scripture. Through the unbroken line of her chief Pastors, from Peter to our Pope today, our Bishops and Priests derive their sacred orders and their right to teach the faithful from the Apostles, who received these powers from Our Lord Himself.

The Office of Peter

To the Apostles Christ said, "Go, teach all nations. He that heareth you heareth Me." And that all might teach the same thing, He put one of them, Peter, over the rest. He made him the visible Head of the Church on earth when He said to him, "Thou art Peter, and upon this rock I will build My Church, and the gates of hell shall not prevail against it; and to thee I will give the keys of the kingdom of heaven."[1] "Feed My lambs; feed My sheep."[2] He also prayed that his faith might never fail, and commanded him to confirm his brethren.[3] Peter was to tend the whole flock; the sheep as well as the lambs, those who have to feed (or the Church teaching) and those to be fed (or the Church taught)—all were to depend on Peter.

---

1 Matt. 16:18, 19.   2 John 21:15, 16, 17.   3 Luke 22:32.

Sursum Corda!

Peter's Office Continued in the Papacy

And as the office of Peter was not to expire with him, his successors have exercised the same supreme authority from his time down to the present day. The Bishop of Rome, the Pope, has ever been regarded as the lawful successor of St. Peter and the visible Head of the Universal Church. A General Council has never been held which was not presided over either by the Pope or by his delegates, nor has a decision of a Council ever been universally accepted unless it has received the Pope's confirmation. "Where Peter is, there is the Church," is an ancient axiom, in which Peter stands for the successor of St. Peter the Pope, the Bishop of Rome. Rome, Peter's See, is the only one of the Sees founded by the Apostles that has kept the Faith, and that has come down to our own days in the unbroken succession of its Bishops. And because God is faithful, He has taken care that Peter and his successors, the Bishops of Rome, shall not lead the flock astray. For the sake of the Church, therefore, the Pope is preserved by God from error whenever he defines a doctrine concerning *faith*—that is, what we have to believe—or *morals*—that is, what we have to do—to be held by the whole Church. *This is what is meant by the Pope's Infallibility.* It does not mean that the Pope cannot do wrong. A Pope might do great wrong; he might even lose his soul. But no Pope can teach wrong when speaking to the whole Church as its Head. Although the doctrine of the Infallibility of the Pope was only defined in 1870, it has always been the implicit teaching of the Church, though not binding on Catholics before 1870. The definition of a doctrine is not the *invention* of a doctrine, but merely its clearer manifestation. The Divinity of Our Lord was not defined till the fifth century, yet, surely, it was held by the Church from the beginning. As new needs and errors arise, the Church declares more fully what has always been part of Catholic truth.

The Communion of Saints

The Church is in Heaven (where it is called the *Church Triumphant*), and in Purgatory (where it is the *Church Suffering*), and on earth (where it is the *Church Militant*, or fighting). All its members, in Heaven, on earth, and in Purgatory, are in communion with each other, as being one body in Jesus Christ—that is, there is a holy friendship between them, a loving intercourse, and an interchange of good offices. The faithful on earth are in communion with each other by professing the same faith, obeying the same authority, and assisting each other by their prayers and good works. We are in communion with the saints in Heaven by honoring them as the glorified members of the Church; and also by our praying to them, and by their praying for us. And we are in communion with the souls in Purgatory by helping them with our prayers and good works. "It is a holy and wholesome thought to pray for the dead that they may be loosed from sins."[1]

---

[1] Macch. 12:46.

Sursum Corda!

Purgatory

We know that there is a place of temporal punishment after death, from the constant teaching of the Church; and from Holy Scripture, which declares that God will render to every man according to his works; that nothing defiled shall enter Heaven; and that some will be saved, "yet so as by fire."[1] Those souls go to Purgatory that depart this life in *venial* sin; or that have not fully paid the debt of *temporal* punishment due to those sins of which the guilt has been forgiven. Temporal punishment is that which will have an end, either in this world or in the world to come.

Sin

Sin is an offence against God, by any thought, word, deed, or omission against the law of God. There are two kinds of sin: *original* and *actual*.

Original sin is the sin of Adam when he ate the forbidden fruit. Every child of Adam—with one exception: the Immaculate Mother of God—has inherited the guilt or stain of original sin from him who was the origin and head of all mankind. *Actual* sin is that which we ourselves commit. Actual sin is either *mortal* or *venial*.

Mortal or deadly sin is so called because it kills the soul by taking away sanctifying grace, which is its supernatural life. The soul has a natural life (which enables us to move, think, and speak), and a supernatural life (which is the friendship

---

[1] 1 Cor. 3:15.

of God, given to it by sanctifying grace). It is its supernatural life that makes it beautiful and pleasing in the sight of God. This is the life that is destroyed by mortal sin. Men see no change after mortal sin; we walk, work, laugh as before. But in the sight of God and His Angels there is a terrible change—our soul has become hideous and loathsome. All the reward laid up for us in Heaven by our good works is forfeited, and no good work done in the state of mortal sin can merit an eternal reward. We deserve eternal punishment, and if we die in this state our soul will fall straight into the flames of hell, where the body will join it on the Last Day.

Three things are required to make a mortal sin: (1) grave matter, (2) full knowledge, and (3) full consent.

(1) GRAVE MATTER—The sinful thought, word, deed, or omission must be something of very great importance, e.g., injuring our neighbor's character in a serious matter, stealing a huge sum, or a small sum from a very poor person.

(2) FULL KNOWLEDGE—Not done by mistake, or before we knew clearly what we were about. The mind must think of the sinfulness of the act at the time it is done.

(3) FULL CONSENT—The will must deliberately agree to the temptation, whether of thought, word, or deed. If there was not full knowledge or full consent, but hesitation in rejecting the temptation, the sin is venial, and the soul is injured but not killed.

Venial sin means pardonable. This sin is so called because it is more easily pardoned than mortal sin. A lie of excuse, or a small injury to our neighbor does not make us enemies of God, or take away sanctifying grace. Nevertheless, venial sin is a great evil—the greatest of all evils after mortal sin—and we should be heartily sorry for it. It deprives us of many graces, it lessens our fear of offending God, and in this way often leads us to mortal sin. No one ever comes to mortal sin except through carelessness about venial sin. Every venial sin will be punished, either in this life or in the next.

❦ HOPE ❧

Besides believing what God has told us, we are commanded to hope for what He has promised us and to show our love for Him by doing what He requires of us. In other words, we have to worship Him by Faith, Hope, and Charity. Because God is infinitely powerful, infinitely good and faithful to His promises, we are bound to hope that He will give us eternal happiness in the life to come, and all things necessary to obtain it, if we do what He requires of us; and that He will provide the things necessary for this life if we ask for them as we ought. Hope brings such brightness and happiness into our lives, that we might have thought a command concerning it would be unnecessary. But God knows how ready we are to despond whenever trouble or difficulty comes in our way. Hence He has laid it upon us as a command to hope in Him and to hope always. More than this, we may not weaken our hope by giving way to discouragement. God is always merciful. He will forgive us whenever we turn to Him with sorrow after falling into sin, and He will never let us be tried beyond our strength.

But we must not sin by presumption. To expect that He will give us Heaven when we are breaking His Commandments, or that He will preserve us from sin when we willfully go into the occasions of sin or live in mortal sin relying on His mercy for the hour of our death—this is not the virtue of hope, but a sin against the First Commandment. We are bound to make acts of hope, especially in time of temptation, and at the hour of death, and to show our hope in God all through life, by

Prayer

To do any good work towards our salvation we need the help of God's grace, which we obtain chiefly by prayer and the holy sacraments. "Ask and you shall receive," says our Blessed Lord. Prayer is the raising up of our mind and heart to God, by thinking of Him, by adoring, praising, and thanking Him, and by begging of Him all blessings for soul and body. Prayer, then, is not all *asking*. To lift up our hearts to God in joy and thankfulness when things go well with us, is prayer. To bow our heads and our hearts in patient resignation in our hours of trouble and of mourning, is prayer. To praise God for what He is in Himself, for His goodness, His glory, His mercy, this is the highest prayer. In the Our Father, the best of all prayers, Our Lord teaches us the chief things to be desired and prayed for.

Sursum Corda!

To pray well we must think of God or of what we say. If our mind wanders we must recall it as well as we can. Willful distractions are sinful, and displease God. This does not mean that we are never to think of our business or our worries when we speak to God. Prayer is a loving conversation with our Heavenly Father, Who bids us ask Him We little children for all we want. If we are tired or anxious, if we cannot see how to make ends meet, if a coming trial frightens us, we may take our trouble straight to Him, Who can and will help us. Above all, we should turn to Him when sin weighs us down. He does not want even mortal sin to hinder us from turning to Him with loving trust. Whatever we have done, and however often we have done it, He loves us still, and forbids us to be discouraged and think it is no use trying. He holds out His arms to us; He calls us back to Him, He promises to forgive us and restore to us all we have lost. However far a sinner may have wandered, he can always pray, and prayer is a certain means of recovering the friendship of GodvTherefore, we must never give up prayer; it is the rope thrown out to the drowning man, to which he must cling if he would be saved. And we must never think God does not hear us because the answer is long in coming. He always hears. But He expects us to wait and to trust. If what we ask is good for us, He will give it sooner or later. If it is not good for us, He will give us something better instead.

The Angels and Saints

Because our prayers are poor and weak, the Church encourages us to ask the Saints and Angels to pray for us. They stand in the presence of God, they are very dear to Him, and He willingly hears their prayer for their poor brethren who are still in the midst of trouble and danger. It is a great joy to them to pray for us, and we should be foolish indeed to neglect such a means of grace.

Some people tell us that they go straight to God. So do Catholics; none go straighter: but sometimes they act like the so-called friends of Job. God was angry with these men for their cruelty to His afflicted servant, and when they went straight to Him for forgiveness, He said to them, "Go to My servant Job, and My servant Job shall pray for you .... And the Lord accepted the face of Job when he prayed for his friends." We go straight to God, but we take the advice of God Himself and go in good company.

Mary, Mother of God

Among our intercessors in Heaven is one whose office, holiness, and power with God place her far above the Angels and Saints. It is Holy Mary, the Mother of God. Mary is truly Mother of God because she is Mother of a Divine Person, because her Son Who took His human nature from her is truly God. In raising Mary to so wonderful a dignity, God has exalted her above all other creatures; the highest angel is His servant; she is His Mother.

Sursum Corda!

Because of her nearness to Him, He was bound for His own sake to save her from all that could displease Him in her, and to enrich her with all the grace that would make her pleasing in His sight, and worthy, as far as a creature could be worthy, of the relation in which she was to stand to Himself. Would He endure sin in one who was to be so closely united to Him? Must He not do for His Mother what He had done for the, angels and for Adam and Eve— create her soul free from sin and in friendship with Himself? The Church teaches that no stain of sin, original or actual, ever touched her. She was brought into being like other children, but, unlike all others, she was preserved from the original stain, and came into existence fair and pleasing in God's sight. The Precious Blood of her Divine Son, that was to win pardon for us, did more for her by preserving her from sin. Christ died for Mary as for us, and so in her hymn of praise she says, "My spirit hath rejoiced in God my Savior." She is the first among the saved, only saved more grandly than any other. This privilege of exemption from original sin is called the Immaculate Conception.

It is God we glorify in honoring Mary. We praise Him for His one perfect creature, for her privileges, her dignity, her holiness, and for the power He has given her with Himself. For He Who came to us by her, has willed to show us favor through her. Because she is so near and dear to Him, the Church would have us reverence and love her, and in all our necessities fly to her as to a mother. This we do whenever we say the Hail Mary. We ask her who is blessed among women to pray for us sinners; to pray for us now, in the needs of the present day and hour; to pray for us above all, in that hour of our death which is to decide our eternity. The Church never separates the Mother from the Son. Three times each day she calls her children by the Angelus bell to thank God for the Incarnation of His Son, and to bless her by whom God made Man was given to us. Thus, in every age and land and tongue, do Catholics fulfill Mary's own prophecy, "All generations shall call me blessed."

❈ CHARITY ❈
The Ten Commandments of God

We are bound to love God because He is infinitely good in Himself and infinitely good to us. The love we are commanded to have is not an affectionate   , but a preference of Him above all things, so that we would not lose His friendship for the love or fear of anything whatsoever. We show that we love God by keeping His Commandments. Of these the first three concern our duty to God, the seven others our duty to our neighbor and to ourselves.

The First Commandment

By the First Commandment we are commanded to worship the one true and living God, by Faith, Hope, Charity, and Religion. The sins against Faith are—all false religions, willful doubt, disbelief, or denial of any article of Faith, and also culpable ignorance of the doctrines of the

Sursum Corda!

Church. We expose ourselves to the danger of losing our Faith by neglecting our spiritual duties—the Sacraments, Mass, morning and night prayers, daily examination of conscience, grace at meals, etc., by reading bad books, going to non-Catholic schools, and taking part in the services or prayers of a false religion.

The sins against Hope are despair and presumption. The chief sins against religion are the worship of false gods or idols, and the giving to any creature whatsoever the honor which belongs to God alone. The First Commandment forbids us to give divine honor to the angels and saints, but we should give them the inferior honor due to them as the special friends of God; and we should give to relics, crucifixes, and holy pictures a relative honor, as they relate to Christ and His Saints, and are memorials of them.

This Commandment forbids all dealing with the devil and superstitious practices, such as consulting spiritualists and fortune-tellers, and trusting to charms, omens, dreams, and suchlike fooleries. We must hold in horror anything that might weaken our Faith. Cheap books that attack the very foundations of Faith—belief in God, the soul, the life to come—are scattered broadcast over the land. Men and women of every class, boys and girls, read them, and to thousands such reading means the loss of all Faith. We should not thus endanger our soul, and risk what is more precious than life. If Hope and Charity are lost, we may recover both by means of Faith. But if Faith itself fails, only a miracle of grace can restore it, and set our feet again in the way of salvation.

The Second Commandment

The Second Commandment requires us to speak with reverence of God and all holy persons and things, and to keep our lawful oaths and vows. It forbids all false, rash, unjust, and unnecessary oaths, as also blaspheming, cursing, and profane words.

The Third Commandment

The Third Commandment requires us to keep the Sunday holy. The Church tells us this is to be done by hearing Mass and resting from servile works. Unless excused by some lawful reason, such as sickness, or grave danger of sickness, the necessity of remaining with little children, very bad weather, or great distance from church, every Catholic, who has come to the use of reason is bound under pain of mortal sin to hear Mass on Sundays and Holydays of Obligation. The duty of hearing Mass is not fulfilled by hearing a part of a Mass or a part of two. We are bound to be present at all the principal parts of one Mass, that is, from the Offertory to the Priest's Communion. It is a venial sin to be absent or late through our own fault during a less important portion of the Mass. Masters and mistresses are bound to see that those dependent on them are able to hear Mass on days of Obligation. Children of seven years of age

Sursum Corda!

are as much bound to hear Mass on Sundays and Holydays as grown-up people. If they miss Mass or are late through their parents' neglect, how can such parents be excused from the guilt of mortal sin?

Of course, it is not enough to be bodily present at Mass. We must unite ourselves in some way with what the priest is doing at the altar and raise our minds and hearts to God in prayer. We may follow the words and actions of the priest, and it is well to unite with him at least at the chief parts of the Mass—the Offertory, Consecration, and Priest's Communion. We may say our beads or other prayers, or think of the sufferings and death of Christ which the Mass commemorates. But there must be reverence, attention, and prayer of one kind or another. It is a sin to talk, laugh, eat, sleep, or allow our minds to be filled with willful distractions.

We are commanded to rest from unnecessary servile work on Sunday. Servile work is that in which the body is chiefly engaged. Liberal works which engage the mind more than the body are not forbidden. Innocent recreation that does not draw us from religious duties or give reasonable scandal is allowed. But we must remember that we are commanded to rest from servile work that we may have time and opportunity for prayer, going to the Sacraments, hearing instructions, and reading good books. Therefore, if we can hear a sermon or go to Benediction it is well to do so. Children who need instruction in Christian doctrine should be sent to Catechism. Priests are obliged to instruct their people, and remind them frequently of the things they are bound to remember if they would save their souls. What, then, is to be said of those who avoid such reminders, and never hear a sermon if they can help it?

The Fourth Commandment

The love of our neighbor proves our love of God. Among those whom we are bound to love, our parents hold the first place. Children who love, honor, and obey their parents are in a marked degree protected and blessed by God. Undutiful children are often signally punished by Him. We have to love our parents not with a natural affection only, because of all they have done for us, but because they hold the place of God, and He commands us to honor and to love them.

We are bound never to sadden our parents by neglect or by unkind behavior. We are forbidden to speak rudely to them, and still more to ridicule, threaten, or strike them. We should hide and excuse their faults, and help them in their needs both of soul and body. In serious sickness we must redouble our care, warn them of their danger, and get them the Sacraments in good time. After their death we should, if we are able, have Masses said for the repose of their souls, and pray much for their deliverance from Purgatory.

Children are bound to obey their parents in all that is not sin. Even when of age, married, or independent, they are bound to love and reverence them. Those commands of parents are of most importance which concern the salvation of the soul, such as religious duties, companions, amusements, late hours, and the like.

Sursum Corda!

We are commanded to obey, not our parents only, but also our Bishops and pastors, the civil authorities, and our lawful superiors. Our Bishop is appointed by the Vicar of Christ to govern the diocese to which we belong; we are bound, therefore, to reverence and obey him as the shepherd of our souls. We owe a like duty to priests sent by the Bishop to administer the Sacraments, to teach us the truths of our Faith, and to guide us to eternal life. The priest makes us children of God by holy Baptism, feeds us with the Bread of Life in Holy Communion, heals the wounds of our souls in the Sacrament of Penance, teaches us in sermons and instructions, comforts us in sorrow, counsels us in doubt, encourages us in temptation, visits our sick bed, and soothes our last moments with the consolations of religion. We are bound to honor him as the minister of God, to treat him and speak of him with respect, to be guided in what concerns our soul by his advice.

Respect and obedience are also due to the civil authorities. We are forbidden to rebel against our rulers, and to belong to any Society that plots against the Church or State, or to any Society that by reason of its secrecy is condemned by the Church. We are bound to pay the taxes, and to obey the laws of our country as long as these are not against the Commandments of God. This duty of obedience to lawful superiors does not cease because those superiors are bad, so long as they do not call on their subjects to do what is bad.

Wives are commanded to be subject to their husbands.

Servants are bound to respect, obedience, and fidelity to those whose service they have entered. They may not be insolent to their master or mistress, or expose their faults or family secrets. They are bound to obey their lawful commands in the duties for which they are engaged, and to take care of all intrusted to them.

Masters and mistresses are bound to treat with kindness those subject to them, to provide them with proper food and lodging, and to give them opportunity for religious instruction, hearing Mass, and going to the Sacraments. They are obliged to protect them from dangerous occasions of sin, to require only reasonable work of them, and to pay them just and reasonable wages.

By the Fourth Commandment parents are bound to provide for their children, to instruct and correct them, to give them good example, and a good Catholic education. A first duty after birth is immediately to have the child baptized. It is a duty that is frightfully neglected. There are mothers who keep a child for days and weeks without baptism, though they know that if it dies without the Sacrament it will never see God. To keep a child without baptism for any length of time, unless for some very grave reason, is a serious sin. The Church says, "Babes are to be brought to the font for baptism as soon as it can possibly be done, that a Sacrament without which no one can be saved may not be put off, to the danger of the child's soul." "As soon as possible" means when there is some one to bring the baby, and the baby can safely be brought.

The training of little children cannot begin too early, and it is a duty on which the salvation of parents as well as of their children may well depend. From their earliest years they

Sursum Corda!

must be taught the law of right and wrong, and be kept as far as possible from seeing or hearing evil. A child begins to notice and to imitate long before it can speak. How terrible will it be for the father or mother whose example has given it is first lesson in wickedness, who have set the little feet on the road that leads straight down to hell! But how happy are those parents who, remembering that God will require a strict account of the precious souls intrusted to them, guard them, from the beginning, from all that could bring them harm! Very early the mother should guide the little hand to make the Sign of the Cross. Very soon should she lead her child to the love of Jesus and Mary. On her knees, from her lips, it should learn its first prayers and the first simple lessons of the Catechism. She must be on the watch as its natural disposition begins to appear. It must be gently but firmly checked as naughty ways show themselves. It must learn that the word of father or mother is to be obeyed at once, that it will not get what it wants by temper or by tears. As it grows older it must be taught its duties as a Catholic—Mass; prayer morning and night; examination of conscience—and be trained to habits of truthfulness, industry, reverence for God and holy things, obedience to the laws of God and the Church. All this it should learn at home, and more by example than by word. When the time comes for First Confession, First Communion, Confirmation, it is the mother's place to see that the child is properly prepared; and she must take care that it afterwards goes regularly to its religious duties. Parents are bound to give their children a good Catholic education, and to guard them against companions, amusements, and reading, that might be occasions of harm. Children should be in bed early, and ought never to be out in the streets at night. In dealing with their children parents should avoid harshness and abuse, dislikes and partiality, and should spare no effort to make a comfortable and happy home for them. Corrections must be just and moderate, not given when the parent is in temper, not injurious to the child. Above all, parents should set an example to their children in the practice of morning and evening prayer, going to Mass and the Sacraments, the observance of honesty, sobriety, and the Church's law of abstinence. Let them avoid quarrelling, bad words, and words that injure their neighbor's character, and remember that what a child learns at home is, good or evil, learned for life.

The Fifth Commandment

This Commandment forbids all willful murder. Except in just war, in self-defense, or in the name of the law, we may not take the life of another. Neither may we take our own, either by direct suicide or by such vices as shorten life. The drunkard sins against this Commandment.

Not murder only, but the sins that lead to it—fighting, quarrelling, anger, hatred, and revenge—are forbidden by the Fifth Commandment. Scandal, also, and bad example, by which is meant any word or deed calculated to lead another into sin. All these come under sins against this Commandment, because they lead to the injury and spiritual death of our neighbor's soul.

The Sixth and Ninth Commandments

These Commandments forbid whatever is contrary to holy purity in thoughts, words, or actions. With regard to thoughts, it is important to remember that what is not willful is not sinful. A thought may haunt us for days, but as long as we would gladly be rid of it, and try to turn our mind away from it, there is no sin. Immodest plays and dances are forbidden by the Sixth Commandment, and it is sinful to look at them. This Commandment also forbids immodest songs, books, and pictures, because they are dangerous to the soul and lead to mortal sin. We must deny ourselves such companions and amusements, such newspapers and novels, as we know to be dangerous. And we must avoid idleness and curiosity.

The Seventh and Tenth Commandments

These Commandments forbid all covetous thoughts and unjust desires of our neighbor's goods and profits, and all unjust taking or keeping what belongs to another; for example, engaging in unjust lawsuits, borrowing with no intention or hope of being able to pay back, extravagance, to the injury of one's family and creditors, the taking of perquisites, without permission, by servants and others, negligence in doing the work which we have undertaken as teachers, workmen, servants, or in fulfilling the conditions of a contract as to time, materials, or manner.

The Seventh Commandment forbids all manner of cheating in buying and selling, such as using false weights and measures, adulterating goods, also the willful destruction of another's goods, the wasting of a master's time or property, and any other way of wronging our neighbor. We are bound to restore ill-gotten goods if we are able, or else the sin will not be forgiven; we must also pay our debts. Those who are careless in paying their debts should remember that of the four sins crying to Heaven for vengeance, two are "Oppression of the poor" and "Defrauding laborers of their wages." Many a poor dressmaker has been ruined by the withholding of the money which she has lost her night's rest to earn.

It will be no excuse to say we did not think of this. The poor are timid, and afraid to press for what belongs to them. But those who, relying on their helplessness, are cruel to them, will have a terrible account to settle when the day of reckoning comes.

As restitution of ill-gotten goods is often a matter of great difficulty, we should consult our confessor on the subject. He knows what human weakness is, he is our friend, always ready to put his knowledge and experience at our service; ways of helping us that we should never have thought of will occur to them—what a mistake to be afraid to ask the counsel that we need!

The Eighth Commandment

This Commandment guards our neighbor's good name. It forbids all false testimony, rash judgment, and lies.

False testimony is saying in a court of justice what we know to be untrue.

Rash judgment is condemning our neighbor in our own mind for a fault for which there is not sufficient evidence.

A lie is any word or act by which we intend to deceive. There are four kinds of lies: jocose lies, those told in jest; lies of excuse, told to escape some evil; malicious lies, told to injure another; sacrilegious lies, told to the Holy Ghost in confession, a false oath. Jocose lies and lies of excuse, that harm on one, are generally venial sins only. Malicious lies are mortal or venial according to the harm intended. Sacrilegious lies are always mortal. If an untruth told in jest is so absurd as to deceive no one, there is, of course, no sin at all.

Calumny, detraction, and tale-bearing are also forbidden by this Commandment.

Calumny is taking away our neighbor's character by telling lies of him. Detraction is making known his secret faults without sufficient cause. To publish a fault that is known to most persons in a place, or to so many that it must soon become public, is not detraction, but it 'may be against charity, because it is not loving our neighbor as ourselves. Any words which harm a person, and not a person only, but an institution, a college, a hospital, by lessening without good reason, the good opinion had of them, are sinful. The guilt of the sin is multiplied by the number of persons who hear the harm said.

It is hardly possible to avoid hearing detraction: sin comes in when we listen to it willingly and encourage it by asking curious questions that bring out the misdoings of others.

We may not be able to prevent an uncharitable conversation, but we may at times be able prudently to change the subject; at least, we can show displeasure by inattention or silence. We should be much on our guard when talk turns on people whom we much dislike or of whom we are jealous. A good practical rule is to try to excuse the absent, and not to say of another what we should not like said of ourselves.

Tale-bearing to make mischief, or from pure love of gossip, is wrong. But if we know of any improper conduct being carried on, we should make it known to those in authority. To neglect to do this might make us answerable for such sins by concealment.

When we have injured our neighbor by speaking ill of him, we are bound to restore his good name as far as we are able. If we have been guilty of calumny, we must tell those to whom we have spoken that what we said was untrue. If we have detracted, we must try to repair the harm we have done our neighbor by saying some good of him. We should beware, however, of bringing up again what is forgotten. On this point it is well to ask the advice of our confessor.

THE COMMANDMENTS OF THE CHURCH

We are bound to obey the Church, because Christ has said to the pastors of the Church, "He that heareth you heareth Me; and he that despiseth you despiseth Me" (Luke 10).

There are six chief Commandments of the Church.

The First Commandment of the Church

The First Commandment of the Church is to keep the Sundays and Holydays of Obligation holy by hearing Mass and resting from servile works. The Holydays of Obligation observed are Christmas Day, Circumcision, Ascension Thursday, the Assumption of Our Lady, and All Saints. Persons who work in places of business are not bound to hear Mass on the eight Holydays of the Church if this would interfere, injuriously to themselves, with their hours of employment.

The Second Commandment of the Church

The Second Commandment of the Church is to keep the days of fasting and abstinence appointed by the Church, that so we may mortify the flesh and satisfy God for our sins.

FASTING

By the law of Fasting we are restricted both as to the quantity and kind of food we may take. It restricts us to *one full meal* a day. We are allowed an evening collation of about eight ounces of solid food, and by approved custom two ounces of *dry bread* and something to drink, as tea, with a little milk, are permitted in the morning. The order of dinner and collation may be reversed.

At the Chief Meal:—Out of Lent flesh-meat is never allowed on Friday unless by special Indult. In Lent it is allowed on all days except Wednesdays and Fridays and

Ember Saturday. Whenever flesh-meat is allowed fish may be taken at the same meal.

Milk, butter, cheese, eggs, dripping, lard, and in some dioceses, suet, are allowed on all days at the principal meal, even on Ash Wednesday and Good Friday.

At Collation:—Flesh-meat is never allowed. The use of milk, butter, cheese, dripping, lard, suet, and fish, depends on the custom sanctioned in each diocese by the Bishop. They are generally allowed in small quantities only, as part of the collation and by way of condiment or seasoning. Dripping and lard are always allowed for cooking.

A drink between meals does not break the fast provided it remains a liquid and is not anything in itself forbidden, as broth, milk, or any such nourishing liquid. A cup of tea or coffee with a little milk may be taken once during the day.

Those who are bound to fast:—Persons over twenty-one years of age are bound to fast unless they are excused by physical or moral impossibility, or by dispensation. Thus the following are excused: those who make their living by hard manual work; those who work hard for the sick out of charity; the sick, the convalescent, and the delicate; very poor people who seldom get a full meal; and those who have reached their sixtieth year.

Times of Fasting: 1. Every day in Lent from Ash Wednesday to Easter, except the Sundays, and after midday on Holy Saturday when the fasting and abstinence of Lent cease.

2. *The Four Vigils,* or Eves of the four great Feasts of Christmas Day, December 24th; of Pentecost; of the Assumption, August 14th; and of All Saints, October 31st; (except when these Feasts fall on a Monday).

3. *The Ember Days:*—Wednesday, Friday, and Saturday in the first full week of Lent; in Whit-week; after September 14th; after December 13th.

ABSTINENCE

The law of Abstinence forbids flesh-meat to be taken, but allows the usual number of meals.

In Lent two days of abstinence are prescribed in each week, Wednesdays and Fridays; the Ember Saturday in Lent is an abstinence day as well.

Times of Abstinence. Out of Lent, fast days and Fridays. But the law of fasting, or of abstinence, or of both, ceases when a fast or an abstinence day falls on any Sunday in the year, or when, out of Lent, it falls on a Holyday of Obligation; hence, if a Feast with a Vigil falls on a Monday, the fasting and abstinence for the Vigil are not to be anticipated on the Saturday.

Those who are bound to abstain:—The law of Abstinence is binding on all who have reached the age of seven years and have come to the use of reason, unless they are excused by a just cause, such as ill-health, poverty, or the nature of their duties. Hence, persons exempt or dispensed from fasting are still bound to abstain from flesh-meat; if unable to do so without grave inconvenience, or in cases of doubt, they should ask their confessor for a dispensation, and should not dispense themselves. Those are guilty of a grave sin who, without sufficient reason, break or willfully cause others to break the laws of fasting or abstinence.

The Third Commandment of the Church

The Third Commandment of the Church is to go to confession at least once a year. Children are bound to go to confession as soon as they have come to the use of reason and are capable of mortal sin. This is generally supposed to be about the age of seven years.

The Fourth Commandment of the Church

The Fourth Commandment of the Church is to receive the Blessed Sacrament at least once a year, and that at Easter or thereabouts. Christians are bound to receive the Blessed Sacrament as soon as they are capable of being instructed in this sacred mystery.

The Fifth Commandment of the Church

The Fifth Commandment of the Church is to contribute to the support of our pastors. It is a duty to contribute to the support of religion according to our means, so that God may be duly honored and worshiped, and the kingdom of His Church extended. How unfair some people are to the priest! We hear them complain that they have not this or that in their church—it is cold or draughty, the vestments are shabby,

Sursum Corda!

the flowers are artificial, the singing is bad. But they do not offer to repair or renew the vestments, or to help in the choir. They do not give to their priest as they ought; nay, for some little grievance, many never give to him at all, never go near him, never speak of him except to injure him in the minds of those he has to help. Yet for their sake he has studied long years, and given up the chance of providing for himself in life; and it is to him they look to bring them the last consolations of the Church when they lie down to die!

The Sixth Commandment of the Church

The Sixth Commandment of the Church is not to marry within certain degrees of kindred, nor to solemnize marriage at the forbidden times, that is, from the first Sunday in Advent till the day after Christmas and from Ash Wednesday till the day after Easter Sunday. A marriage contracted during the forbidden times is valid and even lawful (provided the local laws of the diocese do not forbid it), but it may not be celebrated with the solemn rites of the Church, as nuptial Mass, bells, etc., nor with special public rejoicings.

✥ THE SACRAMENTS ✥

Our soul, like our body, has a life which begins, grows, meets with injury, needs food and medicine. To supply these needs God has provided the Sacraments, which give us spiritual life, strength, feed, and heal our soul, give it the help of the Christian priesthood and of the Christian family, and comfort it in its passage from this world to the next.

All good comes to us from the Precious Blood. Not salvation only, but all we want to save our soul—light to see what we ought to do, strength to overcome temptation, forgiveness of sin, grace to take up our cross daily and follow Christ, courage to bear up against the weariness of well-doing, perseverance to the end. It is by the Sacraments that the merits of the Precious Blood are applied to our souls. They are thus the chief means of our salvation.

There are seven Sacraments—Baptism, Confirmation, Holy Eucharist, Penance, Extreme Unction, Holy Orders, and Matrimony. In every Sacrament there are three things: *the outward sign, the inward grace,* and the *institution of Christ.* The outward sign is something which can be perceived by our senses. It consists of (1) matter and (2) form. The matter is the substance used in giving the Sacrament, as the water in Baptism. The form consists of the words used in applying the matter, as "I baptize thee," etc. The inward grace is the spiritual effect produced. For the Sacraments are not merely signs of grace, they give the grace they signify. A little water is poured on the body and the baby's soul is cleansed from original sin. A few words are said in the confessional, and the chains of sin, which made the soul the slave of Satan, fall off, and it becomes once more the free and happy child of God. God alone can give to an outward sign the power of giving grace. Hence every Sacrament must be instituted by Christ. Because they are His institution there is nothing uncertain about the effects of the Sacrament. As surely as the sun gives light and life, warmth and color to the earth, so surely do the Sacraments give health and spiritual beauty to those who receive them worthily.

Certain dispositions are necessary, but they do not give the grace, they only take away hindrances to the grace the Sacrament gives. When due dispositions are wanting, the Sacrament of Penance is not really received; the Holy Eucharist gives no grace; Baptism in the case of adults, Confirmation, Extreme Unction, Holy Orders, and Matrimony produce no grace till the hindrances to grace are removed.

The Holy Eucharist was instituted at the Last Supper; Penance on the day of Christ's Resurrection; the time of institution of Baptism, Confirmation, Extreme Unction, and Matrimony is not known; probably it was during the forty days after the Resurrection, when Our Lord spoke to the Apostles of the "Kingdom of God." Baptism is the most necessary of the Sacraments, because without it we cannot enter heaven. Penance is necessary for those who have committed mortal sin after Baptism. Confirmation we are obliged to receive if we have the opportunity. The Holy Eucharist must be received about Easter; Extreme Unction when we are dangerously ill. Holy Orders and Matrimony are necessary for the Church as a body, but not for each individual.

Baptism, Holy Orders, Confirmation imprint a character upon the soul, that is, they leave upon it a mark which for all eternity will be for its glory or for its shame. The Sacraments which give a character cannot be repeated.

All the Sacraments give sanctifying grace, which makes the soul pleasing in the sight of God. Baptism and Penance are called Sacraments of the Dead because our souls may be dead in sin when we receive them. In this case they give grace where it was not before. The other Sacraments are called Sacraments of the Living, because our souls must be alive by grace to receive them worthily. These Sacraments increase in the soul the grace they find there. Besides sanctifying grace, each Sacrament gives its own special grace, called Sacramental, and a title to actual graces. An actual grace is a help given in a particular need—at one time strength to profess our faith; at another, sorrow to repent of sin; light to see our way in difficulties, etc.

To receive a Sacrament unworthily, that is, without due dispositions, is a grievous sin, called sacrilege. To receive the Sacraments worthily is the greatest happiness in the world. Hence we should have a great desire to receive them, and prepare ourselves earnestly, for the more fervent our preparation, the greater the grace we shall get, just as a man who takes a large bucket to the well draws more water than another who takes a small one.

❈ BAPTISM ❈

Baptism is a Sacrament which cleanses us from original sin, makes us Christians, children of God, members of the Church, and heirs of heaven.

Baptism also forgives actual sins, that is, the sins which we ourselves commit, and takes away all punishment due

Sursum Corda!

to them when it is received in proper dispositions by those who have been guilty of actual sin. Water is the matter of Baptism. The form is: "I baptize thee in the name of the Father, and of the Son, and of the Holy Ghost." The ordinary minister of Baptism is a priest, but anyone may baptize in case of necessity when a priest cannot be had. Unless when conditional or in danger of death, Baptism must always be "solemn" and conferred by the parish priest of the parents. All should know how to baptize, for any one of us may have to administer the sacrament when a priest is not at hand. How many nurses have opened the gate of heaven to dying infants! And not nurses only. A child in charge of a baby brother suddenly taken with a fit, baptized him. An English soldier out in India used to take his morning walk by the seashore to baptize the numbers of infants left there to be washed away by the tide. He could not save their earthly life, but he could bring them to life everlasting.

Baptism is given by pouring water on the head of the child, saying at the same time these words: "I baptize thee in the name of the Father, and of the Son, and of the Holy Ghost." Notice, the water must touch and flow upon the body; the same person must pour the water and say the words; the words must be said at the same time that the water is poured, not before or after. We must have the intention of doing what the Church does and Christ ordained. To receive Baptism worthily, adults must have the beginnings of faith, sorrow for sin, and the intention of receiving the Sacrament.

There must be a godfather and godmother, or at least one godparent who must be a Catholic, appointed by the parents, and must touch the child at the font. Sponsors undertake to see, as far as practicable, that the child is brought up in the Catholic faith and in the practice of its religion in case the parents die or neglect this duty. When baptized children come to the use of reason, they are bound to carry out the promises made in their name by their godfathers and godmothers. The minister of Baptism and the sponsors contract spiritual relationship with the person baptized, invalidating any subsequent marriage between the baptizer and the baptized, or between the baptized and one of the sponsors.

❈ CONFIRMATION ❈

Confirmation is a Sacrament by which we receive the Holy Ghost in order to make us strong and perfect Christians and soldiers of Jesus Christ.

All Catholics who have come to the use of reason and have the opportunity are bound to receive this Sacrament, for without it few would avoid mortal sin. They must be in a state of grace, and sufficiently instructed in the truths necessary for salvation, and as to the nature of the Sacrament they are going to receive. If possible they should have a good knowledge of the Catechism.

The matter of the Sacrament consists of the imposition of the Bishop's hands and the anointing with holy chrism, a substance composed of olive and balsam, a fragrant plant of Eastern lands. The form is: "I sign thee with the sign of the cross, and I confirm thee with the chrism of salvation, in the name of the Father, and of the Son, and of the Holy Ghost. Amen." As the Bishop says these words he makes the sign of the cross with chrism on our forehead. Then he gives a little blow on the cheek, saying, "Peace be with thee." This is to signify the trials which, as soldiers of Christ, we must expect, and the peace of God which will enable us to bear them with patience. No one must leave the altar till the chrism has been wiped from his forehead.

The special effect of this Sacrament is strength to profess our faith steadfastly, to lead a life worthy of our faith, and to suffer for it if needful. A Patron Saint is chosen at Confirmation. We should often invoke his help, and try to imitate his virtues. One sponsor only is required—a godfather for boys, a godmother for girls. The same spiritual relationship, but not the same impediment of marriage, arises in Confirmation as in Baptism. Sponsors should therefore see, as far as practicable, that their godchildren live up to the practice of their religion.

THE HOLY EUCHARIST

The Holy Eucharist as a Sacrament

The Sacrament of the Holy Eucharist is the true Body and Blood of Jesus Christ, together with His Soul and Divinity, under the appearances of bread and wine.

The matter of this Sacrament is wheaten bread and wine of the grape. The form is: "This is My Body," said over the bread; and "This is My Blood of the new and eternal testament, the mystery of faith, which shall be shed for you and for many unto the remission of sins," said over the wine. The change of the bread and wine into the Body and Blood of Christ takes place by the power of God when the words of consecration ordained by Christ at the Last Supper are pronounced by the priest in the Holy Mass. This change is called Transubstantiation, that is a change—not in figure or appearance, but in reality. Our Lord at the Last Supper said: "*This* is My Body.... *This* is My Blood." What looked like bread and wine were by His word no longer what they appeared to be, but were His precious Body and Blood. After the consecration the bread and wine are gone and on the altar in their stead is He Himself, Body and Blood, and Soul and Divinity, not perceived by our senses, but hidden under the appearances of the' bread and wine which remain after the substance has been taken away. Though there are two appearances, or species, there is only one Sacrament, and under each species Christ is received whole and entire.

This Sacrament exceeds all the other Sacraments in dignity. It was instituted by Our Lord to be a memorial of His love for us especially in His sufferings and death; and to give us not one grace, but every grace we need. He gives Himself to us to be the food and the life of our souls, our Companion and Comforter in the troubles of this world, and that the very body by its union with His may be raised to a glorious life at the Last Day. "He that eateth My Flesh and drinketh My Blood hath everlasting life, and I will raise him up in the last day."

It is a great sin to receive Holy Communion unworthily, that is, in mortal sin. St. Paul says: "He that eateth or drinketh unworthily eateth and drinketh judgment to himself, not discerning the Body of the Lord" (1 Corinthians 11). To receive Holy Communion worthily we must be in a state of grace. If grace has been lost by mortal sin, this must be forgiven by a good confession. We must also be fasting from midnight. This means that from twelve o'clock the night before our Communion we must not eat or drink anything whatsoever by way of food or medicine.

This Sacrament, which is by excellence the Blessed Sacrament, increases sanctifying grace in our souls, forgives venial sin, and preserves us from mortal sin. It weakens our evil inclinations, and is the most powerful means of resisting temptation. The more fervent the dispositions we bring to Holy Communion, the more grace we shall receive from the visit of our Divine Guest.

The Holy Eucharist as a Sacrifice

Sacrifice is the offering to God by a lawful Minister of some object falling under the senses, to acknowledge by its destruction or change God's supreme excellence and power over life and death, and our absolute dependence on Him. Hence sacrifice is the highest act of religion, and can be offered to God alone. In all ages of the world God has commanded men to worship Him by sacrifice, and to pay in this way their fourfold duty and debt to Him.

As His creatures we are bound (1) to adore Him, (2) to thank Him for all His benefits, (3) to beg pardon for our sins, (4) to ask Him for all we need for soul and body.

In the Old Law there were different sacrifices for these different ends. In the New Law there is only one sacrifice but, one of infinite value, for it is the sacrifice of the Body and Blood of Jesus Christ, true God and true man, really present on the altar, and offered to God for the living and the dead. This sacrifice is called the Mass. It is not a different sacrifice from that of the Cross, but the same sacrifice continued or renewed in a different and unbloody manner. This sacrifice was foretold by the prophets. It is the "clean oblation" offered to God by "the Gentiles from the rising to the setting of the sun" (Malachi 1). On the Altar, as on the Cross, Our Lord is both Priest and Victim. But in the Mass Our Lord does not really die. He is the "Lamb standing as it were slain" (Apoc. 5). He offers Himself under the appearances of bread and wine, "a high priest for ever according to the order of Melchisedech" (Psalm 109). He offers Himself by the hands of His priests. "Do this in commemoration of Me," He said to His Apostles at the Last Supper. He gave them power to do what He had done, and to pass on this power of consecrating bread and wine to their successors, so to "show forth the death of the Lord until He come" (1 Corinthians 11).

Sursum Corda!

The Mass, therefore, is not simply a prayer in common, like other public forms of worship. It is an act of awful solemnity—God offering Himself to God, to adore and thank for us, to beg pardon for our sins, and to obtain for us all graces and blessings. Our Blessed Lord does all this in our name. He does perfectly for us what we do so imperfectly ourselves. What matter, then, if we do not understand all the priest is saying at the altar. We know what the invisible High Priest, Jesus Christ, is doing, and we offer ourselves, with all our needs and desires, to God through Him. If we remember what is going on at the altar—that Jesus Christ, Our Lord and Savior, is really there, renewing for us the great Sacrifice of the Cross, and applying to our souls the merit of that Sacrifice; if we remember what we can do by offering this Sacrifice with Him—how we can worship God perfectly, and easily obtain from Him the pardon of our sins, and all we need for ourselves and for those dear to us—we can hardly help hearing Mass well, and drawing down great blessings on ourselves and those we love.

❈ PENANCE ❈

Penance is a Sacrament whereby the sins, whether mortal or venial, which we have committed after baptism are forgiven. Besides forgiving sin, it also increases the grace of God in the soul. Our Lord instituted this Sacrament when He breathed on His Apostles, saying: "Whose sins you shall forgive they are forgiven" (John 20:23).

Of all God's mercies to us the greatest is His ready forgiveness of sin. Whilst our Blessed Lord was on earth He was called "the friend of sinners." He tenderly received those who came to Him for pardon, and He has left in His Church an easy means by which all may obtain forgiveness of sin. However many, however great they may be, the Precious Blood of Jesus will-wash them away if only we are truly sorry for them.

The matter of the Sacrament of Penance consists of the acts of the penitent—contrition, confession, and satisfaction. The form is the absolution pronounced by the priests: "I absolve thee from thy sins, in the name of the Father, and of the Son, and of the Holy Ghost." The effects are to remove all guilt, both mortal and venial; to remit punishment, more or less according to our dispositions; to restore or increase sanctifying grace; to give us back our right to heaven and all past merits, which are lost by one mortal sin. The minister is a priest who has received faculties from the Bishop of the diocese. He forgives sin by the power of God in pronouncing the words of absolution. He is bound, under the most solemn obligation, never to reveal in any way what has been told in confession.

We have four things to do when we are preparing for confession: (1) We must heartily pray to God for His grace to help us; (2) We must carefully examine our conscience; (3) We must take time and care to make a good act of contrition; and (4) We must resolve to renounce our sins and to begin a new life for the future.

Sursum Corda!

(1) We ask the help of God to know our sins, to be truly sorry for them, to confess them as we ought, and to have a firm purpose of avoiding them for the future.

(2) We examine our conscience on the Ten Commandments, on the Six Precepts of the Church, on the Seven Deadly Sins, and on the duties of our state of life. We are bound to confess every mortal sin which, after a careful examination of conscience, we remember. If we leave one out willfully, or through a careless examination of conscience, we make a bad confession; but if, after trying with reasonable care to examine our conscience, we still forget some mortal sin, it is forgiven, only it must be told in the first confession after it is remembered, because every mortal sin must be confessed once. We are also bound to mention any circumstance that changes a venial sin into a mortal one. Though we are only bound to confess mortal sins, it would not be safe to mention those sins only which we know for certain were mortal, because we are so apt to deceive ourselves. The only safe practice is to confess whatever is on our conscience and gives us trouble—certain things as certain, doubtful things as doubtful.

(3) By far the most important part of our preparation is *contrition*. Sin, even mortal, may be forgiven without confession, e. g., if we forget it or are unable to make our confession, but no sin can be forgiven unless we are sorry for it. We must have true sorrow for every mortal sin we have committed. If we confess venial sins only, we must be sorry for at least one of them. And this sorrow must be supernatural, not from any temporal loss or disgrace that sin has

brought upon us, but from some motive suggested by faith. There are two kinds of supernatural sorrow or contrition—imperfect and perfect.

Imperfect contrition is sorrow for sin chiefly for our own sake because we have lost heaven, or deserved hell or purgatory. This sorrow will forgive venial sins, and, when joined with confession and absolution, is sufficient for the forgiveness of mortal sin.

Perfect contrition is sorrow because by sin we have offended so good a God. This is the best of all motives, and is so pleasing to God that by it our sins are forgiven immediately, even before we confess them; but, nevertheless, if they are mortal, we are strictly bound to confess them afterwards. We should often make acts of perfect contrition: O my God, because Thou art so good, I am sorry for having offended Thee." Many a man struck down by an accident has been saved by an act such as this. No one, then, need despair because he is dying without a priest. Let him turn to God with all his heart by an act of perfect contrition and a desire of confession, and his sins will be forgiven.

Both perfect and imperfect contrition remit some of the punishment our sins deserve, more or less according to our dispositions.

We must earnestly ask God to give us a hearty sorrow for our sins, and we must make use of such considerations as may lead us to it, such as the loss of heaven and the eternal punishment of hell which mortal sin deserves; Our Savior's bitter sufferings for our sins in the Garden or on the Cross; the infinite goodness of God in Himself, etc.

(4) Lastly, we must have a firm purpose of amendment; that is, we must determine, with the help of God, to avoid all mortal sin, and the dangerous occasions of mortal sin—the person, place, or thing that usually leads us wrong. If we confess mortal sins, we must have a firm purpose to avoid every one of them for the future. If we confess venial sins only, we must have a firm purpose to avoid at least one of them. If we have any restitution to make to our neighbor, whether of goods or of good name, we must see how this can best be done. It is a useful practice always to accuse ourselves, and to renew our sorrow for some greater sin of our past life already confessed, in order thus to make sure of our contrition and purpose of amendment.

Confession is to accuse ourselves of our sins to a priest approved by the Bishop. A person who willfully conceals a mortal sin in confession is guilty of a great sacrilege, by telling a lie to the Holy Ghost in making a bad confession.

Satisfaction is doing the penance given us by the priest. It is well to perform our penance if possible before leaving the church. This penance helps in a special manner to lessen the temporal punishment our sins have deserved. But as it does not generally make full satisfaction for our sins, we should add to it other good works and try to gain indulgences.

Indulgences

Sin has two effects upon the soul—the guilt or stain which it leaves upon it, and the debt of punishment to be paid in this life or in the next. The guilt of mortal sin is remitted to the Sacrament of Penance or by perfect contrition. The eternal punishment is remitted when the guilt is remitted and part of the temporal punishment into which the eternal has been changed. More or less is remitted according to the dispositions of the penitent. The rest of the punishment must be removed either by works of penance, such as prayers, fasting, and alms-deeds; by the sufferings of this life borne with patience; by the extreme suffering of Purgatory; or by Indulgences.

Good works also have two effects; they produce merit, which is a title to reward, and they make satisfaction for sin. The good works Christ our Lord did on earth and the satisfaction He thereby made for all human sin were of infinite value. These merits belong to the Church and she has power to apply them to our soul for the remission of punishment no less than for the remission of guilt. And because all the members of Christ are bound together in the Communion of Saints, the good works of the Blessed Virgin and of the Saints, and their superabundant satisfactions, are also applied as satisfaction for the debts of each one of us.

No punishment can be remitted till the guilt has been repented of and forgiven. Then, by fulfilling certain conditions, as prayer, works of charity, visits to churches, we can gain a remission of the temporal punishment due to our sins. This remission is called an Indulgence. Hence we see the ignorance and injustice of those who say that an Indulgence is leave to commit sin. An Indulgence has nothing to do with the guilt of sin, but only with its punishment; and no punishment can be remitted by an Indulgence till the sin is forgiven. How much is remitted we cannot tell. The judgments of God are an abyss which we must adore rather than seek to comprehend. We know that indulgences are a means of lessening the rigor of those judgments. This should make us try to gain them. The result of our trying we must leave to God; we cannot know it in this life.

A Plenary Indulgence, if fully gained, remits all the punishment till then due. It remits more or less according to the dispositions of the person gaining the Indulgence. A Partial Indulgence remits a part of the punishment. A Partial Indulgence of a hundred or of forty days remits as much as would have been remitted by the severe canonical penances of former days, but how this is no one knows.

To gain any Indulgence there is required (1) a state of grace; (2) at least a general intention to gain it; (3) performance of the works prescribed—Confession once a fortnight or daily Communion—i. e. practically daily, with the omission of but once or twice a week—suffices to gain all Plenary Indulgences. The prayers for the Pope's intention may be any kind of vocal prayer, but not mental. Indulgences, unless otherwise stated, may be applied by way of suffrage to the Holy Souls in Purgatory, that is, they may be offered to God for the souls we pray for, to pay their debt and procure them release from their sufferings.

⚜ EXTREME UNCTION ⚜

Extreme Unction is the anointing of the sick with holy oil, accompanied with prayer. The matter of this Sacrament is oil of olives, blessed by the Bishop, and the anointing by a priest of the eyes, ears, nostrils, lips, hands, and feet. The form is, "By this holy anointing and of His own most tender mercy, may the Lord forgive thee whatever sins thou hast committed by the sight...by the hearing," etc.

The effects of the Sacrament of Extreme Unction are to comfort and strengthen the soul, to remit sin, and even to restore health when God sees it to be expedient.

A person in danger of death by sickness who refused to receive Extreme Unction, would be guilty of grave temerity.

⚜ HOLY ORDERS ⚜

Holy Orders is the Sacrament by which bishops, priests, and other ministers of the Church are ordained, and receive power and grace to perform their sacred duties. The matter of the Sacrament is the imposition of the hands of the Bishop. The form consists of the words said by the Bishop in administering the Sacrament. This Sacrament impresses a character, and therefore, cannot be repeated.

Sursum Corda!

✠ MATRIMONY ✠

Matrimony is the Sacrament which sanctifies the contract of a Christian marriage, and gives a special grace to those who receive it worthily. No human power can dissolve the bond of marriage, and under no circumstances is it ever lawful for either party to marry again during the lifetime of the other.

The matter of the Sacrament consists of the persons of the contracting parties, and the mutual consent by which they take each other for man and wife. The form consists of the words by which they express this contract. They are bound to be in a state of grace to receive this Sacrament, and should prepare for it by a good confession. The effect is a special grace to enable them to bear the difficulties of their state, to love and be faithful to one another, and to bring up their children in the fear of God.

Those who enter into the contract of marriage are both the ministers and the subjects of the Sacrament. They marry each other. The priest witnesses, ratifies, and blesses the contract.

Betrothal

Since Easter, 1908, no engagement to marry is canonically valid and binding unless it has been contracted in writing and signed by the parties to it, and by a qualified priest, or the Bishop, or at least by two witnesses. None the less, a man not keeping a promise to marry a woman is, of course, bound in conscience to make compensation for any wrong he may thereby have done her.

Marriage

To receive the Sacrament validly both parties must be baptized, and free from any of the impediments called diriment, which by the law of the Church render marriage invalid and null. The principal are (1) Holy Orders; (2) Solemn Religious Vows; (3) Marriage between baptized and unbaptized, e. g., Pagans, Jews, Quakers; (4) Consanguinity, i. e., relationship by blood to the third degree, that is, to second cousins inclusively (unless with dispensation); (5) Affinity, i. e. relationship by marriage to the second degree, so that after the death of husband or wife the survivor cannot (unless with dispensation) marry a relation of the deceased to first cousins inclusively; (6) Spiritual relationship, contracted at Baptism by the minister and the sponsors with the child.

There are other impediments called *impediments*, or forbidding, which render marriage unlawful though the marriage is a real one. These are: (1) Mixed marriages (unless with dispensation); (2) Solemnization of marriage at the forbidden times; (3) Espousals to another person (unless annulled by mutual consent).

Marriage between Catholics, or between a Catholic and a non-Catholic, to be valid, must be contracted before a duly qualified priest, or the Bishop of the place, and two witnesses. When the parties are not able to write, another witness must be added. A qualified priest is (1) the parish priest or the Bishop of the place where the marriage is contracted, or (2) a priest delegated by either. Therefore marriage before a Justice, or in non-Catholic places of worship, or without the presence of a qualified priest, is not only unlawful and sinful, but null and void. However, in case of death, a marriage is valid if celebrated in the presence of two witnesses and of any priest.

For a qualified priest to assist lawfully at a marriage within his own district, one of the contracting parties must have lived in this district for a month, or must be exempted from so doing by his or her Bishop or parish priest. The banns must be published at the principal Mass on three Sundays or Holy-days of Obligation. If the parties belong to different churches, the banns must be published in both. The marriage should be celebrated by the priest in whose parish the bride lives, unless there is some good reason to the contrary.

Catholics ought to know clearly what they have to do in order to receive validly and lawfully the Sacrament of Matrimony, and should understand that although for all *civil* effects marriages are valid in *civil law* if the conditions and requirements of the civil marriage law are fulfilled, they are nevertheless null and void *before God*, and the parties are not in the sight of God husband and wife, if the said marriages are not contracted before the Bishop of the place, or a priest duly authorized for the celebration thereof, and two witnesses.

Mixed Marriages

Mixed marriages are marriages between a Catholic and one who, though baptized, does not profess the Catholic Faith. The Church has always forbidden mixed marriages and considers them in principle unlawful and pernicious. When the Church permits a mixed marriage by granting a dispensation for very grave reasons and under special conditions, there is to be no nuptial Mass, no blessing. Her priest stands sadly by to witness, not to bless. The conditions are: (a) That the Catholic party shall have full liberty for the practice of the Catholic religion, (b) That all the children that may be born of the marriage shall be baptized, and brought up in the Catholic Faith, (c) That the Catholic party shall endeavor, especially by prayer and example, to convert the other to the Catholic Faith, (d) That no religious marriage ceremony shall take place elsewhere than in the Catholic church. It is a sacrilege to contract a marriage in mortal sin, or in disobedience to the laws of the Church; and instead of a blessing, the guilty parties draw down upon themselves the anger of God.

Sacramentals

Sacramentals are sacred objects, words, and actions, by the devout use of which the faithful obtain grace. They are called Sacramentals from a certain resemblance which they bear to the Sacraments. But there is a great difference between the two. The Sacraments were instituted by Our

Sursum Corda!

Lord, and in virtue of His institution give grace by their own power if on obstacle is put in the way. The Sacramentals are instituted by the Church, and for their efficacy depend chiefly on the dispositions of those who use them. Whatever the Church blesses has a salutary effect on those who use it with faith and piety. The Sacraments are necessary for us; the Sacramentals, though powerful means of grace, are not absolutely necessary. The principal Sacramentals are holy water, palms, ashes, crucifixes, rosaries, medals, and scapulars.

Prayer and the Sacraments are the chief means for obtaining the grace of God, without which we can do no good work towards our salvation. Hence our use of these means should be frequent and fervent. By their help we shall be enabled to keep the Commandments, and so enter into life everlasting.

HOLY MASS

INTRODUCTION

With her customary astuteness, Mother Loyola here presents the Holy Sacrifice not as a utilitarian assessment of its parts and its equipment, but with a view toward those things *which we most ought to understand and believe about it.*

Thus she sets out to explain the True Presence of Christ in the Eucharist, the history of Sacrifice in the Old Law and the New, and the Fruits of the Mass with their effects on our souls. Though she does briefly describe the main parts of the Mass and their significance, as well as the reasons why Latin is the language of the Mass, far more energy is directed toward how we can hear Mass with the sort of dispositions that will, in turn, lead to a greater share of the Graces available to us in the Sacrament.

Likewise, while Mother Loyola explains our solemn obligation to hear Mass each Sunday and Holy day, she also exhorts us to assist at Mass more frequently—daily if possible—reasoning that The Mass is truly God's Greatest Gift to us. The more that we appreciate the true meaning and significance of the Mass, the more we will seek the graces to be found there as often as possible.

Contents

Holy Mass

I.	God with Us	275
II.	The Worship of Sacrifice	280
	Sacrifice Ordained by God	280
	Jewish Sacrifices	280
	The Christian Sacrifice	281
III.	The Perpetual Sacrifice	283
	The Bread of Life	284
	The First Mass	286
IV.	Fruits of the Mass	287
	The General Fruit	287
	The Special Fruit	289
	Stipends for Masses	289
	Mass for the Holy Souls	290
V.	Mass on Sundays and Holydays	292
	Mass of Obligation	292
	When We Cannot Hear Mass	293
	Neglect of Mass	294
	Holydays of Obligation	295
	How the Obligation Binds	295

VI.	HOW WE SHOULD HEAR MASS	296
	"Remember the Holy Angels"	296
	"The Acceptable Time"	297
	Why in Latin	299
	Union with the Priest	300
	The Offertory	301
	The Consecration	302
	The Communion	303
	Spiritual Communion	308
	The Memento for the Living	309
	The Memento for the Dead	309
VII.	WEEKDAY MASS	310
	Why We Should Hear Mass Daily	310
	"The Gift of God"	313
VIII.	"BY HIM AND WITH HIM AND IN HIM"	314
	Union with the Holy Sacrifice	314

HOLY MASS

I

GOD WITH US

THERE are those amongst us, who, to the close of a long life, will remember their thrill of awe when it was first told them that Jesus Christ, Who once walked this earth of ours, so worshipped, so hated, and so loved; Who lay on the straw and was glorified by Angels; Who worked in the carpenter's shop, and trod the waves of the sea; Who hung helpless on the Cross, and by His own power rose from the dead—*is with us still.* His going away at the Ascension was not a parting, for as truly as He dwelt at Nazareth and Capharnaum, and was visited by His friends for instruction, or sympathy, or relief, He is with us now. This truth, when it comes—not like the gradual dawn, as to the Catholic child, but like the sudden flash of light from the heavens—makes a moment in life whose memory no length of years can obliterate.

But to all of us it is only the pondering of this wondrous fact that reveals to us what it means; that enables it, little by little, to work its way into our mind, and heart, and life, till we come to see that the Real Presence is, or should be, simply everything to us.

Sursum Corda!

There, on the altar, is He Who for us became Man, and worked for His daily bread, and died a death of shame, and Who for each one of us renews in His Sacramental Life the mysteries of the three and thirty years. No need to look longingly to a past growing dimmer and dimmer in the distance; to days when we might have met Him travel-stained on a dusty road in Galilee; or watched Him in breathless admiration from the water's edge as He taught from Peter's boat; or made our way to Him at night to speak with Him as friend to friend. He is here now, to be to us what He might have been then. He loves us, each one of us, too dearly to shut us out from the mysteries of His blessed life on earth. He would make Bethlehem, and Nazareth, and Calvary realities to us, not only by the memory that recalls them, and the grace laid up in them for us, one by one, to be had for the asking, but by the renewal of them in the abiding marvel of His Real Presence which the Church calls "a remembrance of all His wonderful works."

Is He not as little here as in the Crib where He would have taught us by His own example to be meek and humble of heart? May we not learn of Him here self-sacrifice for the Glory of God and the help of others, and gentle patience, and persevering prayer, as we should have learned by watching Him in His humble home, or at His daily toil, or in the Garden of the Agony? Can we not, like Magdalen, come to Him to have our sins forgiven? The help and consolation His Sacred Person brought to those who saw and heard and touched Him during His life on earth—this indeed is wanting to us. It was this the Apostles craved for when He told them that He was going where they could not follow Him. But to us as to them, He left His real though unseen Self. To us as to them, He says that it is not expedient—that is, not best for us yet—to see and hear and touch Him. This happiness will be ours by and by, as a reward of the faith by which we now believe without seeing, and make our profit of the divine Keepsake He has left, to be a treasury of all good to us, our resource in the cares and temptations and sorrows of life.

A Catholic was trying to impress on a Nonconformist teacher in a Sunday School the necessity of an infallible authority in religious matters. "Suppose," she said, "that one of your class were to ask you point-blank whether Christ, when He said at the Last Supper '*This is My Body,*' meant just what He said, or not—what would you answer?"

"I think," said the other, after a moment's hesitation, "that I should either evade the question, or say we don't know, or that it is better not to discuss difficult questions, but to keep to what is essential and necessary."

What a reply! "Evade the question," or own to ignoranee, when she was there as a teacher; or speak of the Real Presence of Christ in our midst as a detail too trivial to deserve attention! Did it matter to Magdalen whether or not He sat at meat in the house of the Pharisee? Did it concern the fever-stricken of Capharnaum, and the blind and the dumb, that He was coming down the street laying His hands on all? or make any difference to the fishermen on the Lake in their fast-filling boat that He was with them in the storm?

Sursum Corda!

Shall anyone dare tell us it is not necessary to know what Our Lord meant by His plain and most solemn words when He was leaving this world—to know whether His blessed Presence has been withdrawn from us or not? Are we not all of us sinful, and suffering, and storm-tossed? Who that is not utterly heedless of the needs of his own soul and of the needs of others, shall put aside as a thing of no moment the question that is one of life and death to us all—"is Jesus Christ true God and true Man, still on this earth, still within our reach?"

Let no one, quoting Our Lord's words: "It is the spirit that quickeneth, the flesh profiteth nothing," say: "He is with us as God to hear and help at all times." So He was from the beginning. But only since His coming amongst us as man, only by the touch of His sacred virginal flesh, has healing for soul and body gone out from Him in the marvelous way the Gospel story and the history of His Church attest. Because it was His will that this should be, He laid His hands on the eyes of the blind, and touched the lepers' sores. In no way has He shown Himself more truly our Brother, one of the human family, like to us in all things, than in willing to make our contact with His sacred human nature the source of every good to us.

Therefore He has left It always within our reach. Yes, Jesus Christ is with us still—with us all days—even to the end of time.

Holy Mass

When at the Last Supper He held the consecrated Bread before the eyes of the Twelve and said: "This is My Body," He gave them His very Self. And with Himself He gave the faith which—thanks to His mercy—is ours also, the faith which takes Him at His word, and with adoration and thanksgiving and love accepts His Unspeakable Gift.

But in the Blessed Sacrament Our Lord is more to us than Companion, and Friend, and Physician, more even than our Guest, harbored in our very hearts in Holy Communion. He is our High Priest and our Victim, by Whom we can pay to the full all that as creatures we owe to our Creator. To be able to do this worthily and perfectly is our greatest need, as we should feel if our hearts were unspoiled by sin and selfishness.

The Greatness of God, His Almightiness, His Wisdom, His Presence everywhere, His Beauty which shows itself in all His works, call for our adoration. His Goodness by which He has made us for everlasting happiness, claims our deepest thankfulness; whilst the injustice and ingratitude with which we have treated Him, and our many wants of soul and body, oblige us to beg pardon for our sins, and to ask Him to provide us with all we need. These four acts, Adoration, Thanksgiving, Propitiation, and Supplication, are the duty of every human creature, as reason itself shows us.

II

THE WORSHIP OF SACRIFICE

Sacrifice Ordained by God.—But God Himself had to make known to men the way in which they were to discharge this duty and pay their fourfold debt. This He did from the beginning, commanding them to worship Him by an act of supreme homage, which, because it is supreme, can be offered to Him alone. This act is *Sacrifice*. It consists in an offering made to God, by a lawful minister, of something perceptible to the senses, in order to acknowledge by its destruction, or by a change of its nature equal to destruction, that He is the Giver of life and the Lord of all things.

Among heathen nations this highest act of religion has been frightfully perverted. But it is a true instinct found everywhere, even among the most savage tribes, that what is held to be God should receive the homage of sacrifice. "Where is your sacrifice?" is the natural question put to non-Catholic missionaries by the Indians of North America, or the races of Central Africa; a religion without sacrifice seems to them wanting in what they one and all account to be the chief essential in the worship of God.

Jewish Sacrifices.—God has been worshipped in this divinely appointed way from the beginning to the present day. Just Abel offered sacrifice. The Patriarchs offered sacrifice. In the Law God gave by Moses to His chosen people, the sacrifices were of three kinds, answering to the four great duties and needs of man: (1) *Holocausts*, or whole-burnt offerings, in which the victim was slain and then consumed by fire, were for adoration; (2) *Sin-offerings*, to appease the anger of God and to implore His pardon; (3) *Peace-offerings*, in thanksgiving for God's benefits, or to obtain new favors. The offerings were animals—oxen, sheep, doves; or fruits of the earth—oil, wine, frankincense, etc. These sacrifices had no value in themselves. They were acceptable to God because they foreshadowed one to come, the great Sacrifice of the Cross which was of infinite worth.

The Christian Sacrifice.—This Sacrifice of blood by which we were redeemed was offered once for all. But the Prophets who foretold it spoke also of a Sacrifice which should be offered by Christ continually, in every place, and even to the end of time.

King David called Our Lord "a Priest for ever according to the order of Melchisedech," who offered a sacrifice of bread and wine. And Malachias, the last of the Prophets, spoke of a time when the Jewish sacrifices would give place to one pure and holy sacrifice, by which God would be glorified in Gentile lands. "I have no pleasure in you, saith the Lord of hosts, and I will not receive a gift of your hand; for from the rising of the sun even to the going down, My Name is great among the Gentiles, and in every place there is sacrifice and there is offered to My Name a clean oblation; for My Name is great among the Gentiles, saith the Lord of Hosts."[1] Where shall we find a sacrifice like Melchisedech's, a "clean oblation,"

---

1 Malachi 1.

offered in every place from sunrise to sunset, except on the altars of the Catholic Church?

Non-Catholics object: "If the Sacrifice of Calvary was all-sufficient, what need is there of another?" We answer: "The Sacrifice of Calvary was all-sufficient, for it was of infinite value. It fully satisfied the Justice of God. It obtained for us redemption and every grace we need. It can never be repeated. Its merits can never be exhausted.

But they have to be applied. Just as the water of the public fountains is for all, but those only profit by it who take the pains to make it their own and apply it to their needs, so is it with Christ's Sacrifice on Calvary. It was offered for all, to wash away the sins of all, to purchase salvation with every needed grace for all, but no man is saved without his own co-operation. He must exert himself and take hold of the salvation offered him. The Sacrifice of the Mass applies to souls, one by one, what was gained for them by the Sacrifice of the Cross., It is not another Sacrifice but the same perpetually renewed, as the water of an overflowing fountain, falling from the upper basin into others, is all the same water, parted into different channels, and brought down to the reach of those who come to draw.

The Mass is the same Sacrifice as that of Calvary; the Priest and the Victim are the same. But the manner of offering is different. Our Lord sheds His blood and dies, not really but figuratively. He is on the altar as St. John saw Him in heaven, "a Lamb standing *as it were* slain," the separation of His soul from His body being represented by the separate consecration of the bread and wine. He offers

Himself no longer visibly but invisibly through the ministry of His priests. He no longer pays the price of our Redemption, but applies the fruit of that Redemption to our souls.

Like the Sacrifice on Calvary, the Mass is offered for the four great ends of sacrifice. By it we can give to God infinite honor and glory; return Him worthy thanks for all His benefits; offer Him fitting atonement for our sins, and obtain from Him all we need for ourselves and others both living and dead. By offering Him His dearly beloved Son we are able to please Him more than our sins have displeased Him, and to give Him what is of greater worth than any grace or favor that we ask. The value of the Mass is so great, that had Christ so willed, one single Mass would have sufficed to redeem a thousand worlds.

Sacrifice, then, was not to cease with Our Lord's offering of Himself on the Cross. To the end of time God was to be worshipped in the way He had appointed from the beginning. Therefore, on the night before the offering of His bloody Sacrifice, which was to be offered only once, our Blessed Lord instituted the unbloody Sacrifice, which was to be offered in His Church to the end of time.

III

THE PERPETUAL SACRIFICE

It was at the Last Supper that He left us His "Unspeakable Gift." On the morrow He was to give His life for man in the midst of torments so awful that the thought of them brought on Him the agony of death. Men were going to thrust Him out of His own world, to cry: "Away with Him, crucify Him!" They would mock and scourge and spit on Him, and bring Him to the death of the Cross.

And His desire was—not to escape their cruel hands, not to be beyond their reach, but to be with them still. His delights are to be with the children of men, and to content this desire He was going to do what none but He could do—go and prepare a place for them, and stay; give His life for His friends, and remain with them always; offer Himself a bleeding Victim once, and be a Priest and Victim for ever. He was going to invent a means by which to be, not with a few of one generation only, but with all men through all ages, and not in one place only, but wherever there is a Catholic altar throughout the world. Well might St. Paul draw attention to the time when He thus left us this Gift of Himself—that it was "the night on which He was betrayed," and St. John begins his account of the Last Supper with the words: "Jesus having loved His own who were in the world, He loved them unto the end."

The Bread of Life.—Twelve months before, He had fed with five loaves and two fishes five thousand men besides women and children. The report of this miracle had spread far and wide, and the next day an immense multitude gathered about Him in hopes of being fed with the same delicious food. Then, when all eyes were fixed upon Him, and every ear was attentive, He spoke of another bread, a bread from Heaven, better than that bread in the desert, better even than the manna given to their fathers of old, a bread that would give life to the world. Curiosity and desire was aroused: "Lord, give us always this bread," they cried. And Jesus said: "I am the Bread of life. If any man eat of this Bread he shall live for ever, and the Bread that I will give is My flesh for the life of the world."

At these startling words there was a change of feeling in the crowd. "How can this Man give us His flesh to eat?" exclaimed many. "This is a hard saying." And they went away and walked no more with Him. They murmured because they took Him to mean that He would give them as food His very body which they saw before them. He knew this. He saw into their minds and into the minds of all whom in the ages to come this "hard saying" would reach. He knew that taking His words in their plain and literal meaning, the vast majority of believers in Him would worship as very God the Host consecrated on the altars of His Church. Would He, could He, by His own words lead astray all these? To say so would be blasphemy, meaning, explain away what He had said? No. He let them go. He changed nothing of what He had said; He explained nothing. On the contrary, He added words stronger still, words of threat to those who refused the divine Food He offered them, words of blessed promise to those who with thankful hearts accepted it. "Amen, amen, I say unto you,"—a very solemn expression among the Jews— "unless you eat the flesh of the Son of Man and drink His blood, you shall not have life in you. He that eateth My flesh and drinketh My blood hath everlasting life and I will raise him up in the Last Day. For My flesh is meat *indeed* and My blood is drink *indeed.*" Then, turning sadly to the Twelve, He said: "Will you also go away?" And Peter, as spokesman for the rest, answered: "Lord, to whom shall we go? Thou hast the words of eternal life."[1]

The First Mass.—That was a year ago, and now the hour to fulfill His promise had come, the hour He had "desired with desire." Whilst they were at supper, Jesus took bread and blessed and broke and gave to His disciples and said: "Take ye and eat; this is My body which is given for you. Do this for a commemoration of Me." And taking the chalice, He gave thanks and gave to them, saying: "Drink ye all of this. For this is My blood of the New Testament which shall be shed for many."

By the words: "Do this," He made them priests of the New Law. He gave them power to do what He had done—to change bread into His Body and wine into His Blood, and to pass on this power to the priests of His Church till He shall come again; that all who believe in Him, that we when our day should come, may have life in Him and be raised up by Him to a blessed life at the Last Day.

Thus, at the Last Supper, the first Mass was said by Christ Himself. He then instituted both a Sacrament and a Sacrifice. In the Sacrament He dwells with us always as our Companion and Friend, and in Holy Communion as our Guest and the food of our souls. As a Sacrifice, He offers to God in our name a worship of infinite value.

---

1 John 6.

"Do this in commemoration of Me," He said to the Apostles and their successors. The Holy Mass is to keep alive the memory of Calvary, to show forth the death of the Lord until He come."[1] But it is not a commemoration only. It is itself a true and proper Sacrifice, which may be offered for the living and the dead, in satisfaction for sin and for other needs.

The Mass, therefore, is not simply prayer in common like any other form of public worship. It is a most sacred and solemn action, the greatest action that can be done on earth. For by the Mass, the Eternal Son of God becomes present on the altar and offers Himself to God His Father for us, supplying for the defects of our feeble worship by uniting it with His, whilst we kneel by and take part in what He is doing in our name.

IV

THE FRUITS OF THE MASS

The General Fruit.—By every Mass God is worthily adored and thanked by the Church through Jesus Christ, and the Precious Blood of Calvary is, as it were, poured out afresh in order to be applied to the souls of men. By every Mass the Church is extended, protected, and prospered, and each one of her children is helped in ways we shall never know in this life.

---

1 1 Cor 6.

Sursum Corda!

Those who assist at Mass naturally receive a larger share of its blessings than those who are absent. "For those here present, whose faith and devotion are known to Thee," the priest prays again and again. Their prayers, too, being united with those of Christ have a special power with God. They are paying to Him the very highest worship they can. They are making Him a Gift infinitely precious and acceptable, even His own beloved Son. It is Christ Himself Who is asking for them. What wonder that they put up their petitions with unbounded trust, and find time after time by happy experience that "mighty is the prayer that is prayed at Mass."

All who hear Mass properly receive treasures of grace beyond our powers of reckoning and out of all proportion to their dispositions. Nevertheless, the larger the vessel we bring to this overflowing fountain, the more we carry away—spiritual blessings in abundance, and the temporal blessings for which we ask, as far as God sees them to be for our good.

The Mass does not of itself free the soul from mortal sin like the Sacrament of Penance, but it appeases Almighty God and obtains from Him through the Precious Blood graces which lead the sinner to sorrow for sin and to the Sacrament of forgiveness. And so with regard to the venial sins which in our weakness and carelessness we commit daily. By the Mass Almighty God is moved to grant those graces which bring us to the sorrow that obtains forgiveness, either immediately or when we go to confession. It does more still, for through it we obtain, in greater or less measure according to our dispositions, remission of the punishment due to our sins.

The Special Fruit.—A principal fruit of the Mass, which theologians for distinction's sake have called the "most special" (*specialissimus*), i.e., the most individual, belongs to the offerer. The "special" comes to the person or persons for whom in particular the Mass is offered. To receive this special fruit is a great favor which Catholics are glad to secure by causing Mass to be said for their intention. And they are thankful for the greatest favor a priest can show them next to offering the Holy Sacrifice for them—that of making a remembrance of them and their needs in his *Memento* at Mass.

Stipends for Masses.—The practice of offering a small sum to the priest who makes over to us that portion of the fruit of the Holy Sacrifice of which he can thus dispose, is reasonable and approved by the Church. It is not in any sense paying for the Mass, which is of infinite worth and beyond all price. We offer half a crown or five shillings, or whatever may be the amount fixed—not by the priest but by his bishop—as a small contribution towards the maintenance of the priest, not as the price of the Mass, which would be simony.

By the Fifth Commandment of the Church, we are commanded to contribute to the support of our pastors. This was a duty very clearly understood by the early Christians, who were accustomed to offer during Mass not only the bread and wine actually needed for the Sacrifice, but a good deal over and above, for the use of the bishop and his clergy. The offering of a small sum when a priest is asked to say Mass for our intention has taken the place of this ancient custom.

Our priests devote their time, their strength, and their lives to the care of souls, and as a result are unable to provide for their own maintenance. Many of them have no private means, and the expense of keeping up the churches, especially in a country like England, is very great and a source of constant anxiety. It is fitting, then, that, giving to us spiritual benefits, they should receive from us temporal things, as St. Paul says, and that our request to have the fruit of their Mass applied to our special needs should be accompanied by an offering which, in one form or another, is due by the express command of the Church.

Mass may be offered, not for the faithful only, but for non-Catholics, for Jews, pagans, and infidels: "for our salvation and for that of the whole world," the priest says, as he lifts the chalice at the Offertory.

Mass for the Holy Souls.—Above all should it be offered, and offered often, for the Holy Souls in Purgatory, that God may be pleased to accept it in satisfaction for their sins and relieve them from their sufferings. These Holy Souls cannot use the Mass themselves, but their friends on earth can have it offered or can hear it on their behalf. They look to us to show them this charity in their extreme need. "Have pity on me," they cry to us, "have pity on me, at least you my friends, for the hand of the Lord hath touched me!"

Holy Mass

Can we turn a deaf ear to this piteous prayer? Shall we, who promised never to forget them, forsake them now? The greatest kindness we can show our dear ones in Purgatory is to pour out upon them the merits of the Cross through the Holy Mass. Their pains may be keener than all the pains of this life put together, more terrible than any that can be imagined. And these sufferings may last, even in the case of holy people, for very long.

But the Precious Blood can quench those fearful fires and bring the sufferers refreshment, light, and peace. One Mass can give more help than anything we could do by prayer and good works. Our first care, then, when we have lost father, mother, or friend, should be to have Mass said for them if we can, or at least to hear Mass for their relief. And not once only, but from time to time let us do them this charity. It is a mistaken affection that leads us to believe their debts are quickly paid, that after a few days they have no further need of help. Our Catholic forefathers had a truer sense of the severity of the divine Judgments. They knew that the Justice of God, so easily appeased here, is terrible beyond conception when the night has come in which no man can work. They showed both their faith and their charity in providing Masses to be said *for ever*. Catholics should pray throughout a long lifetime for father and mother, husband or wife, brother or sister or friend. These Blessed Souls will show themselves grateful and come in their turn to the help of those who loved them so faithfully. It is in Purgatory

Sursum Corda!

that the words of Our Lord are realized to the full: "Blessed are the merciful, for they shall obtain mercy."

V

MASS ON SUNDAYS AND HOLYDAYS

Mass of Obligation.—It is *well* to hear Mass often, but it is *necessary* to hear it on Sundays and Holydays of Obligation. God has commanded us to keep the Sunday holy, and the Church has ordained that this shall be done by our taking part in that most sacred and solemn act by which perfect worship and infinite glory are rendered to Him.

Every Catholic who has come to the use of reason is bound under pain of mortal sin to hear Mass on Sundays and Holydays of Obligation, unless excused by some lawful reason. Such reasons would be sickness or grave danger of sickness; distance from church—a walk of three miles each way or even less in bad weather; great loss that would result; the necessity of remaining with little children, or of taking care of the house itself. In case of doubt as to the sufficiency of an excuse, one should if possible ask the advice of a priest. Young people are as a rule safe in abiding by the judgment of their parents or superiors.

Parents must bear in mind that children of seven years of age are as much bound to hear Mass on Sundays and Holydays as grown-up people. They must see that their children fulfill this obligation and that they get to church in time. If children miss Mass or are late through the negligence of parents, how can such parents be excused from the guilt of grievous sin?

Servants should try to secure situations where they will be able to hear Mass on Sundays. Should they be in a place where this is an impossibility, they are not bound to give notice at once, at the risk of remaining long out of a situation, but they would do well to make a change as soon as possible.

When we cannot hear Mass.—When circumstances make it impossible to hear Mass, they do not exempt us from the duty of keeping the Sunday holy. We may fulfill this obligation either by saying the prayers of the Mass at home and thus hearing Mass in spirit, or by private prayers, spiritual reading, etc., according to our devotion. Parents, masters and mistresses are bound to see that their children and servants understand their obligation in this respect and that they have the time necessary for discharging it. In the case of young children this is not enough. We should say the prayers with them, and it is well to read to them a chapter out of some spiritual book suited to their age and intelligence, that the duty of sanctifying the Sunday may be deeply engraven in their minds.

All Catholics should realize how necessary Sunday Mass is to the vigor and even to the preservation of their faith, and that the deprivation of Mass, even when this happens without fault on their part, is a grievous spiritual loss. People get accustomed to going without it; they cease to miss it; and too often neglect to supply for it as far as they can by private prayer at home. As a result, they get careless about the practice of their religion, and when through change of circumstances the obligation to hear Mass again binds them, they have become too indifferent to make the necessary effort. Thus, numbers are lost to the Church, for, as every priest will testify, it is the neglect of Mass on Sundays that leads finally to the loss of faith.

It is impossible to insist too strongly on the truth that in the life of a Catholic *it is the Mass that matters*. It is a spiritual barometer. His appreciation of it and his attendance at it—opportunity always supposed—is a fair indication of a Catholic's spiritual state. Does he attend regularly and devoutly on Sundays and Holydays?—he will be the average Catholic who, if he so perseveres, will by God's mercy save his soul. Does he, when occasion offers, hear Mass daily, often at the cost of inconvenience and self-denial?—he will be a fervent Catholic, one who may look for special blessings; spiritual, and, as far as God sees will be for his lasting good and happiness, temporal also; blessings for himself and for those dear to him. Such a one will surely have the crowning grace of a good life, final perseverance, and a large reward in heaven.

Neglect of Mass.—On the other hand, habitual neglect of Mass on Sundays and Holydays is a proof of religious indifference, that shows itself in a selfish, worldly, or irregular life, leading to practical loss of faith, and too often to final impenitence.

Those who neglect Mass on Sundays and let their children play about at home or in the streets instead of sending them to church, draw down upon themselves the terrible anger of God. If it is better for all who scandalize the little ones to be drowned in the depth of the sea, what will be the punishment of parents who, instead of setting a good example in their homes by fidelity to their religious duties, teach their children to despise the laws of God and the Church, destroy the fruit of the religious instruction they receive at school, and, as far as they can, prepare the way for the loss of their faith and the ruin of their immortal souls!

Holydays of Obligation.—The Holydays of Obligation observed in the United States are: Christmas Day, December 25th; the Circumcision, January 1st; Ascension Thursday, forty days after Easter Sunday; the Assumption of Our Lady, August 15th; the Feast of All Saints, November 1st; and the Immaculate Conception, December 8th. Persons who work in places of business are not bound to hear Mass on these six Holydays of the Church if this would interfere, injuriously to themselves, with their hours of employment.

How the Obligation Binds.—The Commandment of the Church is that we hear Mass, not a part of Mass. The duty, therefore, is not fulfilled by hearing a part of one Mass or a part of two. To satisfy the obligation, which binds under grievous sin, we are bound to be present at all the principal parts of one Mass, that is from the Gospel—some say from the Offertory—to the Priest's Communion. But Mass begins with the Psalm at the foot of the altar and ends with the Last Gospel. It is wrong to be absent or late through our own fault during a less important portion of the Mass.

VI

HOW WE SHOULD HEAR MASS

"Remember the Holy Angels."—As to the way in which we are to assist at Mass, nothing is laid down by the Church. Provided we hear it with attention and devotion, we are free to pray in the way we find most helpful and best suited to our actual needs. Attention means that we do our best to dismiss from our minds idle and useless thoughts, and that we refrain from anything out of keeping with the solemn act at which we are assisting. To talk, laugh, eat, sleep, would be irreverent and wrong. And it is surely an irreverence and sinful to go to the Holy Sacrifice so dressed as to be an occasion of distraction to others. "Let nothing," says our countryman, Venerable Bede, "let nothing light or unworthy, nothing calculated to distract our neighbor be done in the House of Prayer where the Body of the Lord is consecrated, and where it is undoubted that the Angels are ever present.... We must make every effort to remember, when we enter the church for Mass, the presence of the Angels, and we ought to acquit ourselves of our heavenly duty with proper fear and veneration, following in this respect the example of the holy women at the Sepulchre, who, on seeing the Angels, 'were afraid and bowed down their countenance towards the ground.'"[1]

Another result of carrying vanity and display into the House of God is that it shames the poor, and by fostering human respect keeps many from Mass on Sundays. How will those who are the cause of this, excuse themselves before God?

We sometimes hear it said that all thoughts of business and earthly things should be laid aside at the time of Mass. Let us see what this means, and what it cannot mean.

Reverence requires that there should be earnest effort to fix our mind on the wonders being wrought at the altar, and that no frivolous thoughts should be willfully entertained. We go to Mass as to Calvary; to unite with our Blessed Lord Who comes down upon the altar to worship God worthily in our name for His Greatness; to thank Him worthily in our name for His Goodness; to beg pardon for our many sins; to ask for all we need for soul and body.

"The Acceptable Time."—Among these needs, those that concern the soul will naturally have the first place—grace to overcome such or such a temptation; to keep clear of this or that occasion of sin; to master our besetting fault, particularly in that circumstance where we are wont to fail; grace to discharge faithfully the duties of our state of life; patience, or guidance in some perplexity; grace to gain much merit for heaven by remembering to offer our work and cares and troubles to God, doing all and bearing all for His sake. Above all, the grace of final perseverance.

---

1 Luke 24:5.

Then there are the spiritual necessities of those dear to us or dependent on us—a conversion to the Faith, a return to God from an evil life, preservation from harm amid dangerous surroundings—which of us has no anxiety of this kind? Now is "the acceptable time," when grace is given more plentifully than at any other. Now is the time for us to ask and receive, for "mighty is the prayer that is prayed at Mass."

The wants of the soul, then, come first. Yet the necessary affairs of this life, our work, our plans, our household difficulties and troubles, the care of providing for those depending on us, these need not be shut out from our thoughts and our prayers when we come to Mass. Whatever brings us happiness, or perplexity, or distress, we may take to God, saying with Peter: "Lord, to whom shall we go?" or with the sorrowing sisters of Bethany: "Lord, come and see."

The wife whose husband is threatened with fatal disease or with heavy loss, the young man whose future depends on a coming examination, the widow who must let her rooms or go to the workhouse—surely these may take their trouble and their need to the altar of God! Jesus is there *for them*. He carries all their necessities in His Heart, and only waits their prayer to give them either the precise form of help they ask, or that which He knows to be better for them and those for whom they pray.

Those best understand and love the Holy Mass who are accustomed to take every joy and care and project to the altar, to unburden their hearts there, to offer up every desire and every sacrifice in union with the Sacrifice of Christ.

Holy Mass

Why in Latin.—This they can do without understanding all the Priest is saying. The Church requires the Mass to be said in a dead language—that is, in one which has ceased to be generally spoken—in order that its sacred words may be guarded against the changes to which every spoken tongue is subject. The meaning of words in a dead language is fixed and cannot change. The Holy Sacrifice is celebrated by the Church in nine different languages, none of them any longer in daily use. Latin is the language of the Mass in the entire West and in a few places in the East.

Another reason for the use of Latin is this. The Catholic Church, being world-wide and for all nations, it is fitting that she should have a universal language binding all together as members of one family, so that her priests and her laity, whatever their nationality, may be at home in any part of the world when they come before the altar to say or to hear Mass.

To be at home. For though the Mass is said in Latin, this does not prevent the people from uniting intelligently with the Priest. The poor and the simple, and the little children of our crowded churches understand the meaning of the familiar words better than is generally supposed. If they like, they can follow the words of the Priest in the translations that are in every prayer book. And even if they do not understand what he is saying, they know what he is *doing*, and may thus join with him in offering the great Sacrifice, which, as he reminds them, is theirs as well as his.

Sursum Corda!

Union with the Priest.—We should unite ourselves in some way with what the Priest is doing at the altar, either by following the very words he is saying, or by using the prayers for Mass, or other suitable devotions which we find in our prayer books. We may use, if we like, the very prayers in which the Catholics of this country were wont to follow the Mass seven hundred years ago.[1] If a book does not help us, we may call to mind the four ends of Sacrifice which Jesus Christ is fulfilling perfectly for us by His Divine Sacrifice of Himself.

We can divide the Mass into four parts, and occupy ourselves with acts of (1) *Adoration*, from the beginning of Mass to the Offertory; (2) *Thanksgiving*, from the Offertory to the Canon; (3) *Propitiation*, from the Canon to the Pater Noster, and (4) *Petition*, from the Pater Noster to the Last Gospel.

Or, bearing in mind Our Lord's touching request at the Last Supper, that what He was then doing should be done again in remembrance of Him, we may think of His sufferings and death, which are here renewed in a real though mystical manner. Some like to say the Sorrowful Mysteries of the Rosary during Mass. A little child who heard Mass daily, without prayer book, rosary, or external help of any sort, was asked what she did all the time. "I look up at the big crucifix," she said, "and think that it was me that did it." A very tiny one, whose picture prayer book represented the various scenes of the Passion, showed her devotion during

---

[1] *The Lay Folk's Mass Book*, Catholic Truth Society.

Mass by digging out with her nails the faces of all whom she saw ill-treating Our Lord!

But in whatever way we assist at Mass, it is well to unite with the Priest, at least at the Offertory, Consecration, and Priest's Communion.

The Offertory.—At the Offertory the Priest makes his intention—that is, he recalls to mind the object to which he intends to apply the special fruit of the Mass. If ever we assist at Mass that is being said *for us,* we should earnestly offer to Almighty God at this moment the Sacrifice which on our behalf the Priest is preparing to offer.

But at all times it is good to have a particular intention when we hear Mass. It is wasting the most precious of our opportunities to come to such an audience chamber with no definite purpose. Those who are to have an audience with the Holy Father prepare for it. They choose carefully the few words they may be able to address to the Vicar of Christ; they make ready the objects they want him to bless, their petitions for themselves, and for their friends. Should we not consider it neglectful, not to say irreverent, to take no pains to profit by such an occasion? At Mass we have an audience, not with His Vicar but with Christ Himself: shall we not make the most of it?

We may offer the Mass for any good end we please. Is there no grace we want for ourselves or for another? Is there no conversion we have at heart, no soul in peril that needs help? Have we no thanksgiving to make? And—to look out upon the world—what needs there are there! The eighty thousand to die to-day, many of them unprepared, many without priest or sacraments; the tempted, the fallen, the downtrodden, the unsuccessful, the little children, the children of bad parents, the poor heathen—oh, let us not draw near the altar to hear Mass with no special object in view, when there are all these souls to be helped! It rouses fervor wonderfully when mind and heart are full of a big need. Some of us make out a list of such needs and go through them regularly, with what fruit to themselves and to others the Last Great Day will show.

The Consecration.—The Consecration is the most solemn moment of the Mass. All that goes before leads up to it by way of preparation, all that follows is thanksgiving. It is the act in which the Sacrifice consists, because it is this act that so alters the bread and wine as to change them into the Body and Blood of Christ. The appearances, called also the "species" or "accidents," remain, but the substance of bread and wine has gone—it has been changed into another substance, the most holy Body and Blood of Jesus Christ.

There is a hush throughout the church as the tremendous moment draws near. The Priest bids us be attentive and expectant by the words: *"Sursum corda,"* Lift up your hearts to God. And we answer, as if needing no reminder: "We have them lifted up to the Lord." Twice the bell rings to warn us to be ready to welcome Christ at His coming, once at the Sanctus, and again after the Memento of the Living, when the Priest bows down and the great moment is close at hand. The Saints tell us that the Sanctuary at this time is filled with Angels, come down to honor the Presence of their Lord and ours.

It is for us He comes and comes gladly, always making it His delight to be in our midst, always with His hands filled with blessings. He looks around to see where He may leave them, where faith and hope and love expect and deserve them. And as He wept over Jerusalem because she had not known the time of her visitation, so He grieves to see willful wandering of mind, indifference, or coldness at this "acceptable time."

The only condition for obtaining the help we need is a very easy one—that we ask for it. At Mass more than at any other time is His promise fulfilled: "Ask and you shall receive." But how many of us deserve the reproach of St. James: "You have not because you ask not." The blind man in the Gospel was wrong when he said: "God does not hear sinners." He hears them willingly, hears them always, and, above all, hears them at Mass. We must not, then, let the thought of our unworthiness paralyze us when we come to pray. The more unworthy we are, the greater is our need and our claim. If the remembrance of our sins discourages us, we must cry out all the more: "Jesus, Son of David, have mercy on me!"

The Communion.—After the Priest's Communion there should be the Communion—Sacramental or Spiritual—of all present.

The Church has always desired that the faithful should approach the Holy Table frequently and even daily. Our

Sursum Corda!

Lord, she tells us, has given Himself to us in the form of food to show that He means us to come to Him often; that as we take our food daily to preserve the body in health and strength, so we must frequently feed our soul with the Bread of the strong to keep up its vigor and activity.

In Apostolic times and for several centuries later, all who heard Mass were accustomed to communicate thereat. During this time of fierce persecution, it was to the body of Christ the martyrs and confessors looked for the strength they needed to confess Him in face of torture and death. It was this that upheld our Catholic forefathers through centuries of trial and gave them courage to bear the loss of all things, and of life itself, for the sake of their Faith.

But as the piety of the early ages declined, the Holy Table became deserted, and the Church was at length obliged in the Fourth General Council of Lateran (1215) to command all the faithful to communicate at least once a year. This command was renewed by the Council of Trent (1545-1563). A hundred years later began the discussion about frequent Communion, which lasted till Pius X in 1905 happily set it at rest for ever.

The Decree of 1905 declares that "daily Communion is in conformity with the desire of Our Lord Himself in the institution of the Blessed Sacrament, which was not principally that He might be honored, but that the faithful by union with God may receive strength to overcome their passions, to expiate the lighter faults of daily occurrence, and to avoid grave sins. Therefore, no one can be prevented from communicating frequently or daily, provided he is in a state of grace and approaches the Holy Table with a right and pious disposition of mind, that is, not through custom, or vanity, or human motives, but with the desire of obeying the Will of God, of becoming more closely united to God by charity, and of making use of that divine medicine as a remedy for one's weaknesses and defects."

To say, then, "I don't deserve to go so often, I am too full of faults and evil tendencies," is to mistake the end of this divine Sacrament. No one can ever deserve to receive It even once. It is medicine, not reward. We are not obliged to be free from venial sin. All that is necessary is (1) freedom from mortal sin, with a firm purpose not to commit it for the future, and (2) the right motive mentioned above, such as to please God, to come to love Him more, to lead a purer and higher life by overcoming our faults, and to live in closer union with Him.

Of course the better our dispositions and the more devout our preparation and thanksgiving, the larger will be the measure of grace we shall receive. Yet, provided we are free from mortal sin, the Sacrament *must* increase the grace of God in our soul.

All who can come to the marriage feast are invited, all who, without neglecting home duties or daily work, are able to come—busy men and women, the heavy-burdened, "whose hands to life's hard work are laid," children who have made their First Communion.

Sursum Corda!

Our Lord seems to be manifesting a special desire to see the little ones at His Table, and to remove any hesitation there might be in admitting them there often and even daily.

Since the Decree of 1905, we come upon instance after instance in England and Ireland of the attraction by which He is drawing these innocent hearts to Himself, so that they even go to the altar rails unbidden and receive Him as it were by stealth, or with no preparation beyond their own ardent desires.

We hear of a dying child who after ten minutes' preparation for First Communion fixed her eyes with such vehemence of love and desire upon the Sacred Host as almost to overpower the priest who held It before her. Of another sick child of four and a half, who, as soon as she heard of the Real Presence, showed so ardent a love of Jesus in the Blessed Sacrament that on Exposition days she would beg to be carried down from the infirmary to "Holy God," and would remain long before the altar in quiet content, the eyes fixed on the monstrance, the tiny hands joined, the pale lips moving in prayer—a sight which those who saw it can never forget.

"A little child shall lead them."[1] Let us not disdain to copy the model Our Lord Himself set before the Twelve. Let the little children both shame and encourage us. Let us be led by them to the love of Jesus, and to the desire of Jesus that will bring us to His Table where we are all wanted, whence no one can be absent without being missed. Our Lord's words to us are: "Come to Me *all*." It is true we

---
1 Isaiah 11.

should ask the advice of our confessor, but confessors are instructed not to keep from frequent or daily Communion those who have the necessary dispositions.

Can we hesitate? Lest His own words were not plain enough or pressing enough, lest we should find some pretext for believing them inapplicable in our own case, lest the conflicting opinions of other days as to the requisite dispositions for frequent Communion should confuse or dishearten us—He has inspired His Vicar to lay down in the clearest terms that the wedding garment of grace is the one condition for being made welcome at His Table. To Pius X He has said in very deed: "*Compel* them to come in that My house may be full."

Shall we not be there when the King comes in to see the guests? The Vicar of Christ takes all responsibility upon himself. He forbids anyone to frighten us away, to make hard what the Lord of the Feast has made so easy.

O blessed age of daily Communion, fresh link between us and the faithful of the Apostolic days! What if dangers abound, and scandals multiply, and the stars are falling from heaven! Can we not do all things in Him Who strengthens us? Can habits now be called inveterate, or labor in the warfare with self be counted too arduous, or sacrifice too hard, when each morning we may feed on the Bread of the strong?

Among the signs that foretell the end, might we not count this supreme revelation of the love of God? Such revelations have increased in tenderness in each succeeding age. But what can be in reserve after this? Can we think the faithful of the future may be more favored than ourselves, who daily at our door hear the Lord knocking?

If we will, life may be made one continuous "Welcome!" to Him, by again and again through the morning hours thanking God with grateful hearts for the "Unspeakable Gift" we have received; and in the afternoon and evening looking forward with loving expectation to His visit on the morrow.

"Surely I come quickly."

"Amen. Come, Lord Jesus."[1]

The Decree allows daily communicants to gain Plenary Indulgences even though they have not made the weekly Confession usually required. And they may use this privilege even though they may have missed Communion once or twice in the week.

Spiritual Communion.—If you cannot make a real—that is, a Sacramental—Communion, make a Spiritual one, which is to eat by desire this Heavenly Bread, and thus by means of faith and love share in the fruits and advantages of Sacramental Communion. The Priest prays specially for the communicants at the Mass, for "as many as shall partake of the most sacred Body and Blood of Thy Son from this altar, that they may be filled with every heavenly grace and blessing."

The Offertory, Consecration, and Priest's Communion are the chief parts of the Mass, but there are two other times when we should do well to unite with the Priest: the Mementos for the Living and for the Dead.

---

1 Apoc. 22.

Holy Mass

The Memento for the Living.—This comes at the beginning of the Canon, and we may take the Sanctus bell as a reminder of it. We should pray for our Holy Father the Pope, for our Bishop, for all our fellow Catholics, and for those who have a special claim upon us: our family, our friends, those who have done us good, those who are in any way dependent on us, any whom we may have harmed by bad example or neglect, any for whom we have been asked to pray, all who at this moment are in sore temptation or in the pains of death. Christ is coming down upon the altar: let us draw all these dear and needy ones round Him to receive His blessing.

The Memento for the Dead comes after the Consecration and Elevation. Now, when Our Lord is really present on the altar, we plead with Him for those who can no longer plead for themselves. They earnestly ask a remembrance at this time: "Have pity on me, have pity on me, at least, you, my friends!" they cry out to us from their place of suffering. Father, mother, wife, husband, brother, sister—if only we could hear those piteous prayers; if only we could see the wistful eyes when this "acceptable time" for them has come! We on earth are apt to consider that the day's work begins after Mass. Daytime in Purgatory, the brightness that breaks in upon their dreary night, is the time of Mass, and in particular this moment of the Memento, when faithful Mother Church who never forgets her suffering children, lifts to the Father His well-beloved Son and prays for those "who are gone before us with the sign of Faith and rest in the sleep of peace." We pray for all who have a special claim upon us in that place of patient waiting but fearful pain. We may pray, too, for any among those holy sufferers who appeal more particularly to our sympathy and pity—for those who may be there on our account; for the soul who has longest to suffer; for the soul that suffers most severely; for those whose friends forget them or who have none to pray for them.

VII

WEEKDAY MASS

Why we should hear Mass daily.—If we believe what the Church teaches about the dignity and the value of the Holy Sacrifice, how is it that so many of us who could hear Mass frequently are never seen assisting at it except on Sundays? Is the Sacrifice of less value on weekdays? Can we believe the Mass to be in very truth the renewal of Calvary, and find it in our hearts to be absent? We think the Apostles who were not with John on Calvary must have grieved bitterly the rest of their lives for such a loss. We believe that if in one only place in the world—somewhere in the Far East—Mass could be offered, and once only every twenty-five years, we should strain every nerve to be present. Would distance, inconvenience, or the cost of the journey, stand in our way? We should scout the idea. Yet a few steps are more than we can attempt when it comes to putting our convictions into practice!

Holy Mass

You say there is no obligation to go to daily Mass. True, but we are not considering what we are bound to do but what is fitting on our part when a walk of a quarter of an hour would bring us to Calvary set up almost at our doors to be to us a daily fount of grace.

Whenever they had the opportunity, our Catholic forefathers in this land and in faithful Ireland risked the loss of goods, of liberty, and of life itself—and not for themselves only, but for those dearer to them than life—in order to have the happiness of hearing Mass. A story is told of an old woman in Wales who, having been for many years unable to hear Mass, was told one day that a priest would be in the neighborhood on the morrow. The joyful news was too much for her and she died during the night.

To have the power of paying to God daily the very highest worship possible; of thanking Him worthily for all His goodness to us; of making abundant reparation for our past sins and daily faults; of laying our needs before Him, and asking in union with Christ for the blessings we have most at heart for ourselves and others—is not this a privilege worth a little effort? What can God refuse us when He sees us daily at the foot of the altar where His Divine Son is offering Himself in our behalf?

No one, whatever be his state before God, can assist devoutly at Mass without obtaining the grace he needs. Those in mortal sin which they cannot bring themselves to give up, will get the strong grace they require to break their chains and find peace in the Sacrament of forgiveness. Those who fall frequently into deliberate venial sins of detraction, vanity or sloth, will obtain the remission of these daily faults and strength to grow in fervor and generosity in the service of God.

There are times when we turn to God in the extremity of need, either for ourselves or others. We want not ordinary grace or help but the "great mercies" of which David speaks. Yet the thought of our sinfulness and selfishness, of our unworthiness to be heard and helped in our distress, paralyzes our prayer; we have no heart to ask for what we have no right to obtain. How we wish in those hours of need that we had the heroic virtues and merits of the Saints to make us pleasing to God and to incline Him favorably towards us! Yet we have more than this; the poorest of us has more than this. For we have the merits of Christ Himself made over to us in the Holy Mass. The adoration and love of all the Angels, the labors, self-sacrifice and constancy of all the Saints, the incomparable holiness and merits of the Blessed Mother of God—all this is less acceptable to God, moves Him less powerfully to show us favor, than one single Mass. For all the merits of creatures are but of finite worth, but the value of one Mass is infinite.

Should we not, then, hear Mass as often as we can? Is it not the want of a lively faith that makes us so afraid of a little exertion or inconvenience, of rising half an hour earlier, of the walk to church, and, perhaps, of the dryness of the half-hour when we get there!

But He Who waits for us on the altar knows all this; every sacrifice that our coming to Him costs us He knows and values and will reward. Most of all does He prize the love that seeks Him for Himself rather than for its own satisfaction. If we cannot *feel* all that we *believe*, if we kneel there like stocks and stones, He counts it all as worship and as love. We bring Him what we can, and bring it at our own cost. And to make up for our shortcomings we offer Him the divine Victim who more than supplies for our insufficiency. What more does He need to make Him look down upon us with love and with favor, however dry and helplessly distracted we may be?

"The Gift of God."—The Host on the altar is to the Church like the sun in the heavens, the source of light and beauty and fruitfulness. Every act of faith, and hope, and thankfulness, and patience; every act of charity towards God and our neighbor; each effort to resist temptation; to begin again without discouragement after a fall; every look of love at our crucifix; every word of love to Mary; every distasteful duty done because it is God's will, and to please Him; the heroism of the martyrs in heathen lands, the steadfastness of many a hidden martyr nearer home—all these supernatural acts, from the least to the highest, derive their inspiration, their merit, and their reward from Jesus in the Blessed Sacrament.

And just as the fruits on a south wall will be the ripest and sweetest, so will the work of grace be richest in souls which abide in the neighborhood of the Sacramental Presence and draw near daily and devoutly to the Fount of grace. Try, and you will find it so. Gradually but steadily the Mass will work a change in your soul. You will find your faith confirmed and your good purposes strengthened. You will begin to see the things of this life and of the next in their true light. When a choice is to be made, you will prefer the goods which last for eternity to those which pass with time. You will be strengthened to bear bravely the burdens and failures of life. The habit of taking all cares and sorrows to the altar and uniting them with the daily Sacrifice of Jesus, has a wonderful power of bracing us for sacrifice and helping us over difficulties. It brings us counsel in doubt, it prospers our plans as far as is good for us—and could we wish it to be farther?—it sanctifies our joys, supports us in temptation, or raises us when we fall. It secures us the crowning grace of final perseverance, and a safe passage out of this world into the eternal happiness of the next.

VIII

"BY HIM AND WITH HIM AND IN HIM"
(Canon of the Mass)

Union with the Holy Sacrifice.—An excellent way of obeying Our Lord's injunction to "Pray always," is to unite with the Holy Sacrifice which on thousands of altars, at every hour of the day and night, is being offered to God. Interrupt your work for an instant now and again to join in the Adoration and Thanksgiving, the Satisfaction and the Supplication which the Sacred Heart is there making in your name and in your behalf.

If you wake in the night, unite again with that faithful Heart which pleads unceasingly for us while we sleep, and obtains for us preservation from harm, and unnumbered blessings which we shall only know when we get to heaven. It is offering Itself for poor sinners who are offending Him, for the dying, and for the Holy Suffering Souls in their extremity of need. Join your prayer with His: "Divine Heart of Jesus, convert sinners, save the dying, deliver the Souls in Purgatory" (300 days, Pius X).

Who would pray alone when he can have his prayer strengthened every instant by the might of that Divine prayer!

"It is the Mass that matters." Yes—and to God Himself. For all that men and Angels and the Blessed Mother of God can do in worship of the Divine Majesty, were their intensest acts prolonged throughout eternity, would fall infinitely short of what is due to Him. But the Mass of one short half-hour gives to God fully sufficient glory, makes Him an offering infinitely acceptable to Him, offers Him a worship absolutely worthy of Him, because God is there offered to God.

"It is the Mass that matters—to us." To pay our debt of adoration and of thanksgiving, to make a fitting return for all God has given us, all He has prepared for us in a happy eternity, we have one means, and only one—the Mass. "What shall I render to the Lord for all He hath rendered to me?" should be the cry of every one of us. And the answer is, "Kneel down before the altar and unite your adoration and

your praise with that which Christ is there offering in your name, and you will have more than repaid the divine Goodness for any blessings It has bestowed or ever will bestow upon you.

When the sense of sin oppresses you, when the thought of God's Judgments frightens you, present to the divine Justice that pure and holy Victim who takes away the sins of the world, and who there offers Himself specially *for you*, in satisfaction *for your sins,* to wipe out the debt of punishment you have heaped up, to secure for you that place in His Father's Kingdom specially prepared for *you*.

And when you are in trouble, when anxiety for one dear to you weighs you down, hasten then to the altar. He is there who knows your pain and has in His Sacrifice the remedy for it. "Pray for my intention," we say to one another in any necessity. "Come to the altar," Our Lord says to us, "and I who know your trouble *will offer Myself* for your intention. *Ask then* and you shall receive, seek *then* and you shall find."

Yes, truly, in every need of soul and body, for ourselves or for others, when temptation presses sorely, when the anger of God is to be appeased, or His Mercy sought in the extremity of distress, then—it is the Mass that matters.

Who know this like the holy suffering Souls in Purgatory? Their distress, their extremity is beyond the power of words to tell. They look to the altar with a piteousness of appeal which would melt our hearts could we see it. They know, as we shall know when we take our place among them, that it is to the Mass they must chiefly look for rest and peace. Therefore they so earnestly ask of those they have left behind to show them this mark of affection, to hear Mass or to have it said for their relief. "Let there be no fuss about my funeral, no flowers for my grave," said a dying girl to her parents, "but Masses, Masses."

Let us not wait till we get to Purgatory to learn the value of Holy Mass, but show by our lives that we truly prize God's Unspeakable Gift. We should not need reminders from without, or to be told by one not of the household of the Faith, that to the life of the Church, and to the vigorous spiritual life of every one of her children—*"it is the Mass that matters."*

WHY MUST I SUFFER?

INTRODUCTION

I could not possibly provide a better introduction for the piece which follows than has Father John A. Ryan, author of the 1906 book *A Living Wage*, in his brief review of the same, which appeared in the Fortnightly Review in 1912. We reprint it here in its entirety:

"In the main the Catholic doctrine on suffering is here presented in the usual terms. The beneficial and meritorious character of suffering, its universality, its prominence in the life of Christ, and its relation to free will, are all clearly and sympathetically set forth. Preceding this discussion, however, is a frank recognition of the unnecessary and harmful suffering endured by a large proportion of the toiling masses, and a plea for the prompt application of adequate remedies. It is this preliminary portion which differentiates the booklet from so many others on the same subject, and which is calculated to win the attention of the toiler to a patient consideration of the more fundamental doctrine which follows."

As noted here, Mother Loyola begins her discourse by empathizing with the sufferers...and she is well-qualified for this task. From what we know of her life, she endured a great deal of sorrow, beginning with the loss of both parents and two siblings to scarlet fever when she was just 9 years old. With both great distance and convent walls between them, she agonized at her inability to console her brother as he lost 3 children in tragic circumstances and succumbed himself to deep depression. And she would go on, long after this essay was written, to endure being bedridden for the last 7 years of her life after a hip fracture. Yet throughout the trials of her life, she never flagged in her missionary zeal to bring souls closer to God—it is said that she continued her work of correspondence and instructing converts in the faith until her last days.

Surely from one such as this, we may learn a great deal about what it is to faithfully carry the cross that is laid upon us, and even to learn to embrace it lovingly as she did.

WHY MUST I SUFFER?
A Talk with the Toilers

PREFATORY NOTE

When the well-to-do preach contentment to the poor, or one in the flush of health sits down by a sick-bed to counsel patience, the first feeling, perhaps, of the party to be benefited is—*irritation*.

"What right have those entrenched in safe retreats to lecture us whose lives are all struggle and trouble?" a wage-earner or "out-of-work" may ask. "Let some one talk who knows what unemployment and misery mean—and we will listen."

There is something, no doubt, in this complaint. But, after all, suffering is common property; no class can monopolize it. To find the safe retreat that is beyond its reach, we must look a good deal higher than this earth of ours. In greater measure or less, it is the lot of every one of us without exception. And to be drawn together, fellow-sufferers need not share precisely the same pain. It is enough that they meet on the common platform:

> "Sorrow with sorrow loves to dwell,
> Mourners their tale to mourners tell"[1]

---
1 F. Oakeley.

Sursum Corda!

As to "lecturing" there is no question of it here. But any one may *talk*. Any fellow-traveller may point on a dull day to where the clouds are breaking and showing a brighter sky. We are brothers and sisters, all of us. Many things have sprung up to make us forget this, to divide us, and to nurture bitter feeling. But now, all the world over, a common desire is being felt by rich and poor, employers and employed, the men and women of every land, to draw together again, and in a fair and friendly spirit talk over their differences and their needs.

No one questions the wrongs and the misery under which so many of us at this moment lie. No one doubts that a remedy must be found, and found quickly. And we shall find it—not by blazoning our wrongs abroad in inflammatory speeches, but by looking our difficulties quietly in the face, by trying to see and judge of them aright, and being willing to be helped to a true and safe solution of them.

September 1911

I

THE CHURCH AND THE TOILERS, IN THE PAST

How ready we are to talk about our troubles! Our aches and pains; our fears, and disappointments, and losses; employment or unemployment; the weather, the Government, the crops—are not our grievances and cares of one kind or another the commonest topics of conversation? Most of the things we say can be traced to our dread of suffering, our misery under it, our joy when it is over. Of the problems discussed by professional men, business men, poor men, capitalists, in the newspapers, on the platforms, in public-houses, in Parliament, in dockyards, in mills, the greater number come to this: "How can we rid life of its pains? How can we add to its pleasures?"

Many answers to this question are pressed upon us, more especially with regard to the problem that is exercising minds in every direction—the sufferings of the working classes.

"Authority," cries the Anarchist, "is the great enemy. Overthrow it, leave every man free to follow all his inclinations, and so bring about a golden age of pleasure and content."

"Nay," replies the Socialist, "so far from destroying the State, make it supreme. The working classes will be better off if private capital is taken from individuals and made over to the State to become the common property of all."

Sursum Corda!

"Feed and clothe and house the people properly," says the Philanthropist; "provide them with the knowledge and the work necessary to make their way in life, and you will have met the need."

Every day and on every side we hear these various views discussed, and our question as Catholics is naturally: "Has the Church anything to say on the great social problems of the day?" We know that she is our infallible guide in faith and morals; but when it comes to Capital and Labour, private property, sweated industries, wages—does she deal with topics such as these? Or is she too much taken up with saving souls to care for the temporal welfare of the masses?

On all matters of faith and morals we must "hear the Church," as our Lord Himself tells us (Mat 18:17). Now, the social problems of the day have their root in principles that affect both belief and conduct. They have the gravest bearing upon our life here and our destiny hereafter. And they are so coloured and distorted by the selfishness, the greed, and the other passions of men, that we have every right to expect the Church to pronounce upon them and tell us what we must believe and what we must do.

And she has not disappointed us. In his Encyclical *On the Condition of the Working Classes*, Pope Leo XIII has declared very clearly the mind of the Church, and shown the way to be followed if society is to be saved. "No one can question," he says, "that a remedy must be found, and quickly found, for the misery which presses so heavily at this moment on the large majority of the very poor."

It is no easy matter, however, to find the remedy, to define the relative rights and mutual duties of rich and poor, of Capital and Labour. Pope Leo knew this and said it. But the way in which he himself handled the difficult problem has won the admiration of all far-sighted and fair-minded men, and wherever his teaching has been acted upon the happiest results have followed.

It took the world by surprise to see a Pope treating so ably such matters as the relations of class to class, the rights of the wage-earner, the necessity of bettering the condition of the poor, and the means to be taken to this end. Catholics, perhaps, were grateful rather than surprised. We know that as God has commanded us to hear the Church, He has bound Himself to see that her guidance of us shall be the safest and best. Moreover, she has had an experience of nearly nineteen hundred years, and has seen, times without number, how right lines of action work out for good in the end, and how wrong and mischievous, though often plausible, schemes bring disappointment and misery. We may trust her, then, when she shows the road to be followed, and when she holds up her finger and says: "Beware! Do nothing rashly. Work for reform and relief, but on safe lines. Let me advise you."

We may trust the Church absolutely, because of the divine promises to her, because of her knowledge of men and their ways, and because of her tender compassion for the poor and suffering. She is so much at home with them, enters with such sympathy into their feelings and their troubles, makes them so welcome when they come to her

Sursum Corda!

for comfort, that it is cast upon her as a reproach that she is pre-eminently the Church of the poor. She accepts the reproach and glories in it. In the days of the Apostles, the care of the poor, the sick, the widow, and the orphan was one of her chief concerns. In every age and country we find her making their cause her own, protecting their interests, and punishing their oppressors. To the Church we owe our first provision for the poor—our hospitals, our asylums of every kind for sheltering and relieving distress. In the Ages of Faith she provided the poor with food, medicine, work, instruction. She threw open to them her schools, admitted them into the ranks of her clergy, set them over churches as bishops, raised them to the Chair of Peter. The monasteries were their resource in every need of soul and body. In and around the great Benedictine abbeys all the crafts of civilization took their rise. The monks were woodmen, masons, carpenters, farmers. They cleared the forests, drained the swamps, brought vast tracts of land under cultivation, made roads, bridges, dykes, as the public need required. More than this: they made men realize that a life of useful toil, so far from being degrading, is elevating and ennobling if the worker chooses to make it such.

To the end that the poor might rise above poverty and wretchedness, the Church banded together for mutual protection and assistance all who practised the same craft. It was she who organized and blessed the Guilds of the Middle Ages, those Trade Unions in which masters and men, all of the same faith and bound by the same laws, met together for the practice of their religious duties and to discuss their labour interests. "The Church protected the workman from excessive labour by her festivals, which gave the needful rest and recreation. On Saturdays and on eves of holy days work ceased at midday. On the holy days no work was done.... The men took a pride in their work and nourished a feeling of loyalty and brotherhood to their masters. Meeting and mingling together as they did at work, at church, at feasts, at processions, there was complete unity of interests.... Consequently, when a workman was conscious of honesty, loyalty, and good conduct, the prospect of distress or destitution did not trouble him. He could look forward to a comfortable and honoured old age: if his own savings or his family could not support him, he had a larger family in the brethren of the Guild, who would furnish comforts for his declining years, and cheer him by visits and talks of the past. Thus the ages of Faith, the days when the Church held sway over the people, were the days when work was favoured and artisans were contented. Wages were unchallenged, strikes were needless, excessive toil was restricted, brotherhood was established, homes were decent, accidents were provided for, few were unemployed, and destitution was rare. What a gulf between then and now! Gone to-day is that personal contact between master and man. Unknown that mutual goodwill. The cause is plainly seen—the spirit of religion is missing. The Trade Unions of to-day, good, necessary as they are, are poor things compared to the Trade Guilds of the Middle

Sursum Corda!

Ages.... It may be that that spirit may one day return—God send that it may!" [1]

It was the Reformers, whom men are beginning to see in their true light as having at heart "not the good but the goods of the Church," who confiscated the property of the guilds, monasteries, hospitals, and almshouses, and gave us pauperism, the poor laws, and the workhouse in exchange.

II

THE CHURCH AND THE TOILERS, TODAY

In the past, then, the Church has always shown herself the friend of the working man. What is she doing now? She is insisting upon grievances and injustice being redressed, and that quickly. She is guiding the movement of sympathy flowing in to the toiler from every side. She is summoning men of all ranks and callings—clergy and laity, rulers and politicians, leaders of labour, and the labourers themselves—to unite in bringing about a reconciliation between Capital and Labour. And she is fostering the associations which are working steadily and successfully to this end.

She would have all help. No matter who or what we are, we may, each in his own place and measure, further the Catholic social movement which in England, as in other countries, is promoting the interests of the industrial classes.

---

1 *Life Through Labour's Eyes*, p. 14: George Milligan.

If we will but work together, shoulder to shoulder, content to do our own part and not envy another's—to do something, even if it seems a little thing—many great things will be done before long.

What, then, does Pope Leo teach us in his great Encyclical?

He reminds all men, rich and poor alike, of those facts which form the basis of human society, and of those principles of right and justice which must be upheld if society is to hold together. He shows that in the differences between the two classes, employers and employed, there are rights and responsibilities on both sides, that neither can hope for any solid and lasting advantage by overreaching the other, and that only by the due adjustment of their several claims can a remedy be found for present evils and for the graver ones that threaten.

"But why two classes?" cries the Socialist. "Men are equal, and have an equal right to the good things of life."

The Pope replies that men are equal, inasmuch as all are children of the same Heavenly Father, all have been redeemed by Jesus Christ, all are provided by God with the necessary means of salvation, and all at the final reckoning day will be rewarded or punished by Him according to their works. But men are unequal in capacity and in the circumstances of their lives, just as the members of the human body differ in their position and functions. It is in the very nature of things that some should be more skillful than others, some stronger, some more favoured by birth, education, or wealth; that there should be princes and subjects, learned and ignorant, leaders and guides, and labourers working with their hands. There will always be the industrious and thrifty who make their way in life, and the indolent and improvident who are left destitute. If all were on a par next Monday morning, there would be a difference before night. And were such a revolution to be brought about, the industrious working man would be the first to suffer. "Shirkers" and "loafers," as their comrades call them, the drunkard and the spendthrift, would eat the bread of idleness, the bread of other men's labour; the hard-working and the frugal would be deprived of their right to dispose of their wages, and thereby of all hope of increasing their store and bettering their condition in life. Hence, "a man with savings is deaf to the voice of the Socialist charmer, charm he never so sweetly," says Bishop Keating.

III

"COME AND HELP"

We must not, then, be led to suppose that Socialists are the only people alive to the sufferings of the industrial classes and prepared to relieve them. "The true remedy for existing troubles," says Pope Leo, "is to be sought in the combined action of the Church, the State, the employers of labour, the wealthy, and the labouring classes themselves." He would have the interests of the wage-earners safeguarded by means of associations and working men's unions, of those especially which consist of workmen and employers together.

He maintains that "remuneration ought to be sufficient to support a frugal and well-behaved wage-earner," and he has raised his voice to condemn the bad housing of the poor, sweated labour, and other forms of oppression. Pius X has shown himself no less zealous in the work of social reform. In accordance with his wish, social instruction on such subjects as unemployment, poverty in towns, the position of women, the wages question, is given in ecclesiastical seminaries and schools. Boys and girls are made to understand the sore spiritual and temporal needs of the poor, and are being trained to practical and useful work in their service.

The efforts made in this direction are full of promise for the future. Social study among Catholics has aroused strenuous energy and devotedness, especially among the young. Lectures to working men have resulted in a great increase of interest in the subject, and the success which in other countries has attended the labours of our fellow Catholics is full of encouragement for us. The Catholics of Germany started with enormous difficulties, and have seen their labours blessed with abundant fruit. The same is true in France and in Belgium. But Christian popular action must be rightly directed; Catholics of all social classes must act, says Pius X, "in complete submission to the Bishops and their representatives." Remedy and relief will surely come, but they must be worked for patiently, and on just and safe lines. They will come as the fruit of conciliation, of men realizing, as in earlier times, that we are all one body, and that in mutual dependence and service alone can the welfare of each and of all be found.

Sursum Corda!

Who should help forward this work of reconciliation if not our Christian women? Women before now have thrown themselves between combatants, and strife has ceased. The perils that in our own day threaten homes and nations are more terrible than in any other period of the world's history. Atheism and universal freemasonry are uniting to overthrow society by attacking all the world over the Christian religion, religious orders, the secular clergy, Christian education, and the rights of parents, sticking at nothing in their determination to seize for their own ends the soul of the child. If society is to be saved, it must be by upholding the principles of morality and the teaching of the Catholic faith, and by safeguarding the dignity and the rights, the peace and the happiness of the Christian home. Under the influence of unbelief, the moral law is losing its hold on the minds of men and women. Suicide, death by anaesthetics, divorce, crime, and corruption of every kind threaten the utter ruin of society and of the race. Who better than—*nay, who but our women* can make head against evils such as these! It needs no learning; it needs but the self-respect, the sense of duty, the irresistible power of her influence, by which woman has again and again rescued nations from destruction, to enable her to come forward now, and save, not nations only, but the world. Never was there a nobler field open to her. She is the mightiest there. There, sooner or later, all must yield to her, if she but take her stand firmly on Christian ground.

And in this fight every woman can help. Let none say she is without social position or means or influence, that she is too poverty-stricken, too beset with daily cares to look beyond her own door. Keep within your own door by all means, do there what you can to uphold your Catholic faith by word and by practice, and you will have taken a noble part, the very noblest in the work of saving society. To wander about in the aimless search for a mission that is to drop down to us from the skies—this is not what is wanted. But to look round upon the scenes and the faces that meet us every day, and within that little circle to cheer and to help—if we would one and all of us do this, what a change there would be around us before many weeks were passed! Those who have no home duties to engross them will seek for labour and serve the cause elsewhere.

But—oh, do remember this! wives, mothers, toilers of every kind, whose lives are one dull round of daily care, daily struggle with the drudgeries of poverty, *you can one and all do great things if you will.* You can stand up for the teachings of your Catechism, and make its lessons respected *in your own home.* And if—God help you!—it is just there that the difficulty and the trouble lies, you can still, by the effort that angels look down upon with admiration, by the grace ready always for those that ask it, bear up trustfully and not unfruitfully till God's hour comes for reward. Do not despond, do not hold back. Your word in season, your influence, your silent prayer, the good cause cannot afford to lose.

In response to the appeal of Pope Leo, women are labouring in every direction to better the condition of the

Sursum Corda!

working classes, and are everywhere realizing two things. First, that as the forces of evil are uniting in all directions against Christianity and the Church, the Catholic women of the entire world must unite to meet the danger. The evil calls for nothing less than a crusade, a combined effort to oppose the destructive doctrines which are making such frightful havoc amongst us and dragging down into the mire our Christian homes. The old ideas of the sacredness of human life, the indissolubility of marriage, reverence and obedience to parents as to the representatives of God, the necessity of religious education, the right of private property against socialistic principles, which open the way to unrest and revolution—all this must be insisted on. Wives and mothers must be restored to their rightful sphere of labour and influence in their own homes; the conditions of labour as to occupations, hours, and environment must be improved in such a way as to raise women from the oppression, degradation, and misery to which as wage-earners so large a proportion of them are condemned, and a friendly-hand must be held out to the lonely and unprotected to fortify them against the temptations to which they are exposed. It was to carry out successfully so vast a programme, to concert measures for developing the social work undertaken by women all the world over, and to guide aright the activity and self-sacrifice of those who are eager to serve in so noble a cause, that the International Federation of Catholic Women's Leagues met at Brussels in the August of 1910.

Why Must I Suffer?

We see, then, with what truth the Catholic Church can say with Christ: "I have compassion on the multitudes." We see that she is to-day what she has ever been, the best friend of those who toil and suffer. And we see that her resolve to soothe their sorrows is thoroughly practical. Pope Leo declares "those Catholics worthy of all praise who take up the cause of the working man, cast in their lot with the wage-earners, and help them to better their condition to the utmost in body, mind, and property. But," adds the Pope, "should all do their utmost, the pains and hardships of life will have no end or cessation on earth.... To suffer and to endure is the lot of humanity. No strength and no artifice will ever succeed in banishing from human life the ills and troubles which beset it. If there are any who pretend differently—who hold out to a hard-pressed people the boon of freedom from pain and trouble, an undisturbed repose, and constant enjoyment—they delude them, and their lying promises will only bring forth evils worse than the present. Nothing is more useful than to look upon the world as it really is, and at the same time to seek elsewhere for the solace to its troubles."

Let us look, then, at the problem of pain from another standpoint, and find another answer, simpler, deeper, and more satisfying, to the question, "Why must I suffer?"

IV

THE BIG QUESTION

The Epistle for the Mass of a Martyr ends with some startling words, and is followed by a response more startling still:

"All who will live godly in Christ Jesus"—it is St. Paul who is speaking—"shall suffer persecution."[1] Thanks be to God!" replies the clerk, cheerfully, and as a matter of course, and in the name of us all.

"Why is this?" we may ask. "Why should suffering be a thing to thank God for? Why is there so much pain in the world, not for the wicked only, who deserve it, but for the good, who are doing their best to serve God and lead honest and useful lives? Nay, how is it that it is the innocent who have often most to bear, while the guilty prosper and have it all their own way? Why has a merciful God created us all to suffer?"

This is a big question, one of the biggest of a questioning age. We must know the whys and the wherefores of everything nowadays, and, because we are rational creatures, the desire within reasonable limits is a lawful one. Only, when questions concern the Infinite God and His dealings with us, we must ask "Why?" not in a captious and querulous, but in a reverent spirit, and, having had a sufficient answer, must be content. There are many problems whose complete

---

1 2 Tim. 3.

solution we must not expect just yet. To us as to Peter our Lord says: "What I do thou knowest not now, but thou shalt know hereafter."[1] One reason why we cannot know now, is that our dispositions are at fault. To understand God's ways with us, we have to be in a right frame of mind for being taught. And this is less easy than heretofore. It supposes a spirit of reverence and docility out of harmony with our times, and often sadly wanting even in our dealings with God. Men in these days call the Almighty to account with an audacity that would have appalled the last generation. Irreverence in speech and in print is so common that it fails to startle us, and even affects us disastrously in spite of ourselves.

To come to the temper of mind needful for looking at things aright, let us get away for awhile from this twentieth century with its wealth and its work, its materialism and its restlessness, its inventions and its competition, its social questions, its self-sufficiency, its forgetfulness of God. Let us go back, back, as far as thought will carry us, to the eternity when the Infinite Almighty God, needing nothing to His happiness, dwelt alone. From eternity He had thus dwelt alone. Then, by an act of His Will, He created—material things all but infinite in number and variety, and intelligent creatures able to know, love, and serve Him, and in reward of this service to enter one day into the joy of their Lord, into a share of the very happiness of their Creator.

---

[1] St. John 13.

Sursum Corda!

But all this vast creation, and all possible creations, are in His sight as nothing. The multitudes of shining worlds we see above us at night and the measureless space in which they move, He holds in the hollow of His hand. On Him every creature depends for all it has and is; unless He upholds it at every instant, it must fall back into its original nothingness; without Him we cannot draw a breath or think a thought.

What must our relations be with such a one as this! what His rights over our understanding, and memory, and will, and affections, over all we have, and are, and can do! The thing we have made we look upon as our own, to be used for the purpose for which we made it. Is not at least the same right to be allowed Him who is not Maker only but Creator?

And he is our Father. "Father" is man's earliest name for Him. It is the name by which God would have all men call Him, since whatever this name implies—tenderness, compassion, provident love—is found as at its source in Him. He knows us through and through. All that there is to know about us, He knows. Because He has made us for Himself, He knows that unless we spend our eternity with Him, we must be everlastingly miserable. Therefore, all that concerns us—birth, and life, and death, our circumstances, and temptations, and trials—His providence has so ordered as to make for our final happiness with Him. By the wrong use of our free-will, by sin, we can, indeed, thwart His designs and turn against ourselves what was adapted to save us. We can, and we do. We can turn against Him and against ourselves all the gifts we have from His hand. We can, alas! and we do. But His will is to save us. He has our happiness at heart, more, a thousand times more, than any earthly father ever had the welfare of an only child. He watches our every step. He sympathizes with our every struggle and pain. If He allows us to suffer for a time, it is as a father here below subjects the child of his hopes to the discipline and training that are to fit him for his inheritance; it is to change labour and trouble and privation, presently, into happiness inconceivable and everlasting.

To those who refuse to recognize God's necessary rights over them as Creator, and who close their hearts to all the advances of their Heavenly Father, life is a mystery indeed. The permission of evil, the triumph of injustice, the inequalities of nature and of fortune, the oppression of the weak, the sufferings of the just—what is there to explain all this? But when we have trained ourselves to see God our Father overruling all things to our final good, we have a clue to the puzzles of life. All is not clear yet. Patience and humility are called for still. We must not expect to understand all the counsels of the Infinite and the Incomprehensible. But there is no room for mistrust, because we know our Almighty Father loves us and that nowhere can we be so safe as in His hand. He has brooded over us, over each one of us—not for a few years, not since our birth only, but from all eternity! As long as He has been God He has loved us and determined to create us, that we may be happy with Him for ever; and with such a happiness!—eye and ear and mind and heart filled to overflowing, satisfied beyond every desire with the delights He has in store for them! The only condition to the enjoyment for ever of all these delights is—that we should *deserve them*. God will not force eternal happiness upon us. The Home made ready there is for His children who have so used His gifts and corresponded with His training as to be able to claim the promised prize. In this it differs from a boy's earthly home, to which he returns as a matter of course when his time of schooling is over. Heaven is no matter of course, though many of us speak as if it were. "He is gone," they say, "to rest and to glory— no more pain and trouble for him—he is with the Saints." Certainly, if reward is his due. If he has won Heaven and glory, they will be given him. He will be with the Saints if he has gone the road of the Saints. But there is no 'of course' about it. The question is: How, during his time of trial on earth, did he use his free-will, God's grandest gift to us? To be the noble creatures we are, God was obliged to give us free-will, the dread power of choice. We can, if we will, frustrate the loving design of our Creator and fling away everlasting happiness. We can, with His help, choose Heaven and work out our salvation, in spite of every difficulty in our way. Poverty, toil, care, sickness, sorrow, disappointment, temptation—all these He has so arranged that they can be used as helps to Heaven. They are being so used by thousands in the world to-day.

V

"WHY?"

"But why," some will ask, "does God send us here to suffer? Why, when He forgave the disobedience of our first Parents and let them off the eternal punishment they had deserved, did He not take away the temporal punishment too, and save us all the suffering sin has brought into the world?"

It might suffice to say: "Because He willed otherwise and whatever He wills must be best." But we may help ourselves very much, by trying in a reverent spirit to see *how* what He has willed is best. We have instincts which point to our noble origin, and show us to be what we are—creatures made in the image and likeness of the All-Just and All-Holy God. One of these instincts is the conviction that goodness ought to be and will be rewarded at last, and that wrongdoing will be punished. Heathens and Christians, the good and the bad alike, feel this. They see tyranny and injustice, and they expect to see punishment; often enough they are impatient because punishment is delayed. That sin means suffering is a law without exception. The Angels—one-third of them—rebelled against God, and fell into Hell. Man imitated them in their rebellion, and would have shared their lot had not God forgiven him his sin and remitted the eternal punishment. Temporal punishment—poverty, privation, pain of body and mind, sickness, death,—a terrible inheritance indeed, but a mere nothing compared with what had been incurred—this remained. But it is all lit up by hope and by the companionship and example of the Son of God, who has come down from Heaven to share it with us and to show us how to profit by it. We are not now convicts undergoing a sentence; we are children at school, learning the lessons and subjected to the wise restraints and experiences that are to fit us for the glorious future prepared for us. We are exiles for a while from our true country, but returning thither, and meantime with materials in our hands for laying up treasure which eternity will not exhaust.

By the way, we may ask those who show surprise that "the Paradise of Pleasure" was not left to us after the forgiveness of Adam's sin, how long they suppose his descendants would have kept it. For free-will would have remained to every one of us. God will have none but His free creatures to share His happiness for ever. Even in the state of innocence, Heaven was a prize to be won. Suppose, then, that Paradise after being forfeited had been restored to us, how long would it have been ours? Do we know ourselves so little as to believe that actual sin would not have followed upon original sin? Which of us can lay his hand on his heart and say that with him at least Eden would have been safe, that suffering in his case, at any rate, is not the well-merited chastisement of sin?

It is this; but, as we have seen, it is much more than this. The troubles of life are not punishment only, but preparation. Heaven is the court of the King of kings. It is a court of dazzling purity. From the great white throne, before which angels bow down in adoration and sing continually, "Holy, holy, holy," to the lowliest place in its glorious precincts—all is spotless. Can we without making ready be admitted there? Or do we honestly believe that any kind of life will suffice as preparation? Surely there must be the clearing away of the stains of earth, either here or in Purgatory!

The process, wherever carried on, is bound to be a painful one, and were the time left to our choice, most of us would say: "Let it be put off as long as possible. Let me enjoy life to the full and then take the consequences in Purgatory." But God loves us too well to leave the matter in our hands. He knows that the consequences of such a life would land us, not in Purgatory, but somewhere else, where pain is not for a time only, but for ever, where it is not remedy or preparation, but simply punishment that does us no good, and that never comes to an end, because the time of probation, when repentance would have availed us, is over. So He mercifully distributes over our life the suffering that is to serve as punishment, and as preparation. He gives us the opportunity of so using pain both of mind and body, that all, even to the least little worry or smart, shall help us heavenward—if we will. For here, again, our free-will must come in. Pain of itself is of no avail, either to pay off our debt of punishment or to make us ready for Heaven. To profit by it, we must understand who sends it, and why, and we must fall in with the intentions of our Heavenly Father, and accept at least with patience what comes to us from His hand.

Sursum Corda!

Borne in this way, trial loses half its pressure. It does not crush, nor exasperate, nor drive us to despair. For beside us and beneath us we feel the support of "the everlasting arms."[1] It is the rebellion of our will against it that is the intolerable part of pain. And we rebel, because we will not see God's hand and God's will in what befalls us. We fix our eyes only on the persons, or the things, or the circumstances through which trouble comes to us, and forget that nothing can touch us but by His permission. Sin and injustice cannot come from Him, but the effects of these things upon us, He allows, and wills for our good. Not to see this, to refuse to look at this, is to defeat God's purpose, and to turn against ourselves what He meant to help us.

Suffering never leaves us as it finds us. Either it drives us to God, draws us closer to Him, purifies, strengthens, and ennobles us, or it drags us down, and embitters us, leads us to compare our lot with others, and repine and rebel. It may even fix a gulf between ourselves and God, which may widen into lifelong estrangement, and end in separation from Him and the loss of Him, which means eternal ruin and despair.

Why will we not trust Him! He told one of His servants that He loves us so dearly, that if it were possible for Him to bring us to Heaven without suffering, He would never let pain of any sort come near us. But as things are, as we ourselves have made them, this is not possible. And so He allows us to suffer for awhile that we may be prepared for the happiness He has in store for us. But He takes care

---
1 1 Deut. 33.

that trial shall never be too hard, and whilst it lasts He supports us with His grace, and if only we cling to Him by patience and submission to His will, He will most certainly provide for us and give us comfort and help. He pities us for that mistrust of Himself, that bitterness and rebellion, which puts a sting into pain He never meant to be there, and makes it at times insupportable. He pities our dismay when at last the mists of earth are cleared away, and we see all things clearly—what earth was meant to be, not home but school; how all that happened to us was planned to work together for our good; how it was the love of God that chose this lot for us rather than that, which led us by a rough, perhaps a very rough way, but brought us safe to Heaven at last. "It was true, then," we shall say; "God has indeed loved me. '*Why must I suffer?*' I asked bitterly again and again. And now I see what I might have seen all along. Oh, what I have missed by mistrusting my Father's love!"

"Why did God make you?" a priest asked a little child.

"God made me," she said, "because He loved me."

"How do you know He loves you?"

"Why, because He made me, Father! If He did not love me, He needn't have made me."

The children see what we fail to see. Their instinct is true which tells them we are here because God loved and loves us.

"But," some will object, "children have not passed through the trials of life which weigh down and perplex and embitter us."

Sursum Corda!

Weigh down, yes, and to the very earth at times. But why embitter and perplex? There are puzzles in life, no doubt: a few for those who know but little, more for those who know more, fewest for those who know most, because these have the clue to the explanation. We are speaking, mind, of perplexities that disquiet us, not of mere difficulties. A hundred difficulties do not make a doubt, says Cardinal Newman. The problems to which a full answer will never be found in this world, need not disturb in the very least our trust in our Father who is in Heaven. Nor need the trials of life embitter us. But they will unless our outlook is a wide one. If to us this world is the beginning and end of all things, life must simply swarm with puzzles, and we may search in vain for an explanation of them. But if we bear in mind that it is only the beginning, the dark narrow tunnel to the wide expanse beyond, then the meaning of its obscurities and its hindrances becomes plain. We understand that these things must be, and hope keeps up our hearts, as we wait in the darkness for the light and air and freedom we shall have directly.

"*Sola fides sufficit,*" we sing at Benediction. Yes, "faith alone suffices." But without faith nothing will enable us to face the mysteries of life without dismay; at times, without despair. It is their faith that must sustain the sweated labourers, the unemployed, the weary, the lonely, the mourners, when the outlook before them is black to the very end. Heaven is beyond. As surely as the hurrying train brings us after a few moments of gloom into the light of day, so is life bearing us swiftly to the eternity that follows, and—if we only will it—to everlasting brightness and joy.

VI

LAYING UP TREASURE

What waste there is in our lives through the neglect of opportunities to lay up treasure in Heaven! We can merit, that is, we can earn an increase of grace here and of glory hereafter by every good work we do. God wants us to go straight to Heaven when our work on earth is done. And He does so want it to be a high place, where we shall see *all*, hear *all*, enjoy *all* the delights He has in store for us. An act of the love of God, of sorrow for sin, of patience, of kindness to another for God's sake, is the work of an instant, yet it will make a difference to our place in Heaven for all eternity. And treasure like this can be gained, not only by works good in themselves, such as hearing Mass, giving an alms, but by actions which in themselves are indifferent, that is, neither morally good nor bad, for instance, eating, working, resting.

Two things only are needed to make these so-called indifferent actions very pleasing to God—that we should be in a state of grace, and that we should supernaturalize them by doing them to please God. A dead soul cannot merit; it can do nothing for Heaven. All the time spent in mortal sin is time lost for ever. This does not mean that prayer and good works done in this state are useless, far from it. They move God to show us mercy and to give us the grace we need to recover His friendship. It is not true to say, "God does not hear sinners." He hears us all and always. Mortal sin, indeed, makes us His enemies, and were we to die in that state He would have to banish us from His presence for ever. But His enmity is not like that between man and man. He bears us no ill-will. He is always seeking reconciliation, holding out His arms to us, inviting us to come back to Him while there is yet time. No matter how frequent or how grievous our falls may be, He is ready to receive us back to His embrace the moment we are sorry. Yes, even before we go to confession. We need not remain a moment in mortal sin, that state of awful peril. The uplifting of our heart to Him in an act of perfect contrition: "My God, I am sorry for my sins, because You are so good," at once restores us to His friendship, provided we mean to confess our sin. And, once His friends, we can begin again to merit for Heaven by every act and every pain, if only we sanctify these by a good intention.

But how many of us neglect to do this? Thousands of undirected letters, we are told, are yearly committed to the flames through the carelessness of the writers. The matter may be excellent, the style perfect, but all is thrown away because they have nowhere to go to. Our work, too, is often lost by not being directed to God. Sometimes we misdirect it, and so cause mischief, but oftener we are to blame simply for negligence in non-direction. The selfsame act may be in one case purely natural, deserving no reward hereafter, and in another supernatural, meriting grace and glory. A man gives his umbrella to a woman in a shower of rain and gets wet through himself. This may be nothing more than a piece of good breeding, or it may be an act of supernatural charity. With God the direction of our work is everything. We are not obliged to do great things to merit reward. "Whether you eat or drink, or whatsoever you do, do it for the glory of God," says St. Paul. What a pity it is, then, to leave our daily actions, like our letters, undirected!

"What do you think about all day as you drive your plough?" a labourer was asked.

"Well, most about nowt," was the answer. What a pity!

The value of work in the eyes of men depends in great measure on the nature of the work. In the eyes of God it depends on the intention with which it is done. He cares more for the workman than for the work. This thought should bring comfort and content to the toilers whom the world reckons only as so many "hands." The mistake of looking upon manual labour as something degrading, and the restless effort to raise ourselves or our children to a certain "position," is responsible for a vast amount of discontent and unhappiness in daily life. Exceptional talent, showing unmistakable aptitude for other tasks, may warrant the endeavour to fit oneself for them; but, seeing that labour with our hands is the lot of most, it is surely unwise to hold it in dishonour, and thus deprive those on whom it must fall, of their self-respect, their peace of mind, and their happiness.

The days are gone by when to earn one's own livelihood was thought demeaning. We are content to be paid as shop-girls, lady typists, secretaries, companions, clerks. But the manual work that begrimes the face and roughens the hands—this remains an abomination still. Why? A life of honest toil dishonours no one, and surely it ill becomes those who worship the Carpenter of Nazareth to despise humble, upright industry. His hands have consecrated it. His example has sweetened it. Shall we who call ourselves His followers sigh after something more "respectable"? A noble man or woman ennobles any calling, whether it be that of a navvy[1], a mill-hand, an architect, or a statesman. We can all make our daily toil dignified and elevating if we choose, by taking it up cheerfully and directing it to the life to come. Of course we cannot offer up to God anything bad, but with this exception we may offer Him all we do, what we like, what we dislike. By every act done for Him we gain a new degree of sanctifying grace to which a new degree of glory corresponds.

Let us see what this means.

God cannot give anything small in Heaven. Everything there is on the grandest scale, worthy of His majesty and generosity. The least reward for the least good thing done, is an unspeakable reward that lasts for ever. It is as if an altogether new Heaven were given us over and above the Heaven due to us before. We shall be a degree nearer to God for all eternity, knowing Him better, loving Him more, and thus enjoying an increase of happiness absolutely

---

[1] Short for *navigator*, a term applied to manual laborers who worked on civil engineering projects, i.e. railways, canals and the like.

inconceivable—and this for ever! How foolish then we should be to neglect so easy a way of laying up treasure in Heaven! To secure it, we shall do well to offer our daily work to God in our morning prayers:

"My God, I offer Thee this day
All I shall think, or do, or say,
Uniting it with what was done
On earth by Jesus Christ, Thy Son."

or,

"O Jesus, through the most pure Heart of Mary, I offer Thee the prayers, work, and sufferings of this day for all the intentions of Thy Divine Heart in the Holy Mass."

VII

THE CROSS

Some people suppose that unless an act is hard, unless there is pain and sacrifice in it, it does not please God. This is a mistake. Nevertheless, sacrifice, by which we mean overcoming our natural inclinations for God's sake, undoubtedly adds to the merit of an action. Borne at least patiently, the Cross is a most powerful means of salvation and sanctification. But what do we mean by the Cross?

Since our Lord came to us as the Man of Sorrows, and those sorrows which were to open Heaven to us reached their height on Calvary, the Cross has been the symbol of pain, of struggle, and of victory. We call everything that

Sursum Corda!

causes us distress of mind or body, and that, bravely borne, will bring us reward in Heaven—our Cross.

Want, always staring them in the face, the working for a pittance no industry or thrift can stretch to the weekly need, to be badly fed, badly clothed, badly housed—this is the Cross of many amongst us. Or it may take a more terrible form still. Work does not come, though we have prayed and prayed; the breadwinner of the family is carried off by death; a husband or child is walking heedlessly amidst dangers where no help but prayer can reach him, and seemingly unanswered prayer begins to weary—this may be our Cross. With very many, their occupation, heavy, ill-paid, monotonous, the burden taken up every morning, and hardly laid down at night, is the Cross that weighs them down. A bad season, losses, injustice, the troubles known to every one and those unseen by any, the pain it costs us to fight our passions and ill habits, to live peaceably with others, to be faithful to our religious duties, to resist the temptations to evil in our daily life—these are but samples of the shape our Cross may take. It may come from the malice or the mistakes of those around us, from good people who are honestly trying like ourselves to serve God. For so long as we are in this world we are all at school. No one is perfect, and the ways of good people may be as trying to us as our ways undoubtedly are to others. No one finishes his education on this side of the grave, and some of us show our want of finish pretty often.

And our Cross may come to us direct from God, who tries us for a little while, that He may be able to reward us throughout eternity. When He hides His face and seems to forget us in our need, when His service is distasteful, when it is hard to submit to His will and to trust His love and care for us—then He himself is laying the Cross upon our shoulders. Whatever, then, runs counter to our liking, whatever goes against self—this is our Cross. Wherever it comes from, of whatever material it is made, it can be the source of untold good to us. For, first:

Suffering expiates our sins and lessens the terrible debt of punishment which to the last farthing must be paid either here or hereafter, either by a little pain borne willingly here, or by a great deal endured in the fires of Purgatory. Secondly:

Suffering leads us to God.—It gives us right views of life. It turns our thoughts Heavenward. We are wayfarers, not having here a lasting city. But a prosperous man is apt to forget this. Earth is so pleasant a place, that he does not look beyond. But trouble comes; other help fails and—he turns to God. When our dear Lord walked upon earth, who was it that were attracted to Him and were His familiar companions? The poor and those in sorrow, either on their own account, as the blind, the deaf, the maimed, or on account of others, as the sisters of Lazarus for their brother. Among the suffering we always find Him, and now, as then. When things go well with us here, we get absorbed in them and forget God. But let sickness threaten us, or failure, or loss, let earth look dark and desolate, and, like the Prodigal Son, we turn to our Home and to our Father. How many has sorrow brought back to God! How many will owe their salvation to a disappointment, a humiliation which all but crushed them at the time! How they will bless God for it throughout eternity!

Suffering proves our Fidelity to God.—The Cross stands as the symbol, not of pain only, but of struggle. It is the Standard that calls upon us to fight. And He said to all: "If any one will come after Me, let him deny himself and take up his cross and follow Me." There is no alternative. There must be patience and self-restraint, submission to the permissions of God's Providence, and war with our rebellious passions. Faithfulness to God is not hard when all goes well with us. But to say: "Thy Will be done" when hard times pinch us, or a crushing blow has fallen, this is the fidelity of His true servants. It is not enough to be Catholics, we must be practical Catholics, ready to live up to our Faith and to suffer for it. This means the having oneself well in hand, the continual making of little sacrifices, which is the daily cross-bearing of the poor.

Sometimes it means more than this. When a man begins to realize that a dangerous habit is forming, he must put such restrictions on himself as will cut off the occasion before indulgence has strengthened the evil. Our Lord's injunction as to this prompt action is very striking: "If thy eye or ear scandalize thee, pluck it out, cut it off, and cast it from thee." Whatever the cost, the work of self-conquest must be carried through, for it is a question of saving our souls. And with God's help, gained by prayer and the Sacraments, it can be done. Habit, perhaps, has grown strong, and our will by self-indulgence, weak. We have not even the strength to will our amendment with real resolution. But God is on our side backing up our weakness. "Fear not," He says, "My grace is sufficient for thee. Even if you fall a hundred times a day, come back to Me with sorrow and a renewed purpose, hold fast to prayer, go to the Sacraments oftener because you need their strength, and you will conquer in the end. Your Faith interferes with your worldly prospects, with an attachment, with what seems to you your chance of happiness in life. Conscience and inclination are in the balance, time and eternity. You say you have not the strength for the right choice. Fear not, My servant, for I am with thee. 'Act like a man, take courage and do, for the Lord thy God is with thee and will not leave thee nor forsake thee.'"[1]

Suffering is the Price of Glory.—Men are so agreed as to this, that in almost every language of the world we find the proverb "No cross, no crown." All know that success in life's work can only be reached by labour and by pain. And because our life's work is before everything else to get to Heaven, we have to remember that by the Cross we purchase our Crown. "Ought not Christ to suffer these things, and so to enter into His glory?"[2] And if He, surely I! for the servant is not above his Master. Why should some be called

---

[1] 1 Par. 28.
[2] St. Luke 24.

upon to give up home, family, livelihood, earthly happiness, for the Faith and for Heaven, and I have to sacrifice nothing! Heaven is given as a reward, that we may taste the joy of having earned it. None know the sweets of repose better than the toiler; none feel the pleasure of recompense like those who have practised severe self-restraint for the sake of the prize.

Yes, the Cross stands finally for victory. Think often of the evening when the tired labourer will meet the Master and lay the sheaves at His feet. Look forward to that smile, to that welcome, to that invitation: "Come, blessed of My Father," and all the sowing in tears now will seem a small price to pay for the reward by and by. "Look out," the Socialist cries, "and see the prizes of life to which you have as good a right as any, and strain every nerve to get them." "Look up," says the Church, "to the prize that, once gained, will be yours for ever. Do what you can by industry, temperance, thrift, to secure for yourself and your family a decent living here, but do not repine at the hardships that are to win for you eternal happiness hereafter."

VIII

"COME TO ME, YOU THAT LABOUR"

Our Lord is the great Consoler—not by freeing us from all sorrow, but by giving us right views about it, above all, by giving us His own example to enlighten, cheer, and strengthen us. He took the largest share of it Himself, and then parcels out the rest amongst us. We all get some; His nearest and dearest often get most. Because He has suffered Himself, He can feel for us in our troubles. He is not one who makes light of smaller pains. His deep wounds do not make Him scorn our little scratches. He has actually felt beforehand all the pain that falls on us. To teach us the dignity of labour, and to encourage us to bear poverty with patience, He has lived the life of a poor man and worked at a poor trade. He knows pain and privation in all its shapes—cold, hunger, thirst, weariness, a hard bed, short sleep. His gentle, tender Heart, so sensitive to kindness and to unkindness, knows the pain of contempt, slander, ingratitude, betrayal by a friend. Could He have done more to encourage us?

The dock labourer who turns wearily from the words of other comforters, will not refuse the sympathy of one who has passed through the same experiences as himself: " 'Oh, brother,' writes a comrade in trouble to the 'out-of-work,' 'you have my sympathy, for these lips have drained that cup of bitterness and this heart has been almost broken with the same unutterable despair.' "[1]

This is the sort of sympathy that goes home to us; it is to such a one as this our heart opens out in trust. Fellow-feeling is what we need in suffering: the heart of a fellow-sufferer to cheer us, the hand of a fellow-sufferer to raise us. Then let us welcome the fellow-feeling of Him who was a

---

[1] *Life Through Labour's Eyes*, p. 59: G. Milligan.

labouring man as one of ourselves, and allow Him what He gave the best part of His life on earth to purchase, the right to comfort us in the way we will accept. We think of Him at Christmas, when the season recalls the stable and the crib. We give Him an occasional glance on Calvary. But do we ever visit Him in His workshop and there hear Him say to us: "Learn of Me"?

Look at Him working patiently at His humble trade, sawing planks, gathering up chips, sweeping His shop, receiving orders, carrying work home. See Him coming forward to welcome us, His face bronzed and flushed, the beads of sweat upon His brow, His outstretched hands hardened with toil, His limbs covered with the dust of labour. Coarse fare and coarse clothing, heavy toil when times were good, distress when work was slack, the monotony of it year after year, as the carpenter of that bit of a place among the hills, the weary going out in the morning, the weary return at night, the fault-finding claimed as their right by those who pay, the beating down of His modest price, the holding out of His hand for the earnings grudgingly given—all this He knows, all this He chooses, that the toilers of all time might turn to Him as to their companion and their friend, that He might have the right to say: "Come to Me, all you that labour, and I will refresh you, by My example, by My pity, by My remembrance of the days when I too was hard pressed and weary. You were My first friends on earth, you are now among My most faithful followers; you have a special nearness to Me in the sufferings of your earthly life; you may, if you will, be near Me in glory throughout eternity." Is it a disgrace, then, to be "only a working man"? Shall we be ashamed to be seen in church in our working clothes?

A traveller, passing one evening through a village, went into the little Catholic church. A bundle of tools lay at the door. Within was their owner in his shirt sleeves, going the round of the Stations. No one else there, only those two—the Master in the tabernacle, and the tired servant coming to lay his day's work at his Master's feet, and gain strength for the morrow by following Him along the Way of the Cross.

IX

NOT "WHY MUST I SUFFER?" BUT "HOW?"

Troubles are the raw material out of which our crown is made, but we have to put them into shape. Pain does not of itself better a man. On the contrary, it may make him worse. Some people, we are told, carry their Cross to Hell, some to Purgatory, some to Heaven. For the rebellious it has a twofold weight. They bear alone and unwillingly what God meant to lighten by His grace and His consolation. What will be the anguish and rage of the lost at the Last Day, to find that in flinging aside the Cross, they have suffered more than the servants of Christ who have taken it up willingly, and so followed their Lord into His kingdom.

Sursum Corda!

Setting rebellion aside, there are three ways in which we may bear the Cross: with mere endurance, because we cannot get rid of it—this is to act like a sensible pagan; with patience and resignation, because we are heirs of Heaven and must go through the training that is to fit us for our inheritance, because, too, we are followers of Christ and must tread in the footsteps of our Leader—this is to suffer as a Christian; with generosity, thanksgiving, and joy—this is to suffer like Christ and His Saints. Since we are not pagans but servants of Christ, the question, then, is—not *if* we will follow Him, but *how closely*.

Much depends on the way in which we carry out our Lord's injunction: "Learn of Me." Some look at Him cross-laden, in a careless, casual way, and His example makes but little impression. Others look closer and oftener, and learn more. They get into the way of supernaturalizing all their troubles, even the least. An inconvenience, a wet day, a disagreeable word from another, all is looked upon with the eye of faith, all is accepted from the hand of God, all is made meritorious by being borne willingly for Christ and with Christ. Their motto is that of the dear faithful Irish: "Welcome be the will of God!" Or the words of our Lord: "Thy will be done. Yea, Father, for so it hath seemed good in Thy sight." All the world over, passing me in the street, working by my side in daily life, living maybe under the same roof with me, are these true followers of Christ Crucified.

And some there are who get nearer to Him still. They have seen a deeper meaning yet in those words: "Learn of Me." They have looked at Him in the crib, in the workshop, on the Cross, till His example has sunk down into their hearts, and kindled there, not patience and resignation only, but the desire to be like Him, to repay Him love for love. "He loved me and delivered Himself for me.[1] I will love Him and show my love by bearing my share of His Cross with generosity, with thankfulness, and with joy." These do not make the best of a trouble, they make the most of it. They do not sit down, fold their hands and be resigned; they spring forward to seize their chance. Their motto is: *"Deo Gratias:* Thanks be to God!" *"They went rejoicing,"* St. Luke says of the Apostles called to suffer for the name of Christ. So the angels say of these.

To reach this highest degree of likeness to Christ, we must begin with little things. It is the greatest mistake to suppose that little things matter little. Nothing is too small to be offered to God, and everything so offered draws us nearer to Him, makes us more pleasing to Him, wins us fresh grace here, and new glory in Heaven. Great gains seldom come in our way. If we wait for them we shall never become rich. And unless we are in the habit of seizing upon the little daily gains as they come, we shall miss the great ones when they offer. What if we were to meet every trouble by a *"Deo Gratias!"* It costs, but it takes the sting out of pain and

---

[1] Gal 2.

gives us God's peace instead. It is not too much to say, that if we can only bring ourselves to take a supernatural view of suffering, we shall have removed the greatest hindrance to our peace and happiness here and the greatest obstacle in our way to Heaven. For this, reflection and effort are needed, as we have seen—and Prayer.

Why, oh why do we not pray more when we are in trouble? We talk to others who, with all their goodwill, can help so little. Why not have it all out with our Heavenly Father? Nothing helps so much as to open our hearts straight out before Him. There is no need for careful words. We may say out to Him, just as it comes, all we feel. Or we need not speak at all. We may be too sore, or too weary to put our trouble into words. But we remember He is there, wherever we are, that He made us, that He loves us, that He knows all, that He wants to help. And so we just lay our heart in its trouble before Him, and wait—we may have to wait a little—for His comfort and His help.

But, unhappily, it is just in time of trouble that we are apt to keep away from Him, and neglect prayer and the Sacraments. When there was trouble in the cotton trade, and the mills had to dismiss their "hands," Cardinal Vaughan made an earnest appeal to his priests: "We hope that the clergy will not cease to preach this truth—that the more miserable, the more neglected, the poorer, the unhappier people are, according to the estimate of this world, the more pressing need have they of the Sacraments. Sad indeed is the thought, that when through poverty and misery men give up this world in despair, they should yield to the temptation of giving up the next world also. The Good Shepherd is never happier than when He carries home upon His shoulders "the poor sheep that is cold and starved, and unable to walk or even to stand without assistance."[1]

Yes, the time of trouble is more than ever the time for prayer, and for united prayer. Pray all together, father, mother, children; such prayer has wonderful power with God. "Gather together the little ones," was His own order to His people of old in time of distress. And when to the prayer of these innocents is joined that of father and mother, God will most surely hear.

Late one Christmas Eve a Sister of Charity entered a miserable garret in Paris. On the floor sat a girl of eleven, her baby brothers, twins, on her lap. The mother had been buried that day. A lad of fourteen, far gone in decline, lay on a heap of straw. He smiled as the Sister came in and looked wistfully at her basket. Alas! it was empty. All her efforts had been fruitless; there had been nothing but rebuffs and threats that day. She had come to the orphans with her hands empty, her heart full. She tried to tell them that very early in the morning she would be sure to bring them food. But the despairing little faces were too much for her, and, bidding the children pray hard to Jesus and Mary, she went out to try again. The girl took her rosary: "Let us say the Sorrowful Mysteries," she said. As she finished them, a thought struck her:

"Let us make a Sixth Mystery—The Hunger and Thirst of Jesus when He was a little boy."

---
1 *Life of Cardinal Vaughan*, vol. i. p. 389: J. G. Snead-Cox.

Sursum Corda!

The Sister too was praying as she hastened aimlessly through this street and that, wondering where she might venture to knock a second time that day. Passing a lordly mansion belonging to one of the bitterest of the anti-clericals, a sudden impulse urged her to try there. It was useless, surely. She would get a sharp refusal, and probably something more. But Charity is bold, bearing all things, hoping all things. She knocked, and asked to see Monsieur N. She gained admittance. She pleaded the orphans' cause, and an hour later, from a well-filled basket, was dividing among the starving little ones the answer to their prayer.

X

MY CROSS

"But *my* Cross!" some one will say despondingly. "All this is true, of course, of crosses in general, but mine is so much heavier than others. See these people and those, how well off they are, how free from care and trouble, how surrounded with comforts and conveniences! Had I their gifts of body or mind, their opportunities, their crosses even, I could serve God well and happily."

You think so? You honestly believe you could arrange better for yourself than your Almighty, All-wise, All-loving Father has arranged for you?

---

1   Gal 2.

Why Must I Suffer?

There was once a boy who quarrelled with his Cross. It was such a particularly disagreeable and objectionable Cross; it was always getting in his way and tripping him up, hindering him, in fact, instead of helping him. Almost all his falls came from tumbling over that Cross.

His Guardian Angel had heard these complaints so often, that he said to him one night:

"My child, since you cannot get to Heaven without a Cross, and the one you have is not to your liking, come with me and choose for yourself."

And lo! in the twinkling of an eye the two were together on a vast plain overstrewn with crosses of all kinds—big and little, rough and polished, crosses with no pretensions to beauty, and crosses artistically wrought, crosses of wood and of lead, crosses of gold and of silver, some so large that they looked as if they must crush any one who should attempt to carry them, some smaller, some very tiny; here a number of little ones heaped together; and there, on a parched and desolate patch of ground, bare and black against the sky, a huge one all alone.

In and out amongst this host of crosses the boy wandered to find one to his taste. There was choice enough, certainly. The moon came out and helped him in his search, and showed him on a grassy mound one of massive gold, sparkling with many coloured gems. This was the very thing for him. He ran up to get a nearer view of it, and looked wistfully in his companion's face:

Sursum Corda!

"It is the Cross of a princess," said the Angel thoughtfully; "try it, if you like."

The boy tried to lift it, and failed, tried again, tried with all his might—and failed. So far from raising, he could not even stir it. He turned round, expecting help. But the Angel only smiled sadly at his flushed face and fruitless efforts. The golden cross was plainly out of the question. But shining in the moonlight was a slender one of silver, so beautiful, it seemed an ornament rather than a burden.

"Dear Angel, may I have this?" he cried.

But oh! how its sharp edges galled his shoulders! A few painful steps and then his courage failed, and it was given up like the rest. Others were tried and abandoned in their turn. They were too heavy, or too rough, too ugly, or too long. Tired and dispirited, the boy looked up almost reproachfully into his Angel's face:

"Dear Angel, won't you help me? You see none of these will do, and I am tired of trying."

The Angel answered gravely: "Child, I could choose nothing better for you than what God Himself has chosen; neither can I help you to carry a Cross which is not of His appointing."

Turning away sorrowful, the boy's eyes fell on a wooden cross lying at his feet. As a last resource, he took it up and laid it on his shoulder. It was light after the others, and there was a certain sweetness about it he had not found in them. Full of surprise and joy he cried out:

---

1 *Life of Cardinal Vaughan*, vol. i. p. 389: J. G. Snead-Cox

"I have found the right one at last. This is just the thing for me; do please let me have it."

The Angel smiled: "Yes, child, it is just the thing for you, as He knows who chose it for you. It is the Cross you have been carrying all this time with so many complaints, with so little generosity and trust. Take it up again now with thankfulness and bear it so even to the end. It will bring you safely into the presence of our God in His kingdom of never-ending joy."

Oh no! with our rule as to suffering—"a little of this, none of that, and not too much of any"—it would never do for us to have the choosing of our Cross. We must leave it all to Him whose love for us is too wise, too far-seeing to make any mistake about it. Why can we not bring ourselves to trust Him? Who can show us a single reason why we should fight shy of Him whose love of us had no beginning, and is so persevering in spite of all we have been, and are? Why not surrender ourselves to Him—at last? Why not throw ourselves into His arms and say:

"O my Father, my Heavenly Father, help me to trust You as You deserve! I thank You for Your eternal love of me. I thank You for all You have done to bring about my salvation. I thank You for my life *as You have planned it*, with its joys and its difficulties; its opportunities, if I will but use them; its helps, if I will but ask for them and stretch out my hand to get them. I offer You my life, or all that remains of it. Make me remember always that there is another life to follow, and make me live for that other eternal life. What

Sursum Corda!

matter is it how much I suffer here so I reach the happiness You have in store for me! Let me so trust You that I may be willing to wait for the explanation of many things I cannot understand now. Let me so live that it may be a joy to look back upon life from my place in Heaven."

XI

THE CROWN

Those who saw Wellington, grim, unwashed, smoke-blackened, the night after Waterloo was won, say that as he sat at supper, his few surviving officers about him, he repeatedly leaned back in his chair, rubbing his hands convulsively, and exclaiming: "Thank God I have met him! Thank God I have met him!" The effort had been tremendous; the tension, the fatigue, the anxiety, the sense of what depended on that day's fight, overpowering. But it was over, and the end was—Victory. And, looking back, the one thought that absorbed all others in the great soldier's mind was thankfulness.

So will it be with us when, weary but victorious, we come out of the fray. Thankfulness, as we hear from the lips of Jesus at our judgement the blessed sentence: "Come!" Thankfulness, as we enter the prison of Purgatory, that we are "saved, yet so as by fire." Thankfulness, when the debt is paid at last, and we are called to the joys that eye has not seen, nor ear heard, nor heart conceived.

It is to be rest at last after labour, triumph after the battle, the plenty of our Fathers House after the hunger and the hardship that were our lot on earth. *Oh, what will Heaven be to the poor!* What will be their surprise who wanted everything on earth, to find themselves so rich, so abounding with delights, so satisfied! All life through they had to check their desires, to understand that they might not have and do and enjoy as others, that the things which made life easy and pleasant were not for them—and now, how all is changed! Restraint and privation were only for a little while, and they have gone by, never to return. The time of schooling is over, and they are at Home. No more need for patience and for hope. God has wiped away all tears from their eyes. He has received them into His House, not as honoured guests only, but as His children, who have a right to have and do and enjoy as they will.

All is for them. "The former things have passed away."[1] Only the memory of them remains, to be a source of unspeakable joy for ever. We might have rebelled at our lot, and we tried to be patient. We might have coveted and sought to get unjustly the pleasant things our station in life had denied us. We might have shut our hearts against God in bitterness and despair. But we lifted our eyes and our hearts above the trials of our life. We remembered how quickly they were passing, and the reward that patience would bring. We made them drive us, not away from God, but into His arms. He was all we had, and we would not

---

1 Apoc 21.

part with Him. If He had denied us what others had, it was because the road of want is safer by far than the road of wealth, and He would not let us run the risks of the more dangerous way. It was only for a time, we kept saying to ourselves: He would make it all up to us soon.

So we trusted Him and clung to Him in our pain. We strengthened our hearts with prayer and the help His Sacraments brought us. And now, He has brought us safe—*to this!* He has made us welcome to all He has. We may take all, enjoy all, for all is ours. We may go here and there as we will, in and out among the great Saints of God, and not feel strange. The shyness and shrinking from notice of days gone by, the fear of intruding or giving offence, the shamefacedness, the constraint—all has passed away for ever. There is perfect freedom and ease in our intercourse with the highest here, for all are brothers and sisters in our Father's House.

And yet we are aware of a difference. We notice that whilst all the Blessed treat one another with loving reverence, there is special honour shown to those who shared on earth the lot of the Son of God. All in Heaven are like Christ, but there are degrees of likeness, and the glory of each is in proportion to this resemblance. We on earth were more like Him than others, and so He treats us as brethren in a quite special way; there is an affectionate familiarity and a tenderness in His ways with us, that amazes us and makes us bless a thousand thousand times the poverty we once thought so hard. "Thou also wert with Jesus of Nazareth" was the reproach once made to Peter. And he was ashamed and denied his Master. That we were with Jesus of Nazareth all the days of our life—oh! what a joy it is to us now! What a nearness to Him, what glory and happiness it has brought us here! The courtesy He shows to all His elect is specially *for us*, and the whole Court of Heaven follows the lead of its King.

Yes, we are at Home! We are treated now as children whose school-days are over and who can be taken into confidence. Our Father shows us now the reasons of what perplexed us in the past, the answer to the many "Whys?" we asked in days gone by. How clear everything is from this height! We look back upon the road by which we have come, and see why we were led this way, not that. We look back upon our troubles, and see what they have done for us, and how our Father was watching always to see that trial should never be too hard. We see how He has brought good out of evil, how He has made everything work together for our good.

O my Father! how well Thou hast cared for me through it all! How well Thou hast kept Thy promise: "What I do thou knowest not now, but thou shalt know hereafter." How well I see now the answer to my question of long ago:

Why must I suffer?

ABBA, FATHER!

INTRODUCTION

After serving as Mother Superior of the Bar Convent from 1883 to 1891, Mother Loyola took up the task of Mistress of Novices in 1897, serving in this position until a fall in 1923 shattered her hip and confined her to bed for her remaining years. Anecdotes from her letters, as well as the memories of her charges, give us to understand that this task was at times a heavy cross.

It might reasonably be supposed, then, that Mother Loyola knew quite intimately the difficulties and perils entailed with the role of Religious Superior. The extent to which this is true can be amply shown in the following CTS pamphlet from 1912.

The title of this Litany for Religious Superiors sets the tone for the rest: *Abba, Father!* This familiar term used by Our Lord when calling upon His Father in Heaven invites us to enter into a more intimate relationship with God the Father, as his own child. Just so, Mother Loyola's petitions seek a kind, fatherly guidance in the important work of shepherding souls.

ABBA FATHER
A Litnany for Relgious Superiors

Lord have mercy on us.
Christ have mercy on us.
Lord have mercy on us.
Christ hear us.
Christ graciously hear us.
God the Father of Heaven,
God the Son, Redeemer of the world,
God the Holy Ghost;
Holy Trinity, one God,
Wisdom of God, that reachest from end to end mightily, and orderest all things sweetly,[1]
That hast chosen the foolish things of the world to confound the wise, and the weak things of the world to confound the strong, and the base things and the things that are not, to bring to nought things that are, that no flesh should glory in Thy sight,[2]
That in the days of old didst appoint Gideon and Deborah to be the rulers of Thy people, and art still pleased to choose for Thy instruments the ignorant and the weak,

Have mercy on us.

---

1 Wisdom 8:1.   2 1 Cor 1:27

I

WISDOM

Give me, O Lord, heavenly wisdom, that I may attend to things eternal, and cleave not to those which pass with time.

Give me, for the guidance of my charge, and for my own sanctification, the spirit of wisdom and of understanding, the spirit of counsel and of fortitude, the spirit of knowledge and of godliness, and fill me with the spirit of the fear of the Lord.[1]

Give me the high thoughts of the children of God, the aim of one whose heart is fixed on Thee alone, and whose one desire is to promote Thy greater glory.

Let me look at everything in the light of God.

Let Thy praise, reverence, and service be the motive of all my actions.

May I do all things purely for Thee, resting in Thee as in my Last End.

May I have confidence in the Lord with all my heart, and lean not upon my own prudence.[2]

Give me the hearing ear and the seeing eye, but let my words be few.[3]

In all my works let the true word go before me, and steady counsel before every act.[4]

---

1 Isaias 11:2.   2 Prov. 3:5.   3 Prov. 10:12.
4 Eccli. 37:20.

II

HUMILITY

May I not be high-minded, but fear.

May I distrust my own views, and look to Thee always for light and guidance.

Let me rely so little on myself as to draw down Thy help, that thus out of the depths of my helplessness my help may come.

Let my heart be ever crying to Thee, *Abba, Father!* [1]

Take me by the hand, and say to me, "Fear not, I have helped thee." [2]

Let abyss call upon abyss, and the very excess of my poverty draw down on me the riches of Thy mercy. [3]

Let me attribute nothing of good to myself, but faithfully refer all things to Thee from whom all good proceeds.

Let me know by happy experience that Thy grace is sufficient for me, and that power is made perfect in infirmity. [4]

Let me find, amidst all my weakness and ignorance, that I can do all things in Him that strengtheneth me. [5]

Grant that in silence and in hope my strength may be. [6]

---

1 Gal. 4:6   2 Isaias 41:13.   3 Psalm 41:8.
4 2 Cor. 12:9.   5 Philipp. 4:13.   6 Isaias 30:15.

Sursum Corda!

III

RESIGNATION TO GOD'S WILL

Make me cast all my care upon Thee.[1]

In all plans, directions, desires, let my one thought be to seek and to accomplish Thy holy Will.

In failure and disappointment, let me be content with Thy knowledge of my desires, O God, my Inward Witness.

Let my heart be at peace when trouble comes, knowing that Thy providence, O Father, governeth it.[2]

Let me not fail, nor swerve, either in prosperity or adversity, that I be not lifted up by the one, nor cast down by the other.

Let me not be solicitous, saying; What shall we eat, ... or wherewith shall we be clothed, for Thou, Father, knowest we have need of all these things.[3]

Let me not be disturbed by the loss of things temporal, but place my treasure and my joy in Heaven, where nothing is lost.

In every trial and trouble of soul, let me wait on God with patience, let me join myself to God, and endure.[4]

---

[1] Psalm 54:23 [2] Wisdom 14:3. [3] Matt. 6:31, 32
[4] Eccli. 2:3.

IV

ZEAL

Give me an insatiable thirst for gaining souls to Thee, and willingness to endure for their salvation, labour, contradictions, and troubles.

Give me grace to consider, not what may be advantageous to myself, but what may be profitable to many.

Help me to reprove without anger, to love without dissimulation, to edify by word and example without ostentation, to suffer without complaint.

Give me an ever-watchful eye, an upright and a tender heart.

Give me the love that is strong, patient, faithful and prudent; the love that is humble, long-suffering, courageous, and never seeking itself.

Let me rouse the tepid, indifferent, encourage the fervent, support the strong, and compassionate the weak.

Give me the grace to comfort, assist, instruct, admonish, according to the Heart of Jesus.

Father, keep them in Thy Name, whom Thou hast given me.[1]

Make them to be "followers of God as most dear children."[2]

---

[1] John 17:11.   [2] Eph. 5:1.

Sursum Corda!

V

CHARITY

Help me in all things to put *souls* before *self*.

Help me to be gentle in commanding, mild in reproving, indulgent without weakness or excess.

Let me rejoice with those that rejoice, and weep with those that weep, not minding high things, but consenting to the humble.[1]

Let me become all things to all, that I may save all.[2]

Let all who are Thine be dear to me for Thy sake, and Thou, my God, dear above them all.

Let me love with a supernatural tenderness all whom Thou hast confided to me.

Make me bountiful and open-hearted, judging it "more blessed to give than to receive."[3]

Give me, O Lord, the charity that is patient, is kind, that envieth not, dealeth not perversely, is not puffed up. That is not ambitious, seeketh not her own, is not provoked to anger, thinketh no evil. That rejoiceth not in iniquity, but rejoiceth with the truth. That beareth all things, believeth all things, hopeth all things, endureth all things.[4]

---

[1] Romans 12:16. [2] 1 Cor. 9:22. [3] Acts 20:35.
[4] 1 Cor. 13:4.

Abba, Father!

VI

COURAGE

Help me to govern myself in all things, great and small, by lofty motives, to keep my soul always in peace, and to manifest amid all vicissitudes an imperturbable calm.

Keep my heart free and raised upwards to Thee, knowing that I have not here a lasting city.[1]

Grant that I may be prudent, yet magnanimous, in all my undertakings.

Help me to be vigilant and diligent in Thy service, courageous to suffer, and constant to persevere.

Help me to bear my crosses bravely, and give me an unconquerable spirit which no tribulation can crush or quell.

Give me freedom of heart, that I may pass through many cares, as it were, without care.

In opposition from the world, give me fortitude that I may stand my ground, patience that I may endure, and constancy that I may persevere.

Let me feel that outside of Thee there is no powerful help, nor profitable counsel, nor lasting remedy.

Let me remember that when Thou seemest far from me Thou art often nearest to me.

Let me fly to Thee in all tribulations and anguish, remembering Thy tender promise: "I will have mercy on thee more than a mother,"[2]

---

1 Hebrews 13:14.   2 Eccli. 4:11.

Sursum Corda!

VII

IN ANY NECESSITY

In my affliction I called upon the Lord and I cried to my God. My God is my Helper, and in Him will I put my trust.[1]

O God, my God, look upon me, why hast Thou forsaken me?[2]

Lord, when wilt Thou look upon me?[3] Look Thou upon me and have mercy on me, for I am alone and poor.[4] How long, O Lord, wilt Thou forget me? How long dost Thou turn away Thy Face from me?...Consider, and hear me, O Lord, my God.[5]

Show forth Thy wonderful mercies, Thou who savest those that trust in Thee.... Protect me under the shadow of Thy wings.[6] Be Thou my Helper, forsake me not.[7]

Hear me, O Lord, for Thy mercy is kind...turn not away Thy Face from Thy servant for I am in trouble.[8] Hear my prayer, O Lord, and my supplication, give ear to my tears.[9]

I ask one petition of Thee, turn not away my face. I desire one small petition of Thee, do not put me to confusion.[10] Thou, Lord, art rich enough to give me much more than this.[11]

---

1 Ps. 17.   2 Ps. 21.   3 Ps. 34.
4 Ps. 24.   5 Ps. 12.   6 Ps. 16.
7 Ps. 26.   8 Ps. 67.   9 Ps. 38,
10 3 Kings 2.   11 2 Par. 25.

Abba, Father!

And now, O Lord, think of me.[1] Let Thy eyes, I beseech Thee, be open, and let Thy ears be attentive to my prayer.[2]

O God, who art mighty above all,[3] bow down Thy ear to me;[4] to the work of Thy hands reach out Thy right hand.[5]

Remember me, O my God, according to the multitude of Thy tender mercies...remember me unto good. Amen.[6]

I will humbly wait for Thy consolation.[7] I will stay patiently awhile to see Thy great power.[8] I will have patience even until Thy visitation.[9]

---

1 Tobias 3. 2 2 Par. 6. 3 Esther 14.
4 Ps .30. 5 Job 14. 6 2 Esdras 13.
7 Judith 8. 8 2 Mach, 7, 9 Eccli. 2.

VIII

TRUST

In every need let me come to Thee with the humble trust of the Canaanite, saying, "Lord, help me!"

In all my doubts and perplexities,

In hours of loneliness, weariness, and trial,

In the failure of my plans, in disappointment and trouble of soul,

When things are not well with me, and I come to Thee,

When all others fail me, and Thy help alone can avail me,

When I throw myself on Thy tender Fatherhood,

When my heart is tempted to be cast down at seeing no fruit,

When I am ill, and the head and the hand cannot work,

Always, always, in spite of failures, falls, shortcomings of every kind,

Lord help me

Abba, Father!

Holy Mary, Mother of God and our Mother,
Mother of Good Counsel,
Mother of Perpetual Succour,
Seat of Wisdom,
St. Joseph, least in merit in the Holy House of Nazareth, and Superior there,
St. Peter, Chief Shepherd of the Flock of Christ,
Whose daring and impetuous love endeared thee to thy Master,
Who didst learn by thy own weakness to compassion the weak,
Whose greater love deserved the reward of greater service, greater labours, greater sufferings, and death for Christ,
St. Paul, Vessel of Election and Apostle of the Gentiles,
Whom neither death, nor life, nor any other creature could separate from the love of Christ,[1]
Who wouldst be an anathema from Christ for thy brethren,[2]
Who didst become all things to all men that thou mightest save all,[3]
In whom power was made perfect in infirmity,[4]
St. Michael, Prince of the hosts of Heaven, and of all the souls to be received,
All ye holy Angels, guardians of Religious Orders,
All ye holy founders of Religious Orders,

Pray for us.

---

[1] Romans 8:35.   [2] Romans 9:3.   [3] 1 Cor. 9:22.
[4] 2 Cor. 12:9.

Sursum Corda!

St. Anthony,
St. Basil,
St. Augustine,
St. Columba,
St. Benedict,
St. Scholastica,
St. Bernard,
St. Bruno,
St. Norbert,
St. Gilbert of Sempringham,
St. Francis of Assisi,
St. Clare,
St. Dominic,
St. Catherine of Siena,
St. Ignatius,
St. Teresa,
St. Francis of Sales,
St. Jane Frances de Chantal,
St. Alphonsus Liguori,
St. Vincent of Paul,
St. Paul of the Cross,

} *Pray for us.*

All ye holy servants of God, Superiors of Religious Houses, who have borne the burden of the day and the heats,[1]

V. Give me, O Lord, wisdom that sitteth by Thy throne.[2]

R. That she may be with me and may labour with me that I may know what is acceptable with Thee.[3]

---

1 Matt, 20:12.   2 Wisdom 9:4.   3 Wisdom 9:10.

Abba, Father!

Let us pray:

1. O God, the Faithful and True, Who in appointing Thy servants to the dangerous and difficult office of superiority, dost grant them all needful grace to discharge its duties, give me, I beseech Thee, that grace without which I can do nothing. Stand *before* me in all my undertakings that I may look to Thee alone and to Thy greater reverence, service, and praise. Stand *beside* me to direct my eyes, my ears, my hand, my tongue, every movement of my body, every faculty of my soul, every affection of my heart. Stand *behind* me that I may have Thy strength to fall back upon always, Thy arms to support me always, Thy bosom, O Father, to rest on always—for this is sufficient for me.

2. Give me, my God, a constant dependence on Thee, not speculative only, but true and practical, a reliance on Thee in all things and for all things. Let me be strictly united to Thee in prayer and in all my actions, that I may obtain from Thee as from the Fountain of all good, abundant gifts and graces for the Institute, and efficacy for all my efforts for the help of souls. Give me grace to sustain my charge by prayer and holy desires; to watch with solicitude over all confided to me; to see that fervour is maintained by the observance of the Rules and Constitutions, preventing and remedying what is harmful, as the good of each and all shall require; to preserve among Ours fraternal charity; and to help them in the way of perfection according to the design of our Institute.

Sursum Corda!

3. Let me "imitate in my government the charity, meekness, and government of Christ, our Lord, by example rather than by word leading Ours in the way of perfection." Give me grace to order with modesty and circumspection; to temper needful severity with mildness, and to tend with solicitude all under my charge, that all may confidently have recourse to me. Help me to unite strength with sweetness, to belong to all, to be ready for all without partiality, to remember that I am Superior, not for my own advantage, but to dilate souls and give them to God. Let me be the servant of all, but with the strength of religion behind me.

4. Let my sweetness be the tenderness of charity, not human respect seeking popularity, nor weakness. Give me strength to attain the end, sweetness in allotting the means. Let me remember that as Superior I have three burdens: my own, my community's, and that of each soul entrusted to me. Give me the patient charity that bears with defects, that takes into account repugnances, character, temperament, health. Help me to give these souls their promised hundredfold—for where else are they to get it—to comfort, to encourage, to listen to troubles and to provide all with the remedies their need requires.

5. Give me that one good thing which will bring all other good things—union with Thee, familiarity, intimacy with Thee, my Heavenly Father. Help me to unite my soul with Thee easily, even in the midst of business. Make me willing "to leave God for God"—to leave Thee in Thy Sacramental Presence to find Thee in Thy creatures and in

Thy works. But let there be a sense of relief when I may put all aside to be alone with Thee.

6. Watch over me, my God, that I may not be so distracted by the work of government as to grow lukewarm in prayer. Give me a great and steadfast soul to expect from the Divine goodness that all necessary temporal things will be added to us, if we but seek first the Kingdom of God and His justice.[1]

7. And at last, when I am to render an account of my stewardship and of the souls confided to me, let it be with joy and not with grief.[2] Say to me then with gladness: Well done, good and faithful servant,[3] of those whom I entrusted to thee thou hast not lost one, enter thou into the joy of thy Lord.

---

1 Matt. 6:33.   2 Hebrews 13:17.   3 Matt. 25:23.

ITA PATER!

INTRODUCTION

The title of this piece, *Ita Pater!* can be translated from the Latin as "Yes Father!" What a particularly appropriate name for this short prose-poem, which was issued by the Catholic Truth Society at the same time as *Abba, Father!* Here, a series of short acts of submission to the Will of God is followed by a brief meditation on the same subject, beginning with the line from the *Our Father*: "Thy Will be done on Earth as it is in Heaven."

ITA PATER!

I

WILL OF GOD

My First Love, I praise Thee,
My Last End, I reverence Thee,
Alpha and Omega, I serve Thee in union with the praise,
    reverence, and service rendered Thee by the Word
    Incarnate, and to be rendered to Thee by all creatures
    throughout eternity.

High Will of God, I desire Thee,
Holy Will of God, I adore Thee,
Hard Will of God, I welcome Thee,
   Dear Will of God, I love Thee.

Beautiful Will of God, I praise Thee,
Blessed Will of God, I reverence Thee,
Best Will of God, I serve Thee,
   Dear Will of God, I love Thee.

Sursum Corda!

Fatherly Will of God, I confide in Thee,
Faithful Will of God, I count on Thee,
Each and every Will of God, kneeling I receive Thee,
   Dear Will of God, I love Thee.

Sovereign Will of God, I submit to Thee,
Strong Will of God, I lean upon Thee,
Satisfying Will of God, I content myself with Thee,
   Dear Will of God, I love Thee.

Stern Will of God, I embrace Thee,
Safe Will of God, I trust Thee,
Sweet Will of God, I bless Thee,
   Dear Will of God, I love Thee.

Eternal Will of God, I annihilate myself before Thee,
Omnipotent Will of God, I fear Thee,
Inscrutable Will of God, I magnify Thee,
   Dear Will of God, I love Thee.

Kind Will of God, I thank Thee,
Tender Will of God, I cling to Thee,
Patient Will of God, I wait with Thee,
   Dear Will of God, I love Thee.

Just Will of God, I side with Thee,
Wise Will of God, I acknowledge Thee,
Calm Will of God, I rest in Thee,
   Dear Will of God, I love Thee.

Ita Pater!

Perfect Will of God, I worship Thee,
Pitiful Will of God, I confess to Thee,
Prevailing Will of God, I rejoice for Thee,
   Dear Will of God, I love Thee.

Blasphemed Will of God, I weep over Thee,
Mistrusted Will of God, I grieve for Thee,
Disappointed Will of God, I condole with Thee,
   Dear Will of God, I love Thee.

Despised Will of God, I reverence Thee,
Rejected Will of God, I own Thee,
Hidden Will of God, I seek Thee,
   Dear Will of God, I love Thee.

Accomplished Will of God, I congratulate and rejoice with Thee,
Provident Will of God, I cast my care on Thee.
Purifying Will of God, I surrender myself to Thee,
   Dear Will of God, I love Thee.

Great Will of God, I delight in Thee,
Glorious Will of God, I extol Thee,
Gentle Will of God, I bless Thee,
   Dear Will of God, I love Thee.

Merciful Will of God, I cast myself upon Thee,
Mighty Will of God, I exult in Thee,
My Own Will of God, I choose Thee and bless Thee
   and abandon myself wholly to Thee and to Thy
     Designs over me,
   Dear Will of God, I love Thee.

Sursum Corda!

> Subduing Will of God, I subject all that is Thine to Thee,
> Loveable Will of God, I give myself and all that is mine to Thee,
> Royal Will of God, I enthrone Thee in my inmost soul, and there offer my loyalty to Thee,
>   Dear Will of God, I love Thee.
>
> Will of God, my Stronghold, I climb for safety into Thee,
> Will of God, my Treasury, I seek all help in Thee,
> Will of God, my First Love, knocking always at the door of my heart, I rise and open to Thee,
>   Dear Will of God, I love Thee.
>
> Will of God, dear and bright Ocean of all good, I lose myself in Thee,
> Will of my Heavenly Father, I lay my will alongside of Thee,
> Will of God, ever Blessed, I rejoice that neither I nor any creature of Thine can prevail against Thee,
>   Dear Will of God, I love Thee.
>
> I consecrate to Thee myself and all creatures to praise, reverence, and serve Thee.
> I offer to Thee The Incarnate Word to praise, reverence, and serve Thee adequately.
> I offer to Thee Thy Own Dear Perfections to praise Thee eternally and sufficiently.
> May the most high, the most just, the most loveable Will of God be done, praised, and eternally exalted in all things. Amen.

II

"Thy Will be done on Earth as it is in Heaven"

We say this every day, and all life through—say it in all manner of moods, say it with difficulty at times, say it with tears, say it without adverting to what it means, above all without reflecting on the gladness with which the Will of our Father is done in Heaven. Let us think sometimes how the Blessed, as they look back upon the trials of life, say with overflowing gratitude and joy: "*Ita Pater*—Yea, Father, for so it hath seemed good in Thy sight."

One of the joys of Heaven will be that retrospect. Safe by our Father's side, we know now the whys and wherefores of all the happenings in the past. We know, not by the view of faith, but by the act of sight: "With the hearing of the ear I have heard, but now my eye seeth." We look, and listen, and wonder, as He shows us how here, there, everywhere, His Hand and His Love directed all.

"See, child! Was it well for you that I set your path here, not there; that I kept out of your way pleasant things with which you would have hurt yourself, and put in your way, instead, the daily trials which have brought you hither?"

"Yes, Father!"

"Was it well that I laid upon you that pain of body, that anguish of soul, that life of monotonous labour, and care, and struggle, and the harder toil of strife with self, up to the very last? When I permitted that injustice, broke that friendship, left you weeping by the grave that held all you loved and leaned on—was even that well, My child?"

Sursum Corda!

"Yes, Father, I see it all now. Oh! that I had seen it sooner, and given Thee the childlike trust Thy love deserved."

"The succour which came so opportunely, the answer to prayer which took you by surprise, the consolation which refreshed you from time to time and showed you I was with you—do you see My Hand in all this? And when I hid My Face from you, and upheld you—not by the sweetness of My Presence but by the sheer strength of faith and the might of My Grace—was love, the love that purifies, the secret of it all?"

"O my Father, forgive me for my mistrust of Thee in the past! Let me hide my face in Thy bosom, and own, now though so late, that Thou hast indeed done all things well for me."

" 'Thy Will be done on earth as it is in Heaven,' " I said. "And now I see the Fatherliness of that Will which at times seemed to me hard. I see that for a little while there must be trial for Thy elect. They must lament and weep 'whilst the world rejoices.'[1] But 'God shall wipe away all tears from their eyes,'[2] and they 'shall remember misery only as waters that are passed away.' "[3]

Let me think of this when the Cross presses, and try to do Thy Will, not with submission only, but with joy here on earth, as through Thy mercy, I shall do it throughout eternity in Heaven.

---

1 John 16. 2 Apoc. 21. 3 Job 11.

ON HIS MAJESTY'S SERVICE

INTRODUCTION

In 1916 the world had for two years been tearing itself apart in a conflagration the likes of which had never before been seen or imagined. Nothing remained the same as it had been such a short time before. Beginning in late February of that year, the German and French forces launched the longest and bloodiest battle ever fought at Verdun, while the British prepared to attack at the Somme. It was at this time that Mother Loyola took up her pen to bring before the eyes of all the vision of the cross and its meaning for the war-weary world, as both chastisement and remedy.

The themes developed here clearly formed the germ for *Blessed are They That Mourn*, which followed it six months later, as the casualties of the Somme mounted to over 400,000 and scarcely a woman was to be found in England that had not lost a son, a brother, a husband or a friend.

In the midst of what seemed like Armageddon, there was a desperate need to make sense of the endless slaughter, and where reason stood no chance, only faith could suffice. Christ, the Man of Sorrows, has shown us the way of the Cross, and for the sake of both atonement and of healing, that path had now to be trod with firmness of belief of what lies beyond death—redemption and the promise of the Resurrection.

ON HIS MAJESTY'S SERVICE
A Talk with our Wounded

I

TURNING over the pages of our illustrated papers, we come time after time upon the same picture—the surroundings different, but the main fact the same—a crucifix standing or lying amid ruins. Here, it is propped up on the pavement of a desecrated church. There, it hangs on the battered wall of a Belgian cottage. Further on, it is standing unhurt in a wayside shrine, with the havoc made by bursting shells all around. There is no lack of evidence for the fact. Letters from the Front, and our wounded at home, bear witness to it and to the impression it has made. Describing a church in an almost obliterated village through which his men were marching, the correspondent of an English paper says:

> "Leaning forward from what remains of a wall at one end, is a pale figure with arms widely extended, and a wreath of thorns on its head. The shells have smashed away from it the wooden cross to which the arms were nailed; they seem now opened wide in a gesture of entreaty.... In the very earliest days of the war, when Belgium was being made a terror to all who would not bow to Baal, the preservation of these figures of the Christ

from the willful ruin of torch and shell was so remarkable as to be deemed a miracle. Since then, over and over again, amid villages pounded almost to powder, and within churches reduced, as was this one, to a battered skeleton of arches, one has come with a shock of bewilderment upon that same figure with its outspread arms, looking down unscarred upon the desolation of the stricken world about it. In Loos, after a bombardment which deprived men of their senses and left scarcely a roof or a tree unshattered, the figure of Christ, with its face of enduring patience, still looked down, unscathed, upon the cross roads, as the men of our most Christian nation, masked like demons, dashed past it with reddened bayonets in pursuit of their foe. Perhaps it is not surprising that the country folk find something of miracle in the oft-repeated preservation of that figure on the cross, even though they have paid but little heed to the miracle it commemorates. They kneel now before that relic from destruction who never kneeled before."[1]

How are we to account for this "miracle of the crucifixes"? Many will hesitate to call it chance. Still less will it be set down to reverence on the part of the enemy, for whom the churches have been a target from the first. The faith of the simple folk about supplies at least a possible answer. We do not hear them crying out: "Why does God allow these horrors? Why is the world turned into a slaughterhouse?" No. The crucifix has a message for them, and they are not turning a deaf ear to its reproach, its warning, and its comfort. It speaks to them of sin, and of the justice of God. It speaks of love and of sacrifice; of the final triumph

---

[1] Mr. H. F. Prevost Battersby, special correspondent of *The Morning Post* at the British headquarters in France.

of right over wrong; of a resurrection to follow upon defeat and death.

And not to them only does it speak. Its message is to the whole world. We all need the lesson and the warning. We need the example, and the encouragement, the strong faith and hope that will bear us safely over this time of universal mourning and desolation. The world to-day is terror-stricken. All that it counted stable is shaken to its foundation. Of the magnitude of the war and its issues, Mr. Lloyd George says: "It is not a spell of bad weather. It is the deluge. It is a convulsion of nature. . . . It is an earthquake which is upheaving the very rocks of European life."[1] Men and women are asking in consternation where they are to turn for safety and for hope. And their eyes meet the outstretched arms of the crucifix.

II

Our Lord calls Himself "the Son of Man." His Cross He calls "the sign of the Son of Man." And because by His Cross He redeemed us and won back for us the Heaven we had lost, this sign is very dear to Him. He has made it the standard round which He rallies His followers: "And I, if I be lifted up from earth will draw all things to Myself."[2] When the Apostles asked Him: "What shall be the sign of Thy coming and of the consummation of the world?"

---

[1] Words to Clyde Workers in Glasgow, Dec. 31, 1915.   [2] John 12:32.

Sursum Corda!

He answered: "You shall hear of wars and rumours of wars.[1] Nation shall rise against nation and kingdom against kingdom. And there shall be great earthquakes in divers places, and pestilences, and famines, and terrors from heaven, and there shall be great signs[2] in the sun and in the moon and in the stars, and upon the earth distress of nations, by reason of the confusion of the roaring of the sea and of the waves[3]. All these are the beginnings of sorrows.[4] And then shall appear the sign of the Son of Man in heaven."[5] "I saw," says St. John, "another Angel ascending from the rising of the sun, having the sign of the living God, and he cried with a loud voice to the four Angels to whom it was given to hurt the earth and the sea, saying: Hurt not the earth and the sea till we sign the servants of our God in their foreheads."[6]

Very early in the history of the Church, the sign of the Cross became the sign of the Christian. "We Christians wear out our foreheads with the sign of the Cross," said Tertullian in the first half of the third century: "When we come in or go out, when we sit down to table, when we light up lamps, we make on our foreheads the sign of the Cross." And St. Augustine says that by the sign of the Cross and the invocation of the Name of Jesus all things are sanctified and consecrated to God. As early as the first half of the third century, Christians were known as "devotees of the Cross."

---

1 Matt. 24:6. 2 Luke 21:11. 3 Luke 21:25.
4 Matt. 24:8. 5 Matt. 24:30. 6 Apoc. 8:2, 3.

It was this saving sign that sustained the martyrs during three hundred years of persecution.

Then came a change. As Constantine marched to battle, the Cross blazed out in the heavens, with the words: "In this sign thou shalt conquer." After his victory and the discovery of the true Cross by St. Helena, the Emperor's mother, it entered on a new stage in its history. In the hands of missionaries it travelled to the ends of the earth. Barbarians were brought to Christ, not by the scattering broadcast of a written Gospel, but by the sight of the crucifix and the preaching of Christ crucified. The sign of the Son of Man appeared everywhere in a world that was now Christian—not only on altars, vestments, and bells, on the royal crown and the coinage of princes, but on lamps, toys, spoons, on all kinds of objects, the noblest and the meanest. It was prefixed to signatures, and it still stands for the name of those who cannot write. Relics of the true Cross were distributed throughout the world; pilgrimages to the Holy Places of Palestine became frequent, and for a century and a half the Crusades bore testimony to the resolve of Christian Europe to wrest from the infidel the sacred scenes of Christ's life and death.

Thus it was that men showed their love for their Saviour in the ages of faith. The sixteenth century brought the so-called Reformation—and another change. Like Him who hung upon it, the Cross now became "a sign to be contradicted." Throughout northern and central Europe,

Sursum Corda!

wherever Protestantism became the religion of the land, a clean sweep was made of the crosses and crucifixes so long venerated by the people. In our own days and in our own country a reaction has set in, and in many places they are being restored to their place of honour; but abroad—in France before the war, in Belgium and northern France to-day, Christian men, by outrage and desecration worthy of infidels, are openly proclaiming themselves "enemies of the Cross of Christ."[1]

This was to be expected. The Cross stands for the religion of Jesus Christ. It stands for His infinite love of man, for His Redemption, His teaching, His influence through His Church to the end of time. It stands for Christian civilisation which it created and fostered, for the final victory of right over wrong, of Christ over sin and hell.

Therefore, when religion and civilisation are assailed as they have never been before, the Cross becomes anew a sign to be contradicted. If this greatest of wars is indeed to prove the greatest event in history since the Incarnation, may we not expect to see all the forces of evil arrayed against the Cross? And might we not even look for divine intervention in its behalf, such as this almost miraculous preservation of the crucifix? Why—when hell is allowed "to scourge the world for sin"—should shells and fire spare it, but for a divine purpose, because it has a special message for the world at a turning-point of the world's history!

---
1 Phil. 3:18.

III

Shutting their eyes to the miracles they witnessed daily, the Jews of our Lord's time were always asking Him for a sign. He reproached them with it: "You know how to discern the face of the sky and can you not know the signs of the times?... And He left them and went away."[1]

What if we deserve the same reproof! Do we not see enough, hear enough of wars and rumours of wars, of nation rising against nation and kingdom against kingdom, of earthquakes in divers places, of the distress of nations by reason of the confusion of the roaring of the sea and of the waves, of pestilences and famines—to ask ourselves if these things may not, indeed be the "beginnings of sorrows"?

"He left them and went away." The Heart of Christ is wrung with grief when men shut their eyes and are dull of hearing lest they should see with their eyes and hear with their ears, and be converted, and He should heal them. He would have us see and hear to some purpose. The justice of God has overtaken the world. It is being punished for sin, for the sins of each and all. He would have us understand this and be converted—that is, turn to Him in the sorrow that is being brought home to every one of us—and say, as we strike our breasts: "We indeed receive the due reward of our deeds."

Our Lord speaks of the world as having to be "convinced of sin, and of justice, and of judgement."[2] How much convincing it takes! How hard we find it to bring the evil of

---

1 Matt. 16:3, 4.   2 John 16:8,

Sursum Corda!

sin home to us, to think of it as anything that really matters very much! What God is, what His rights are, we scarcely advert to in this life. The rights of an earthly king are outraged, the guarantees for the preservation of justice and order are trampled under foot, and the world rises in indignation. Armies are created as if by magic. Volunteers from East and West pour their thousands on to the battlefields of Europe—princes and peasants, boys straight from school, and men whose work in life seemed done, clamouring one and all to be allowed to sacrifice themselves for a cause dearer than life itself, whilst wives and mothers, far from holding them back, spur them on by brave and noble words. There is to be no peace nor truce till the wrong is avenged and justice done.

But the rights of God may be infringed and His commandments despised as a mere scrap of paper, and no one feels aggrieved or even surprised. He is "King of kings and Lord of lords, a powerful King and greatly to be feared."[1] "Thousands of thousands minister to Him, and ten thousand times a hundred thousand stand before Him."[2] And we defraud Him without scruple, quite as a matter of course, of what is His by every right. He does not overstate His claims or press them harshly. If He lays commandments upon us, it is to save us from the ruin our unchecked passions would bring about. If He would have us love Him with all our heart, and soul, and mind, and strength, it is because He alone can satisfy and make us happy. And we

---

[1] Ecclus. 1:8.   [2] Dan. 8:10.

rebel. We will not fall in with His designs for us. There are those who resent the action of His omnipotence, which brought them into being for a happiness which it has not entered into the heart of man to conceive. There are millions who have never thanked Him for life, or health, or any blessing they enjoy; who every day and every hour repay His love with insult, and His forbearance with bolder sin.

"I have brought up children and exalted them, but they have despised Me."[1] "Thou hast forsaken the God that begot thee and hast forgotten the Lord that created thee.... Is this the return thou makest to the Lord, O foolish and senseless people? Is not He thy Father that hath possessed thee, and made thee, and created thee?... The Lord saw and was moved to wrath because His own sons and daughters provoked Him."[2] Which of us has not deserved these tender reproaches!

The word "frightfulness" has taken on a new meaning since the autumn of 1914. It stands now for the subversion of all law and order, of all that the moral sense approves as right and just. Now this is what sin is, what we shall one and all see it to be, when the mists of this life are cleared away—something *frightful*, the only evil which in the light of eternity deserves the name of frightfulness. And as our indignation against lawlessness is coupled with the conviction that right and order must triumph in the end, and evil be finally overthrown, so must we recognise that sin, which is law-breaking, must be punished sooner or later. When the punishment comes even to our own door, we shall see in

---

[1] Isaias 1:2.   [2] Deut. 32.

Sursum Corda!

it Divine justice vindicating its own rights, and humbly bow down before it.

"Thou hast forsaken Me, saith the Lord, thou hast gone backward, and I will stretch out My hand against thee.... I am weary of entreating thee.... I have killed and destroyed My people, and yet they are not returned from their ways. Their widows are multiplied above the sands of the sea; I have brought upon them against the mother of the young man a spoiler at noonday: I have cast a terror upon the cities."[1] "Howl, O ye ships of the sea, for your strength is laid waste."[2] "Surely thou wilt fear Me and wilt receive correction."[3]

God will not be ignored in His chastisements. So long as we refuse to acknowledge them as such, so long will His hand be heavy upon us. We must confess our sinfulness if we want to obtain mercy. The servants of God under the Old Law always humbled themselves before Him in times of national calamity:

"Thou art just, O Lord, in all that Thou hast done to us...and all thy ways are right...for Thou hast exercised true judgements in all the things that Thou hast brought upon us...for our sins. For we have sinned and committed iniquity, departing from Thee. And we have not hearkened to Thy commandments that it might go well with us. Wherefore all that Thou hast brought upon us and everything Thou hast done to us Thou hast done in true

---

1 Jerem. 15.   2 Isaias 23:14.   3 Wisd. 3:7.

judgement.... Nevertheless, in a contrite heart and humble spirit, let us be accepted."¹

"Let us humble our souls before Him. Let us ask the Lord with tears that according to His will He would show His mercy to us.... Let us humbly wait for His consolation...and He will humble all the nations that shall rise up against us, and bring them to disgrace. Esteeming these punishments to be less than our sins deserve, let us believe that these scourges of the Lord with which we are chastised, have happened for our amendment and not for our destruction."² "Remember, O Lord, and show Thyself to us in the time of our tribulation.... O God who art mighty above all, hear the voice of them that have no other hope."³ "For we suffer thus for our sins. And though the Lord God is angry with us a little while for our chastisement and correction, yet He will be reconciled again to His servants."⁴

We notice how it is insisted on that the purpose of God in His chastisements is our correction. In this life it is always so. Punishment is never simply pain and penalty. If we will, it may be Purgatory, that is atonement. And even—what the Purgatory after death is not—it may be meritorious, deserving of eternal reward. All depends upon the dispositions in which we take it; the grace of God, to take it as we should, will never be wanting to us.

---

1 Dan. 3:27-39.   2 Judith 8.   3 Esther 14.

4 2 Machabees 7:32, 33.

Sursum Corda!

IV

The misery of the world to-day may well bring home to us the evil of sin. Yet not with the force of the Crucifix. In the slaughter which is turning Europe into a graveyard, we see its effects on sinful man. In the crucifix we see the havoc it wrought on the only-begotten Son of God. Today, if ever, the Crucifix is convincing the world of sin, is holding up to the world the frightfulness of sin.

But more than this. The darkness that shrouded the Cross on Calvary that first Good Friday cleared away. And not many hours later the sun shone out again, and the glad disciples were hastening here and there with the news that their Master was risen. "You now indeed have sorrow," He had said to them on the eve of His death. "But I will see you again and your heart shall rejoice, and your joy no man shall take from you."[1] Even the darkness of Calvary was not utter blackness. "It is finished," Jesus said, as He bowed His head in death. The work He came to do was done; the chastisement of sin borne; the Atonement made; the price of our "plentiful Redemption" paid; Heaven reopened, and the way cleared for us.

So now. Both for the present life and for the next, this time of trouble has its consolation. It is for our correction, not for our destruction that it has come. Forces were at work in our modern society which foretold some tremendous

---
[1] John 16:22.

catastrophe. Luxury and self-indulgence, the worship of material goods, of prosperity, and of pleasure, forgetfulness of God, and of a day of reckoning to come—these were undermining the foundations of states and empires. To go no farther than our own land, the signs of degeneracy were on every side. The canker of effeminacy was destroying the manhood and the womanhood of the country. What had proved the ruin of other empires was bringing about the downfall of England. The best that those who loved her could wish was a national calamity so severe as to imperil her very existence, if so she might be roused to a sense of her impending fall. And it has come. In this war we may see not only the chastisement of our sins, and above all of our forgetfulness of God, but the proof of His remembrance of us and His care for us still. He will not in His justice withhold from us and from the world the terrible scourge which is to be our salvation by bringing us back to Him.

The Cross, then, stands for many things, for many contrary things, even: for the rage of the enemy of God against the standard of Christ which brought him defeat; for the anger of God against sin, and for the chastising of sin in the Divine Victim who "His own self bore our sins in His body on the tree."[1] Also, for the atonement made to God by the Cross; for our reconciliation to Him through Jesus crucified; and for all suffering borne by the members of Christ in union with their Head. This is one side of the

---

[1] Peter 2:24.

Sursum Corda!

Cross. But it has another. For suffering meekly borne is not only the payment of a debt. It is merit gained for Heaven and will have an eternal reward. The side of the Cross that faces us now is dark and frightening; the other side, bright and beautiful, will be the Cross glorified, as we shall see it coming in the eastern sky, borne by angels, His standard before the King.

"Of that day and hour no one knoweth," says our Lord. What we do know is that the hour of our death, on which everything for us depends, is not far off. Our call may come at any moment. Therefore, the command of the Leader is: "Watch!" Our men in the trenches know the need of alertness. The sky above, the earth beneath, everything around, is full of peril. They watch. They take precautions against surprise. They study the enemy. They keep their weapons in order. So must we. "Be ready," is our Leader's command. In the firing line, thank God, our men are ready for whatever may come. There is no need to urge them to go to the Sacraments. They realise then the value of absolution, of an act of contrition. We may hope that before going into action every one of them is prepared to meet death. But what about the soldiers not yet called up; what about the convalescents in hospital? The time for those waiting, for the wounded, and for the discharged, is not without its dangers.

V

In spite of care and comforts, the man in hospital may find his position more trying in many ways than in the firing line. There is the pain of his wounds, renewed by the daily dressings. And—harder to bear than physical suffering—the distress that comes of inaction, monotony, and uncertainty as to the future. The wounded soldier needs a friendly hand to be stretched out to him in his trouble. Happy will he be if his eye meet or his thoughts turn to the crucifix. The wide-stretched arms invite him; the wounded hands and feet appeal to him; the pierced Heart is that of a comrade in suffering, and draws him by its sympathy.

He who hangs there is God *and Man*. He knows all our sorrows—and shares them. He knows by experience the fiercest pangs of soul and body. He has made Himself one of us that He may be at our side in all the trials of life, and give us in all, the fellow-feeling of His Sacred human Heart. In this hour of universal distress He enters as the most devoted of friends into the special sorrow of each—of mother, and wife, and fiancée at home, of each and every one of our men at the front and in hospital. Our eyes and our thoughts are on the battlefield. So are His. Our prayers and our tenderest care are for the dying and the wounded. So are His. Each one of the millions engaged in this terrific struggle is more to Him than our nearest and dearest are to us. And for each one He has gone through the anguish of mind and body which the Crucifix sets before us:

"All you who pass by the way, attend and see if there be any sorrow like to My sorrow."[1]

"The whole head is sick and the whole heart is sad."[2]

"From the sole of the foot unto the top of the head there is no soundness therein: wounds and bruises, and swelling sores."[3]

"Surely He hath borne our infirmities and carried our sorrows ... and by His bruises we are healed."[4]

But a man may say: "All this does not appeal to me. I've not been much of a reader or a prayer, not much of a Catholic for the matter of that. I've been to Mass on a Sunday and that's about all. At the front I felt different, more like most of the Catholics there. But that's all over. I've done my bit and don't know what's coming, whether I shall be sent back or discharged. When the war's over, we shall be heroes for a day, and then—not wanted, only in the way."

Are you down-hearted, then? Surely, no. It is a great thing to have done your bit. Christ our Lord has called you to be on His side in the greatest conflict the world has ever seen. You have freely chosen to follow His call. You have made the sacrifice of all a man holds dear. Think how He must prize that choice of yours, what a reward He has in store for you! You did not perhaps recognise the voice of God in the call of King and Country. Your thought was only to do your duty: "I ought

---

[1] Lament. 1:12.   [2] Isaias 1:5.   [3] Ibid. 1:6.

[4] *Ibid.* 53:4, 5.

to go," you said. That, in other words, is: "God wants me," as theory of the Crusaders of old was: "God wills it!"

This war is a crusade. Never was so much at stake. We are fighting for the Christianity and the salvation of the world, for all that the Cross brought to the world—justice, civilisation, brotherly love between man and man. Therefore the Crucifix is aimed at by the powers of evil, and is being preserved as the standard of Christ by the providence of God. You have enlisted under that standard. Your motto, "On His Majesty's Service," is a noble one, charged with a loftier meaning than is suspected at Downing Street or Whitehall. God looks upon you as His soldier, and counts upon you for the loyalty in His service which you have shown in the cause of King and country. His aims for you go beyond this life and any recognition or reward you can receive here. If you labour and fight for Him, and persevere in His service till death, your reward hereafter is certain. A purely natural motive, it is true, cannot deserve a supernatural and eternal reward. But in that resolve to do your duty, there will have been reference to God, at least in a confused way. Duty means what is due to God, and to do one's duty is to be faithful to conscience and to God. This motive will have made your great purpose meritorious in His sight, and when you went to the Sacraments you will have renewed that purpose, at least indirectly, and in a state of grace. We may even hope that our men who have given their lives in the cause of God will have a merit which has been compared with that of martyrdom, and a

Sursum Corda!

corresponding reward : "Greater love than this no man hath, that a man lay down his life for his friends."[1]

For the wounded and disabled there will be a longer route to victory and reward, and there will be dangers on the way. Convalescence is a critical period and calls for vigilance. Rest and relaxation are a necessity; cigarettes, magazines, dainties, music and songs, motor drives, entertainments—all that affection and gratitude can devise to give comfort and pleasure to the brave fellows who need our care, must be provided as a matter of course. But we have to bear in mind that the soul no less than the body needs attention, and that our men appreciate the higher charity that looks after the needs of both.

"Can you spare time to come into the ward for morning prayers? It's the last time, you know," said a Sister, as she passed through the room where the men were completing their toilet before changing quarters that day.[2] "Yes, last time, worse luck!" exclaimed a poor fellow, as he limped after her into the ward. A comrade who followed, added: "We shan't have anyone to care about our prayers where we're going."

"Do not wholly neglect thyself," is the gentle counsel of Thomas à Kempis when the body is weighing down the soul. Short morning prayers, the offering to God of the day with its pleasures, pain, or monotony, will secure for every thought, word, and act an everlasting recompense, assuming of course the state of grace which with the help of God we

---
1 John 25:13.
2 The Concert Hall of the Convent had been converted into a military hospital.

can always secure. We need never wait till we can get to confession. A hearty act of perfect contrition—"My God, I am sorry for all my sins because Thou art so good"—may, if it is really genuine, obtain forgiveness of *all* sin, provided there is the desire of confession and the resolve to go when opportunity offers. At night a short examination of conscience and a hearty act of sorrow will obtain pardon for the faults of the day. On Sunday, if you cannot hear Mass, take care to say some prayers instead.[1] And might you not well ask for some Catholic book more profitable and satisfying than the magazines brought by kindly visitors?

If you are wise you will take advantage of every occasion of going to the Sacraments, whether you are returning to the front or not. A time of rest may easily become a time of slackness, and in the matter of religious duties it will be far easier to hold your ground now than to recover it later. But effort will be needed to do even this much. Such duties, when they have been dropped through negligence, are hard to pick up. The effect of feeding the mind exclusively on sensational or frivolous books is to disgust it with anything more solid. Human respect—the fear of what those around will say or think—may unnerve many a man who has bravely faced "Big Willie"[2] or "Black Maria."[3]

---

1 Should you want a prayer-book, apply to any convent near for the *Simple Prayer-Book* of the Catholic Truth Society. Requests of this kind, e.g. for rosaries, scapulars, medals, meet with a ready answer.

2 Big Willie was one of the main trenches in the German defensive line at the Battle of Loos in October 1915, over which much blood was shed.

3 Black Maria was a slang term for the German shells that would leave behind huge clouds of dense black smoke after exploding.

Sursum Corda!

But your military training will help here. You have found by experience that in the making of a soldier much more is involved than the majority of civilians imagine. Habits of discipline, obedience, and punctuality have to be formed. Courage, cheerfulness, a sense of honour, readiness to undergo hardship, fatigue, and danger, to endure as well as to fight, to act in conjunction with comrades, to sacrifice oneself for others, to fight and continue to fight as long as one can hold a weapon—all this is insisted on. This develops a soldierly spirit in the recruit.

But it does more. It not only makes him fit for the field, but it furnishes the raw material on which grace may work. Grace takes nature for its foundation. It raises natural virtue to the supernatural and makes it deserving of eternal reward. It will supernaturalize the good habits your military training has formed, if your co-operation now is not wanting. Do not let such valuable work done go to waste.

The great war is exemplifying once more the truth that God draws good out of evil. In eternity you will see that it has been the chance of your life. It has made you what otherwise you would never have been. You have in you now the makings of a strong—nay, of an heroic servant of God, and this, with His help, you will remain to the end. Let the war's stern lessons bear fruit in a life stamped clearly with the inscription: "On His Majesty's Service." Do not suffer them to be frustrated by habits which would unman you, by a life unworthy of a volunteer in this war. You have sacrificed too much, you have gained too much, for this. Life, for us all, will soon be over. Whether you live to see the return of peace or not, life will be over soon. Let us make the best use of what remains.

Whatever happens after the war, the world can never be the same as before. However things may settle down, it can never be in the old grooves. We must prepare ourselves—and God be thanked for it—to lead simpler, harder, and therefore healthier lives. The Cross, which will be raised again in the churches and wayside shrines of Belgium and France, will be found too in the daily lives of every one of us. Hundreds of thousands of women, who before the war had never done a stroke of manual work, will have learned to labour, and will still have to labour with their hands. And though generous provision will, we trust, be made for our wounded and disabled men, they will have to content themselves with such employment as the circumstances of their case and the altered conditions of the times allow. But what of that? Is not the soldier's grandest quality endurance? A glance down the columns of *The Military Mail* shows that not "conspicuous gallantry" only, but "courage and devotion to duty," are singled out for honourable mention. Such, too, is the nation's appreciation of the work done by our silent, steadfast fleet. And—which matters most—such, too, is God's estimate of greatness. The grandest courage is endurance.

Speaking of the men at the front, an officer says: "This war will change many characters and the aftermath will be crowded with opportunities....In the weakest of men

Sursum Corda!

there is such manhood and character as I never hoped for."[1] "Crowded with opportunities." Yes. It will not be all loss and gloom. As war-time has brought its compensations and special graces, so will the after-time. God will be there. England will be a very different country from the England of 1913. Nothing for any of us will be as easy as it was before—trade, social life, organisations of every kind will be dislocated when the men come back from the trenches. A period of intense excitement may be looked for, and popular discontent, and industrial trouble, as is the experience after all wars. To some people this will seem a gloomy, not to say an alarming prospect. To others, the outlook is stimulating, rousing all that is keenest and most vital in the nation's character, opening up new possibilities, in an era of "peace, betterment, and Christian regeneration."[2] But whatever may be thought of the situation, it will have to be faced. In whatever way the conflict ends, everything will be different—work, duties, temptations, trials, and—*our own selves!* There is consolation for us here. By the experiences through which we are passing now, Divine Providence will have prepared us for the new world into which we shall step.

Those who have stood in the firing line may well come back different men. They have been too near the other world not to feel its action upon them still. In spite of the careless gaiety that hides what is within, the man in the convalescent ward knows he can never be quite the same again. He feels the needs of his soul as he never felt them before. He finds

---

[1] *Military Mail,* Feb. 25, 1916.
[2] Letter of the Archbishop of Paris to Cardinal Mercier, Jan., 1916.

himself facing grave questions with a concern quite new to him—"Am I ready for death and for judgement? What must I do to get ready—to save my soul?" A Catholic will know the answer to these questions. A Catholic knows the value of his faith when shells are falling all around. Non-Catholics feel the all-importance of a definite creed in the face of death and eternity. "Give us," they say, "what the Catholics have, what sends them so calm and plucky into the fight." A French officer, killed in the terrible battle of Verdun, wrote to his wife before setting out: "How often must a man pray that at his last hour nothing should disturb his conscience. Am I ready? If I am, death is nothing."[3]

VI

No, those who have been through this war can never be the same as before. Thousands have heard the voice of God above the roar of the guns. There are thousands who need almost the touch of death and the summons to judgement to induce them to prepare for either. They refuse to go to the Sacraments whilst danger is still remote. There is time yet, they say. They will wait till they get abroad and take what chances they may find at the front. But, once there, all is changed. They need no pressing then. Now, if this carelessness in the affairs of the soul is the disposition of numbers before going into action, it will probably be the same with

---

[3] Colonel Desgrées, *Daily Mail*, Feb. 29, 1916.

many who come out of battle, more or less disabled for life. Impressions, however vivid, fade with time. Old thoughts and ways will seek to regain their hold. Unless he is on his guard, a man will be—what he was before? No, but more indifferent and careless. *And more responsible* because of neglected grace. To expect impressions to remain and *of themselves* to change a man permanently for the better, would be absurd illusion. Such a change must be the fruit, not of feeling, however strong, but of conviction *and of prayer.* The influences of this solemn time and the resolutions to which they give rise, are a grace which must result in practice, and that without delay, or they will die down and the last state of a man will be worse than the first.

Hence the need to take up, or to keep up, the habit of regular prayer, morning and night. Sunday Mass, of course. Benediction when you can. Confession and Communion at regular intervals. It will cost, because a reaction has set in. But what of that? When the charge sounds, does a soldier in the firing line hesitate or count the cost? Bring to the service of God that alertness, that cheerful discharge of duty, however distasteful, which your military training has developed. Your fight for Him will not end with the war. He will have a claim upon your fidelity and you upon His as long as life shall last. And His help will never fail you. The grace which has enabled so many to die a hero's death on the field, will not desert in their still greater need the heroes whom death has spared. But they must do their part. Pray for strength and perseverance to show at home the generosity which has done such good service abroad.

And make a friend of the Crucifix. A wounded soldier can turn to Christ "wounded for our iniquities and bruised for our sins"[1] as to a fellow-sufferer for comfort and for help. The wounded understand each other. There is a sympathy between them such as no bystander can ever feel. In the weary monotony of the day, in the hours of lonely suffering at night, there is no companion like the crucifix. Not all at once, but gradually, as we pass from wound to wound—from the thorn-crowned head to the bruised, disfigured face, the disjointed limbs, the torn hands and feet, we come to realise the meaning of the words: "He loved me and delivered Himself for me."[2] "He is not far from every one of us,"[3] but we have to call to mind His presence for it to be helpful to us. "I have a heart as well as you,"[4] He says to His wounded soldiers, volunteers like Himself who "was offered because He willed it."[5] It is for them to bring home to themselves that sympathy and to have recourse to that pitying human Heart.

In its praise of a hero of long ago, Holy Scripture says: "Choosing rather a most glorious death than a hateful life, he went forward voluntarily."[6] Millions, thank God, in our own day are doing the like. "It is a great glory to follow the Lord,"[7] to have fought under the standard of Christ in this

---

1 Isaias 53:5. 2 Galat. 2:20. 3 Acts 17:27.
4 Job 12:3. 5 Isaias 53:7. 6 2 Machabees 6:19.
7 Ecclus. 23:38.

greatest of wars. It is a glory to have laid down one's life in such a cause. And may not their merit be equal in God's sight who have returned from the field of battle to complete their sacrifice by a fervent Catholic life, and have so persevered to the end, "faithful unto death" On His Majesty's Service!

Soldier of Christ, lay well to heart the Leader's final charge to you:

"I know thy works and thy labour and thy patience... thou hast endured for My name, and hast not fainted."[1]

"Hold fast that which thou hast that no man take thy crown."[2]

"Hold fast," He says, *"that which thou hast."* In prayer and the Sacraments we have within our grasp what will carry us safely through this time of crisis, through every trial to the end of life. In the lives of all there is a turning-point. Two ways open out before us. We must choose between them, and on the choice our future here and hereafter may depend. Such a crisis is upon us now. We shall be the better for this war or we shall be worse, but we shall not be the same as before. "Hold fast till I come."[3]

"Behold I come quickly and My reward is with Me."[4]

"Be thou faithful unto death and I will give thee the crown of life."[5]

---

1 Apoc. 2:2, 3.   2 *Ibid.* 3:11.   3 Apoc. 2:25.

4 *Ibid.* 22:12.   5 *Ibid.* 2:10.

To Soldiers Going into Action

We have to face the fact that any moment may bring us before the Judgement Seat of God:

We must be Ready.

Hearty sorrow for sin because it offends God who is so good, will obtain forgiveness of all sin.

Say this Act of Sorrow from your heart every night, before going into Action, and in any danger:

My God, I am heartily sorry for all my sins because Thou art so good.

MARY WARD

INTRODUCTION

The two selections which follow belong to a somewhat tangled history.

From her earliest days at the Bar Convent, Mother Loyola had been involved, either directly or indirectly, with rehabilitating the status of Mary Ward as foundress of the Institute of the Blessed Virgin Mary. Several biographies of her life had been written over the course of those years by members of the Institute, most notably the two-volume *Life of Mary Ward* by Sister Catherine Chambers in 1885, and *Mary Ward, A Foundress of the Seventeenth Century* by Mother Mary Salome in 1901. In addition, the Catholic Truth Society had published in 1910 a pamphlet version of her Life written by Mother Joseph Edwards, and Mother Loyola had contributed a brief biographical sketch for the Catholic Encyclopedia in 1912.

As the early 1920s approached, the possibility of opening a Cause for the beatification of Mary Ward began to be a reality. Opinions were sought, costs were discussed, and the favor of Cardinals was sought to help forward the Cause. Eager to renew interest once more in the Life which was so dear to her beloved Institute, Mother Loyola wrote yet another short biography for the Catholic Women's League, which she subsequently offered to the Catholic Truth Society in August 1921 to replace Mother Joseph's biography, which had fallen out of print.

James Britten, the editor of the CTS at the time, had a well-established relationship with Mother Loyola, which we can date back as far as at least 1890 and her writing of "How to Help the Sick and Dying." Nevertheless, he respectfully declined to print it, stating that they had stereotyped the 1910 pamphlet and would prefer to make use of that at some future date. He proposed, in the meantime, that they might print a booklet containing some of Mary Ward's wise maxims, for which Mother Loyola could write a brief preface summarizing her life.

During this same period, however, the Catholic Truth Society was undergoing major changes and expansion with the help of the American William Reed-Lewis. On his own authority, and without consulting Mr. Britten, he communicated to Mother Loyola that he wished to act on the printing of her Catholic Women's League biography at once. He hoped that she might ask either Cardinal Bourne or Cardinal Gasquet for a preface, in order to lend more weight to the work. Not realizing that he was not working in concert with Mr. Britten, Mother Loyola did as he asked.

Naturally some dispute ensued. Thankfully, with the help of Mother Loyola's longtime editor and dear friend, Father Herbert Thurston, S.J., it was amicably resolved, and both pamphlets were printed in late 1921.

PREFACE

By H. E. Cardinal Bourne

At the beginning of 1919 I passed a few days in the capital of Rumania, Bucharest. In the visits that I made, under the kindly guidance of the Archbishop, to the various Catholic institutions of the city, I was greatly impressed by the splendid schools taught by the "English Ladies," not one of whom was English. In my sermon at the Cathedral it seemed a duty to recall how all these flourishing institutes owed their origin to the brave Englishwoman, Mary Ward.

It is no less a duty of gratitude to recall continually to the Catholics of England, and indeed of the whole United Kingdom, as well as to all the teaching orders of religious women throughout the world, that the very existence of the modern educational and charitable congregations, such as we know them in their almost countless multiplicity, was made possible by the supernatural foresight, the heroic perseverance, and the terrible disappointments and sufferings of Mary Ward. She waged the battle, to the point of apparent defeat, of which they are reaping the victory. To no one after their own special founders do they owe greater gratitude than to Mary Ward.

St. Francis of Sales had made the same attempt, and failed; God allowing that failure, so generously accepted, to be the source of the special graces and privileges which characterize the Order of the Visitation.

St. Vincent of Paul shrank from any similar attempt, and boldly proclaimed, in accents proudly treasured and repeated by his children, that the "Daughters of Charity" are not religious in the canonical sense; thus gaining for them a necessary freedom of action of which, in the existing conditions, they would otherwise have been deprived.

We in England have a very special duty to the memory of Mary Ward, for while she was persecuted abroad, our forefathers also failed to understand her providential mission, and she had to suffer much from the misconceptions of some, even, of the Vicars Apostolic.

May an increased knowledge of her life lead to greater appreciation of her work; may it be the means of uniting into one great organisation the widely scattered branches of her Institute; may it bring about in God's own day her publicly authorized invocation.

FRANCIS CARDINAL BOURNE
Archbishop of Westminster
September 1921

MARY WARD
(1585-1654)

FOUNDRESS OF THE INSTITUTE OF THE B. V. MARY

THE STORY of Mary Ward's life has been often told. That the toil and zeal of men of the highest character and greatest research should have been spent upon it, and that some of its most stirring incidents were portrayed a few years after her death in a series of fifty large oil paintings, still preserved, are proofs of the interest it inspired in her own day and of that which a true instinct predicted for it in the times to come.

It was a life of sixty years, and covered one of the most eventful periods of English history. Persecution raged throughout England, and Yorkshire was distinguished for the sufferings and the constancy of its Catholics.

Mary Ward was born at Mulwith Manor, near Ripon, on January 23rd, 1585, a year after the cruel death at York of Margaret Clitherow. Her parents, Marmaduke Ward, of Givendale, and Ursula Wright, of Ploughland, were connected by blood with most of the great Catholic families of Yorkshire, and, like others of their station, lived under the constant shadow of the penalties to which those were subjected who refused to conform to the new religion. Marmaduke had often to flee from his home, providing for the safety of his family as best he might. From her fifth to her tenth year we find the little Mary living with her grandmother, Ursula Wright, who, as a recusant, had spent fourteen years in a common gaol with the lowest criminals. It was from this confessor of the faith that the child learned that tender compassion for the poor and suffering, and those habits of prayer and self-denial which characterized her throughout life.

At the age of fifteen, Mary tells us, "it pleased our loving Lord to lead me to religious life in general, for I had no instruction touching any particular Order nor means to inform myself in that." But she knew what such a call implies; and with characteristic vigour began to attack her faults, in particular a love of esteem, setting herself to acquire humility and meekness by practices little short of heroic.

Mary was singularly attractive; the uncommon beauty of her character and the combination of gifts with which she was endowed—above all, her sweetness and affability—exercised a fascination which none could resist. It is written of her that "her features were exquisite, her look angelic, and her modesty sweet and graceful." We are not surprised, therefore, to learn that her intention of becoming a nun met with a storm of opposition. But prayer and confidence in God removed all obstacles; and in 1606, leaving behind all she held dear, she crossed the sea, and, alone in a foreign land, entered on those years of suspense as to God's designs regarding her which she declared afterwards to have been the most painful of her trials.

In the Convent of Poor Clares at St. Omer and in her own foundation of the Order at Gravelines, Mary tried her vocation to a contemplative life. Finding this was not "what God desired," she returned to her native land in 1609 and there began to labour for the salvation of souls among rich and poor, strengthening Catholics in the Faith, reclaiming the lapsed, helping and comforting all "in her wonted mild, sweet manner." "No prison did she dread to visit or danger to pass," says her dearly loved companion and biographer, Winefrid Wigmore, whom we shall often quote; "God gave her an admirable power over wickedness in man or devil." Later experience enabled Winefrid to add: "The devil was ever a coward where Mary Ward personally was concerned, waiting until her back was turned to begin his mischiefs."

It was during this stay in England that Mary found her first companions. Drawn by her power of attracting others, which led parents to entrust their children, priests their penitents, to her care, seven young girls of her own rank determined to cast in their lot with hers, and under her guidance to labour for the help of souls in whatever way God's Providence should point out. With joy and thankfulness Mary welcomed the little company and with them returned to St. Omer, where she opened a school for rich and poor.

At length, after ten years' patient prayer for guidance, a heavenly light streamed into her soul, showing that her life was to be given to God, not, as she had long desired, by martyrdom, but by earnest labour for religious perfection and by the education of children of her own sex, under the Rule of St. Ignatius, so far as this could be practised by women. From that day forward her way was clear. All suspense was over, all anxiety as to God's will. "Trials, opposition, persecution, failure—all these came; but doubt as to God's Will regarding her Institute—never."

The state of England must have been the cause of bitter anguish to the little band of chosen souls at St. Omer, and Mary longed that she and hers might do some little thing at least to prevent the religion of their forefathers from dying out, to save the hundreds of Catholics whose faith was in danger, and especially to preserve the young from the snares from which there seemed to be no escape. Though so young, she had outgrown the popular notion that "women did not know how to do good except to themselves—a penuriousness which I resented," she says. A patriot and a pioneer, she felt that if the Catholic faith was to be saved to her native land in days when the craving to know was spreading far and wide, the Catholic education of its daughters, no less than that of its sons, was of the first importance. What men were doing for the Church in the Society of Jesus, she felt women in their proper sphere might do; and with the insight, the fearlessness and self-devotion of a pioneer, she offered herself for the work. It was no rash resolve. That an Institute of women, organised as far as might be on the lines of the Society, was feasible, she inferred from the words she believed to have heard in prayer: "Take the same of the Society" *i.e.*, the Rule: that it would arouse opposition on every side, she was prepared for.

Her scheme involved freedom from inclosure; from the obligation of choir; from wearing a religious habit; from the jurisdiction of the diocesan. It petitioned for subjection to the Holy See alone, and for government by a Chief Superior elected for life. To us there is nothing very startling in these propositions, but longstanding principles and traditions were against them. St. Pius V had declared strict papal inclosure to be essential to all communities of religious women; hence, the project of a society devoted to the education of girls, sanctioned by the Holy See, with an approved Rule, was deemed by many a dangerous innovation, and, with the exception of Bishop Blaise, of St. Omer, few gave it any encouragement.

We have to bear in mind that in the beginning of the 17th century it was an almost unheard-of thing for religious women to have schools for young girls. A few years previously a pious confraternity had been formed in the south of France for the education of children, and had adapted to its use the Rules of St. Ignatius. The Ursulines, too, had some large educational establishments where they were doing successful work. But these places of education were little accessible to the general public; for in all convents of the time, inclosure was strictly observed, according to which a child entering a convent as a pupil became for the time of its stay as bound to inclosure as the nuns themselves. Thus day-schools were impossible, and comparatively few parents were able or willing to send their children away, as it were for good.

But this was one only of Mary's difficulties; another concerned the Rule. Her determination to "take the same of the Society" brought her much suffering, not from her enemies alone but from her best friends. Why could she not take a Rule already approved for women? it was urged. Among the Fathers of the Society itself, some were opposed to her in this respect. Lessius and Suarez had both praised the way of life of the new Institute; but, while retaining a deep veneration for the Foundress, the Jesuits were anxious to disclaim any special connection with her Congregation, the "Jesuitesses," as their enemies called them. In its early days, before restrictions had been issued by the General of the Society, some of the Fathers were Mary's ablest advisers. Like her, they saw the necessities of the times, and thought that such an Institute as hers would meet the need. As the plans developed, they withdrew more and more from all responsibility, and in the time of her greatest need the Foundress was left to stand alone.

But it was from those whom it was her life's desire to serve—the oppressed Catholics of England—that Mary had most to suffer. Harassed by unrelenting persecution from without, they had no certain guidance on many of the difficult problems of the day. There were unfortunate differences between confessors of the Faith in the same prison, between the secular clergy and the religious orders. The Society of

Jesus in particular was an object of mistrust to many; and the fact that Mary Ward proposed to borrow so much from it for her Institute, caused her to be pursued by an animosity on the part of the English secular clergy which was never satisfied till it saw the destruction of her work.

In 1616 Mary drew up a Memorial of her projected Institute, which was presented to Pope Paul V. The result was a Brief addressed to Bishop Blaise, in which the labours of its members were praised and hope of Confirmation later was held out. In 1621 Mary made her first journey to Rome, and with a recommendatory letter from the celebrated Carmelite, Father Domenico di Gesù Maria, already venerated as a saint, appeared before Pope Gregory XI to plead her cause. "He received her with singular benevolence and with all fatherly and benign expressions, so far as to say, 'God had in good time provided for His Church,' alluding to the profit which was to come by her labours."

The main charges against the "English ladies"—"that they deter others from entering any communities but their own; that they call themselves religious women; that they undertake apostolic missions in England," had been refuted by Bishop Blaise, their constant friend and defender. But the misrepresentations of their enemies appear to have been credited in Rome, for it was intimated to the Foundress that the Cardinals appointed to examine the case were agreed to decide it against her. Without any attempt to disprove the charges brought forward, she asked permission to remain with her companions in Rome that on its own

Sursum Corda!

merits her Institute might stand, or fall. Her petition was granted and her work in Rome began—not began only but was well watched, seeing that Cardinal Mellino, Vicar of Rome, "himself told our dear Mother that he kept not one but twenty-five spies over her, inasmuch as there was not one passed in or out of the house that he had not notice of."

Foundations had by this time been made in London, Liège, Cologne, and Treves. In London the fruit of Mary's labours was so great that Abbot, Archbishop of Canterbury, had special search made for her, saying she alone did more harm than six Jesuits. Twice she was seized and imprisoned; "sentence of death was passed upon her, but there was no execution for fear of odium."

After the foundation of the Roman house, the Institute spread to Naples and Perugia. The Infanta Isabella, daughter of Philip II, and her husband, the Archduke Albert of Austria, were from the first among Mary Ward's devoted patrons and friends. The Elector Maximilian I of Bavaria and the Emperor Ferdinand of Austria welcomed her to their dominions, a foundation being made in Munich in 1626, and one in Vienna in 1627. Men eminent for learning and holiness—as Cardinal Federigo Borromeo, Fra Domenico di Gesù Maria, Fr. Mutius Vitelleschi, General of the Society of Jesus—held the Foundress in singular veneration; and everywhere her children's virtue, their zeal for souls, and their fruitful labours were the best refutation of calumny.

Gregory XV died after a short pontificate and was succeeded in 1623 by Urban VIII. Like his predecessor, the new Pope gave Mary a kind reception, and at her request called together a Congregation of four Cardinals to examine her petition. "She herself was to be present at their meeting, and to declare what she desired, and her reasons."

With so many powerful, so many saintly friends, it seems strange indeed that "loneliness" should have been one of her keenest sufferings at this critical time. That it was so, we know from herself. In a paper headed "The Loneliness," she writes: "It occurred to me that perhaps I might find more difficulties and crosses in the passages of my life than I did imagine. I then offered myself to suffer with love and gladness whatsoever trouble or contrariety should happen in my doing of His will—were His will whatsoever. It appeared to me that there was some great trouble to happen about the confirmation of our course... and I begged of Him that the prayer I now made might serve as a petition for His grace at that time."

Who can doubt that that prayer was heard?

It was the lot of Mary Ward to have no one near her at this critical time to whom she could turn for guidance or protection, or on whose judgement she could fully rely. There was no one at work in her behalf. Her truest friends in Rome were foreigners, and it was a voice from among her own people that she needed. But that voice failed her. None of her countrymen for whom she was toiling came forward to bear testimony to the value of her labours. Truly she was "lonely," as she had foreseen, and there was no human "help or comfort" for her. She had no skilled advocate to defend her cause. We hear of no friendly intervention, nor of any effort made in her behalf; of nothing, in fact, beyond her own diligent application to all in authority in Rome.

In person Mary pleaded before the Cardinals; her relation lasted for three quarters of an-hour, during the whole of which time she was not interrupted. But neither the irreproachable lives of her children, nor the favour shown her by Paul V, Gregory XI, and so many bishops and Catholic Sovereigns, could avail to save her work from destruction. Had she been willing to concede one point only, that of inclosure, she would probably have obtained all she desired. But concession on this point would have been fatal to her ideal. On the other hand, she "did not wonder," says Winefrid, "that Holy Church made difficulty in a thing that was new: contrarywise, she did profoundly reverence that vigilancy of theirs.... If, therefore, His Holiness and their Eminences thought it good that she should desist, she should at once humbly submit to their decision, as the will of God to her; but she could not in fidelity to Him, change her plan or undertake others in its room. She placed herself in their hands. So that the will of God were fulfilled in her and her companions she was content. She and they had no haste, what was not done in one year could be done in another. She could attend God Almighty His time and leisure, for man had to follow, not go before Him."

The Cardinals were much moved by Mary's simple words and humble demeanour. Cardinal Borgia, the first among them, on relating the whole to the Pope, added "that he held it to be of God, and that he neither could nor durst be against it, nor was his power enough to assist it, such and so powerful were her enemies. Therefore he humbly entreated His Holiness he might deal no more in it."

Mary's persistence in adhering to this feature of her design in its entirety has been called obstinacy. But it must never be lost sight of that she did not found primarily for foreign countries—she founded for England. Her ideas and her heart were large enough to embrace the whole world, and through the whole world her Institute has spread in its subsequent form. She always believed that God had given her her vocation for her own country's sake, and it was therefore a matter of fidelity to Him not to allow of anything which would prevent the Institute from taking root there.

With regard to her plea for government by a head directly subject to the Pope himself, it was practically admitted by Clement XI in the next century. His *Lasciate governare le donne dalle donne*—"Let women be governed by women"—said by him of the office of General Superior as it then existed in the Institute of Mary, became the word of authority for self-government among religious, by which the modern Congregations of women have benefitted. As to these two points, therefore, her fidelity and fortitude have had their reward. If she laboured, as it seemed in vain, others have entered into the fruits of her labours—fruits which she was not permitted to see in this world. Unsuccessful herself for the time, and having in consequence to suffer what few women have been called to endure, she has done a great work to last on to all generations.

Her last word said, Mary left Rome, and awaited in Vienna the decision which she foresaw. She wrote a circular letter desiring her companions to yield prompt obedience to the Holy Father, and gave directions to her secretary to forward it to all the houses of the Institute as soon as the Bull was actually published, should she herself be unable to see to the matter. Rome moves slowly, and more than eighteen months of suspense passed before the decision of the Congregation was made known.

In 1031 the Bull of Suppression was signed: the ten flourishing houses of the Institute were dissolved; its schools broken up; and the two or three hundred women who composed it, disbanded and sent adrift on the world.

To some this measure may appear drastic, calamitous, even cruel. Those familiar with the lives of the Saints will see in it, rather, one of those Divine ways, inscrutable to human wisdom but "justified in themselves," by which God perfects His elect, conforming the members of Christ Crucified to their Head here, in order to glorify them with Him hereafter.

"It must not surprise us," says Father Coleridge, "if schemes were set aside by the prudence of authority as untried, which now receive the sanction of the same authority after their principles have been proved by experience. The unerring insight of the Church does not exempt her from the duty of caution, nor is it any argument that measures would have been wise and safe in the 17th century, that their safety and wisdom are recognised in the 19th. No middle course, such as deferring the decision of the question, was open to the Roman authorities. They had either to approve the Institute of Mary Ward, or, as her opponents urged, suppress it." And whatever the merits of her case, her scheme was too novel, the opposition to it too strong, to make approbation possible at that time. It came later, as Mary Ward knew it would come. Meanwhile, the work of nearly thirty years was destroyed. Her enemies had triumphed, and wrote: "Their schole is tooke away: they shall stay in Rome if they will: but their habit shall be tooke away, their houses at Perugia and at Naples shall be undone."

By a Decree of the Holy Office Mary Ward was arrested and imprisoned. Nine weeks of close confinement brought her to death's door, and she wrote to her forlorn companions: "If God would have me die I would not live: it is but to pay the rent a little before the day, and to love and suffer for God, or die and go to Him, are both singular graces and such I merit not, and one of the two I trust in the mercy of God will fall to my happy lot. Meanwhile, I would have you not the least troubled, but beg hard that He Himself would do what Himself would have done."

Before allowing her to receive the last Sacraments, the Dean of Munich required her to sign a paper to the purport that "if she had ever said or done anything contrary to faith or Holy Church, she repented her and was sorry for it." Humble and submissive, but equally firm where principle was concerned, Mary, on the point, as it seemed, of entering her agony, asked if His Holiness or the Holy Office required such a thing; and finding that no such command was laid

Sursum Corda!

upon her, she said: "God forbid that I, to cancel venial sins, which through God's mercies are all I have to accuse myself of, should commit a mortal, and cast so great a blot upon so many innocent and deserving persons, by saying '*If* I have done or said anything against Holy Church.' My 'If,' with what is already acted by my adversaries, would give just cause to the world to believe I suffer justly. No, no, I will cast myself, rather, on the mercy of Jesus Christ and die without the Sacraments." She then asked for paper and ink and wrote in Italian what follows:

> I have never done or said anything, either great or small, against His Holiness (whose holy will I have offered myself, and do now offer myself, wholly to obey), or the authority of Holy Church. But on the contrary, my feeble powers and labours have been for twenty-six years, entirely, and as far as was possible to me, employed for the honour and service of both, as, I hope by the mercy of God, and the benignity of His Holiness, will be manifested in due time and place. Nor would I now for a thousand worlds, or for the gain of whatever present or future seeming good, do the least thing unfitting the dutiful service of a true Catholic and a most obedient daughter of Holy Church. Nevertheless, if that which was at the first allowed and authorized by the Supreme Pontiffs, or Sacred Congregations of Cardinals, in which according to my poor capacity I have desired and sought to serve Holy Church, should be by those to whom the decision of such things belongs, determined (the whole truth being heard), to have been in any way repugnant to the duty of a true Christian and to the obedience due to His Holiness, or to Holy Church, I am, and ever shall be, with the help

of God's grace, most ready to acknowledge my fault, to ask pardon for the offence, and together with the public dishonour already laid upon me, to offer my poor and brief life in satisfaction of the said sin.

MARIA DELLA GUARDIA
Munich March 27, 1631.

The desired leave was given and Mary received the last Sacraments. Meantime, her companions had not been idle. In a direct appeal to Pope Urban, they told him of the treatment she had received and the state to which she was reduced, ending with the following words: "Vouchsafe, then, to call her to Rome, give her leave at least once to speak her own cause, the case being made so public, and that of which she is accused, and for which she is thus treated, so enormous."

The appeal had immediate effect. The Pope summoned a special Congregation of Cardinals to investigate the matter, declared that he had been kept in entire ignorance of her arrest and imprisonment, and ordered her immediate release. The authors of her imprisonment, we are told, knowing her influence in Rome, and her favour with Pope Urban, and desiring to forestall the efforts for any fresh religious work to which they rightly supposed her resolute soul would prompt her, endeavoured to prevent her return to the City by requiring her to defray herself the expenses of the journey. Moreover, she was to appear on a certain day, and, as one in disgrace, to be accompanied by a Commissary appointed by the Dean of Munich. Mary saw the snare, and with her usual simplicity appealed straight to the Pope, laying before him the impossibility of complying with this order in her state of health and impoverished condition. The answer she received must have left her free as to her movements; and "God turned all to her glory," says Mary Pointz, her constant companion, as appeared by the singular favours done her by all the princes along her way, by more than their accustomed marks of kindness by their Eminences the Cardinals on her arrival in Rome, and, finally, by the grant of an immediate private audience by the Pope.

Very touching is the way in which Mary hastened to his presence and opened her heart to him—who had just signed away all her hopes—with the same simplicity and trust with which she had at first commended her Institute to his care; telling him that God had given her indubitable promise of promoting and perfecting it, and assurance that it should remain in the Church of God until the end of the world. Kneeling at his feet she said: "Holy Father, I neither am nor ever have been a heretic." With paternal kindness the Pope interrupted her, saying: "We believe it, We believe it. We need no other proofs. We and the Cardinals are well informed as to yourself and your habits, and your exemplary conduct. We and they all are not only satisfied but edified, and we know that you have carried on your Institute well. We have nevertheless permitted the trial of your virtues, nor must you think it much to have been proved as you have been, and as other Popes, our predecessors, have done in similar cases, who have exercised the endurance of the servants of God."

Thus encouraged, Mary went on to ask permission that the ladies who still wished to live under her guidance might do so under the protection of the Holy See. The Pope acquiesced at once. Her fast friend, Maximilian I, was allowed to shelter a certain number in the *Paradeiser Haus*, Munich, whence some of the younger ones were transferred by the Pope's desire to Rome, to live with Mary Ward and be trained by her in the religious life. "We are glad," he said, "that they should come and we will take them under our protection."

The work of Mary Ward, then, was not wrecked. In Rome, under the supervision and protection of the Apostolic See, it revived gradually and developed, following the general lines of the first scheme. The second Institute was approved as to its Rule by Clement XI in 1703, and as an Institute by Pius IX in 1877.

To return to Mary Ward personally. How did she receive the blow so long expected when at last it fell? Winefrid tells us that she "enjoyed as much peace as if the thing had been of her own procuring... Nor was there seen the least change in word or look, the smallest appearance of conflict or trouble when by the Bull she beheld the ruin of her labour past, the loss of so many houses which with so great toil she had established... What but conformity to the Divine Will could have made her, without the slightest disturbance or sadness, see and rise above the total destruction of the work of nearly thirty years?"

Sursum Corda!

"She had indeed stripped herself of everything both spiritual and temporal, as to herself and her Institute which she loved so well; and given all back into His hands in perfect peace who had bestowed them." Thirteen years before, some sight had been given her of the dark waters through which the Institute had to pass in the future and of the solitary and singular vocation which she herself was to fulfil. "I besought our Lord with tears," she said, "for grace to bear it; I saw that there was no help or comfort for me but to cleave fast to Him, and so I did, for He was there to help me."

Added to these trials from without, were disaffection and discord in certain houses of the Institute, due to the jealousy of those whom Mary had loved and trusted. And even sufferings such as these were as nothing compared with the severer spiritual trials with which God proved His faithful servant. During the whole of the two years, when her affairs had reached their gravest crisis in Rome, her soul was in a state of the darkest desolation. She believed herself abandoned and forsaken by God. Prayer and the sacraments no longer brought sensible joy and strength. But the opportunity of proving faith, and hope, and trust—this they brought, and this she faithfully used. Her daily Communions were never intermitted, and, like her Lord and Master, being in agony she prayed the longer.

The rest of Mary Ward's story is soon told. In 1639, with letters of introduction from Pope Urban to Queen Henrietta Maria, she returned to England and established herself in London. In 1642 she journeyed northward with her household and took up her abode at Heworth, near York, where she died, January 30th, 1645.

"On that bitter night," says Mary Pointz, the first of the faithful little band who had joined her at St. Omer and followed her through the vicissitudes of her eventful life, "pitying their desolate condition, she said to her companions: 'God will assist you...and when God shall enable me to be in place, I will serve you.'" All through her life, joy was one of Mary's chief characteristics: it never escaped her altogether, even in time of grievous trouble and pain. She taught it to her spiritual children. It runs through all her conversation and letters. Not even round her death-bed would she let them grieve. "Oh, fie, fie!" she said. "Come, let us rather sing and praise God for all His infinite loving kindness." She sang the hymn they had often sung together. As the night advanced, a great agony came on, but in the intervals her face was lit up with heavenly joy. When morning dawned, she drew each one of them into her arms and kissed her tenderly: "then seemed to mind us no more," says Mary Pointz, kissed the crucifix, pronounced the name of Jesus three times, then, without sigh or groan, bowed her head in death.

The end of that strenuous life had come. "There was no apparent victory over her enemies, no great triumph in this world. She closed her eyes in an out-of-the-way part of England, without priest or sacraments, with only a few of her most devoted children round her. Yet she enjoyed to the end that wonderful peace of soul and rest of mind which comes only from a conformity to the Will of God such as hers."

Mary Ward was a pioneer and had the characteristics and the trials of a pioneer. A gallant spirit, fitted for the times in which her lot was cast and for the arduous vocation given her by God; a greatness of soul that made her—practical and energetic though she was—detached from the affairs of this passing life and at home only amid the things of eternity; a lofty courage and confidence in God that opposition and failure did but strengthen; the joyousness and peace that come of seeing God's hand in all things; and above all, a love of Him so steadfast and supreme, that when all else was taken away, He alone sufficed her—this was her equipment for her task in life. It was a life noble in its aim, and noble in the spirit in which its vicissitudes were met. Mary spent all the resources of her rich nature on a work for God and for souls that she knew was to end in failure. She accepted its overthrow for herself and for those she loved, with unquestioning obedience and loyalty. And on the ruins of this, her life's work, and under the very eye of him who had suppressed it, she laid, in confidence in God and in His Church, the foundations of the second Institute that was to have so full a share of blessing.

This is the life and these are the merits as to which the children of Mary Ward await in hope the judgement of the Church, that after long years of waiting they may see her, not vindicated only, but glorified, and may "rise up and call her Blessed."

Almost with the eye of prophecy, Mary Ward appears to have seen what women would do in the time to come. In her early days she "resented the penuriousness" of the notion that they could do good to none but themselves. Some disparaging remarks of a priest, later, drew from her an indignant protest. Addressing her community, she said: "Hearing how much our course was esteemed in Rome, he answered: 'It is true, while they are in their first fervour, but fervour will decay, and when all is done, they are but women!' I would know what you all think he meant by this speech of his, 'but women' and what 'fervour' is. Fervour is a will to do good. Fervour is not placed in feelings but in a will to do well, which women may have as well as men. There is no such difference between men and women that women may not do great things, as we have seen by example of many saints who have done great things. And I hope in God it will be seen that women in time to come will do much. Wherein are we so inferior to other creatures that they should term us 'but women'? I would to God that all men understood this truth, that women if they will be perfect, and if they would not make us believe that we can do nothing and that we are but women, might do great matters. What can this profit you to tell you you are but women, weak and able to do nothing, and that fervour will decay? I say, what does this profit you but to bring you to

Sursum Corda!

dejection. It is true fervour doth many times grow cold, but what is the cause? Is it because we are women? No, but because we are imperfect women."

How must Mary Ward rejoice to see the triumphant vindication of her claim for the recognition of women's powers which the world-war has brought! With what sympathy must she behold the effort to enlist in the cause of Religion and of mankind the organised service of Catholic women throughout the world! Her words to her little community in France three hundred years ago might have been a far distant hailing of the many-sided activities which are to-day giving abundant and worldwide proof that urged by the charity of Christ, "women may do great things."

MAXIMS OF MARY WARD

INTRODUCTION

The following collection of proverbs is the only piece in this anthology not actually written by Mother Loyola, with the exception of its preface. Nevertheless the spirituality of Mary Ward, as expressed in these Maxims, permeated the Institute of the Blessed Virgin Mary and its daughters, particularly Mother Mary Loyola, who had a special affection for the Foundress and her fellow Recusants. Thus it seems appropriate to include here the entire compilation, rather than merely Mother Loyola's preface.

MAXIMS OF MARY WARD
Introduction

"Inquire not who said this, but attend to what is said," is a wise injunction. None the less is it a tribute to the instinct that prompts us to prize deeds above words, that would test the soundness of a counsel before accepting it, and consider the worth of a man and the example of his life before appreciating his sayings. Our Lord tells us that out of the abundance of the heart the mouth speaketh. But He also warns us that not everyone saying: "Lord, Lord," shall enter into the Kingdom of Heaven, for there are those who say and do not.

It is not superfluous, then, to prefix to these *Maxims of Mary Ward* a few words as to the aim and work of one whose history has not only engaged the attention of men eminent for virtue and learning, but is brought vividly before us in a series of fifty large oil paintings preserved to our own time.

The life of Mary Ward covers one of the most eventful periods of English history (1585-1645). During the whole of that time the Catholics of England were subjected to a persecution so severe as to threaten the survival of Faith in the land. Not only, however, did it survive, but it has given birth to a multitude of educational and charitable Congregations which minister to-day to every variety of spiritual and temporal need; and these, Cardinal Bourne tells us, owe their very existence to the providential mission, the supernatural foresight, and the heroic perseverance of Mary Ward.

Even as a girl she grasped the needs of her time and of after-time. She felt that women no less than men—nay, even more than men—must do their part, if the flood of evils let loose by the new heresies were not to submerge the world. Schools for girls, unhampered by restrictions hitherto in force, must be provided, and, acting as she believed on a Divine call, she resolved to supply the want.

Her personal charm and the fascination of her character drew around her a band of devoted companions whom she inspired with her own aims and gradually formed into a Congregation under simple vows, unenclosed and without the obligation of choir. They were to go wherever need required and to be under a Mother-General elected for life. The venture proved a success. Schools for rich and poor were set up, and the rapidity with which her Institute spread in the Low Countries, Bavaria, Austria and Italy, under the patronage of the respective rulers seemed to augur well for the undertaking. But other influences were at work. The novelty of the experiment roused opposition in many quarters, where it was regarded as a dangerous innovation, and where, as in England, it was resented by those who might well have seen in it a useful ally—the hunted Catholic priests.

Complaints were sent to Rome, and alarming results predicted if the "Jesuitesses" remained unchecked. The silence of Mary's friends in her hour of need, the misrepresentations of her enemies, and her own application, not for toleration only but for approbation of her Institute, obliged the Holy See to take some step. Four Cardinals were appointed by Pope Urban VIII to examine her petition and in person she pleaded before them. But a design so much at variance with all precedent, and so vehemently denounced by many, could not at that time receive formal approbation. And judgement being given against her, no course remained open but suppression.

And it came, as Mary long years before knew it would come. In a moment the work of thirty years was destroyed, ten flourishing houses were broken up, and their two or three hundred members sent adrift on the world. The schools were closed and—unknown to Pope Urban—Mary herself was imprisoned. She had previously taken the precaution of ensuring, by letters to the various houses, prompt and complete submission to the decree which she had foreseen.

As soon as the Pope was made aware of her imprisonment he ordered her immediate release. She hastened to his feet, and, to the amazement of her so far triumphant enemies, was not only received with fatherly kindness, but allowed to resume her manner of life under his own eyes. In Rome, then, her second Institute took shape. It was approved as to its Rule by Clement XI in 1703, and as an Institute by Pius IX in 1877. Mary returned to England in

Sursum Corda!

1639 and established herself in London. In 1642 she journeyed northward with her household and took up her abode at Heworth near York, where she died, January 30, 1645.

Entrusted with a providential mission towards her own and future times, Mary Ward was richly dowered both by nature and grace. Her character was remarkable at once for its many-sidedness and for its simplicity. Vehement desire of martyrdom coupled with a patience that no years of weary waiting for the manifestation of God's designs could exhaust; meekness in the face of contradiction and ill-will, united with the zeal of the Boanerges where the honour and interests of God were concerned; a cleaving to God's Will that at the voice of authority abandoned with perfect serenity the very plans inspired by Him; acute bodily and mental suffering overmastered by energy of will that was always ready with a playful word to sustain the courage of her children—these are beautiful traits, not always found united, we venture to say, even in God's holy ones.

In her own day Pope Urban was accustomed to speak of Mary Ward as "a great servant of God." Cardinal Federigo Borromeo and the celebrated Carmelite Fra Domenico di Gesù Maria held her in singular veneration. Bishop Hedley called her "a great Englishwoman," and Cardinal Bourne considers it a "duty of gratitude to recall her memory continually to the Catholics of England, and indeed of the whole United Kingdom, as well as to all the teaching Orders of religious women throughout the world."

The *Maxims* which reveal the guiding principles of her life we owe to the devoted companions drawn to her in girlhood and faithful to her till death. A brief record of her life and work may be found in a recent publication of the Catholic Truth Society.[1]

INSTRUCTIONS HOW WE ARE TO CONDUCT OURSELVES TOWARDS GOD, OUR NEIGHBOUR, AND OURSELVES.

BY MARY WARD

I. How we are to conduct ourselves towards God.

Be not content only to love God, but strive to be wholly lost in His love. Give thyself entirely to thy Creator, and lend thyself only, so to speak, to creatures.

Diligently attend to all occupations and offices for the honour of God, and the salvation of thy neighbour, but desire and seek after none. We have but one occupation, namely, to fulfil the will of God in every work.

It very ill becomes a religious person to be faint-hearted; for she knows well that God is omnipotent, and that He loves her infinitely, and therefore will permit nothing which could hurt her.

---

[1] *Mary Ward, Foundress of the Institute of the B.VM.*, with a Preface by H. E. Cardinal Bourne. [Editor's note: this text has been provided in this volume.]

Sursum Corda!

The true children of this Company shall accustom themselves to act not out of fear, but solely from love, because they are called by God to a vocation of love.

A troubled dejected spirit will never love God perfectly, nor do much good to His honour.

Whoever wishes to do much good in this Company for the honour of God and the salvation of her neighbour must place the common profit before her own.

The best way to bear troubles with equanimity is to thank God heartily for them.

We must so wholly devote ourselves to His Divine Will—that we are as it were enclosed in it, and therefore cannot on any side withdraw from it.

Whoever would work much good in this Company must have an entire mistrust in herself and great confidence in God.

We ought only so far to desire the favour of secular persons and seek to please them, as may be profitable for our calling; which requires that we endeavour to draw all men, with ourselves, to God, by the fulfilment of the Divine Will, and thereby to true happiness.

We should, out of love to God, not only willingly let pass all impermissible joys, but those also which are allowable; and rejoice if they are taken from us through others, against our own will.

We cannot always attend to the service of God and to our own health, therefore we must not care if our body has to suffer something. Indeed, we should not desire to live, except thereby to be able to serve God, and our neighbour for God.

Prize thy honour higher than thy life, but esteem it little to lose both for the love of Jesus Christ.

We ought to work and suffer for God; and for the rest, let Him make use of us according to His good pleasure, for the fulfilment of His most holy Will should be our sole wish and only desire.

Our greatness and strength consist not in the favour of princes and great personages, but in this—that we have free and open access to God, from whom all greatness and strength come.

Exercise thyself daily in the love of God, and rejoice that the will of God should be done in thee, although that which happens should be contrary to thy will.

Desire nothing else, however good it may appear, but according to the rule of the Divine Will.

Desire not the least thing which is contrary to God and thy conscience under the pretext and in the hope of attaining a great good.

Do not, like the slothful servant in the Gospel, bury thy talents, which God has lent thee to be expended in His service.

Sursum Corda!

If an opportunity offers of advancing the honour of God, be not content that others busy themselves about it, but, if it is fitting for thee, do thou also take part in it, after the example of St. Mary Magdalen, who was not content that St. Joseph of Arimathea anointed the Body of Christ, but would perform this office to Him also.

Be ashamed to say that anything appears hard to thee in the service of God; for to those who love all is light.

Satisfy thyself with nothing which is less than God.

Remain steadfastly in the service of God until the end, and do not trouble where thou wilt close thy life; for it little matters whether it is behind a hedge, or in a ditch, or in thy bed, if only thou art found faithful.

Be not too much troubled about temporal things; remember our dear Lord has said that we must seek first the Kingdom of God and His justice and then all other things will be given to us.

Divine love is like fire, which will not let itself be shut up; for it is impossible to love God and not to labour to extend His honour.

Show thyself at all times glad and joyful, for Almighty God loves a cheerful giver.

The happiness of a man consists in the Divine good pleasure, therefore we should seek this alone in all our doings.

The spirit of God is not ill-mannered, but teaches all courteousness.

We should desire nothing unconditionally from God, but that His most holy Will may be done in and through us; for in this petition we cannot do amiss, because in it not only our own contentment but our sanctification is also included.

Always receive the Blessed Sacrament of the Altar with such devotion, as if It were to be thy Viaticum, and offer It with this intention.

Mistrust in God ties, as it were, His hands, so that He cannot bestow upon us His blessing and His Divine gifts.

If something sweet and pleasant happens to thee, turn thyself immediately with thanksgiving to God, who has granted this sweetness, and remember that it is to be found infinitely more perfect in Him.

If you think that some one has neglected to co-operate with the gift of God's graces, and is therefore in danger of losing them, ask Him in His mercy to make ready your heart so that it may be worthy to receive them instead. For the Blessed Mother of God has said in her Canticle that "He fills the hungry with good things, and sends the rich empty away."

When you desire a grace from God, offer your petition with great humility; and if it appear as though He would not listen to you, yet, like the Canaanite woman in the Gospel, persevere in your prayer and say: "Lord Jesus although it is not good that the bread of the children should be thrown to dogs, yet the whelps eat of the crumbs that fall from the table of their masters." And so perhaps you too may merit to hear, as that woman did: "Great is thy faith, be it done to thee as thou wilt."

Sursum Corda!

Accustom thyself in all doubts to cry out with the holy Apostle Paul, "Lord, what wilt Thou have me to do?" and when thou learnest the will of God, set aside all self-love and fulfil it perfectly.

In order that *ours* may not only by their own perfection advance the greater honour of God, but also by the salvation of their neighbour, they shall spare neither trouble nor diligence to find both fitting persons and the necessary means, yet without being troubled at the want of both.

Perform all thy employments with order and diligence and be not content to appear good in the eyes of men only, but strive also to be so in God's eyes.

Care not for what concerns thy own person, but stand up zealously for whatever touches God and His honour.

We ought to seek God alone in our works, and therefore to fulfil all as faithfully and carefully, though no one sees us, as if we had the whole world as spectators.

Ours ought often to desire of God the true spirit of their calling, and the grace to exercise themselves in the virtues which are befitting it; for what is praiseworthy in one state of life is often reprehensible in another.

Prize thy calling highly, and love it before all others, since our Lord has said in the Gospel that he who keeps and teaches the Commandments shall be great in the Kingdom of Heaven.

It is impossible to serve God and the world at the same time, for our dear Lord says, "He who is not with Me is against Me."

Do not let the foolish world persuade thee that virtue is difficult, for the Eternal Truth says: "My yoke is easy and My burden light."

If it appear to thee hard and painful to overcome thyself and to break thy will, remember that our Lord requires this of thee by virtue of thy calling; for He says, "If any one will come after Me, let him take up his cross daily and follow Me." By regarding only what is His Will, all that is burdensome will be turned into sweetness and thou wilt cry out with the Prophet David, "I have run in the way of Thy commandments, when Thou didst enlarge my heart."

Whoever will serve God according to her state in this Institute must of necessity love the Cross, and be ready to suffer much for Christ's sake.

Make to thyself friends in Heaven, and have the whole heavenly host for thy intercessors.

II. How we are to conduct ourselves towards our neighbour.

Do not endeavour so much to please thy neighbour as to be of use to him.

Thou wilt never attain to true perfection if thou payest attention to other people's doings, which concern thee not.

If thou see anything blamable in another, thou shouldst strive to replace it through thy own well doing. Yet thou must not in the least degree despise the person who has

Sursum Corda!

failed, but rather feel compassion towards him, stirring up a wholesome fear within thee, when thou hast in remembrance that Holy Scripture says: "Let him that thinketh he standeth take heed lest he fall."

Ours shall most diligently be on their guard that they never speak of the defects of other people, and especially not of those of religious. They shall not complain of one another, but preserve charity indissolubly as the peculiar virtue of our Company.

Listen willingly to good counsel; but be not too confidential, unless thou knowest the person to be such that thou mayest hope to derive profit.

If thou showest service to any one, do it willingly, and not with such repugnance that he who receives it should be with justice discontented.

If any one gives thee trouble, meet him with friendly words, for so thou wilt soften both thyself and him.

We should zealously endeavour to be grateful to our benefactors, loving towards our enemies, obliging to our companions, and courteous towards every one.

If we see a fault in our neighbour, we should certainly dislike the fault, but not the person: we must blame the fault but not the man who has committed it, remembering how dearly God loves him, and how just it is therefore that we should love him.

Ours should be as courteous towards each other as if they were strangers, but at the same time as gentle and amiable as they are accustomed to be with their most intimate friends.

Strive more to merit the praise and love of others than to receive it.

Let thy love be at all times rooted in God, and then remain faithful to thy friend, and value him highly, even more highly than thy life.

Be all things to all men, that so thou mayest win all for God; and be careful as much as thou canst to satisfy all.

Pray earnestly for thy departed friends, for it is in a time of need that true friendship is proved.

Thy conversation shall at all times be such that all who hear it may derive profit; yet it shall be so ordered, that it may not appear as if thou soughtest thereby to instruct others.

In all thy ways show a recollected mind and do not be too careful to stand upon thy rights with any who ought to yield to thee; still less allow thyself to dispute or quarrel with them, if they oppose and contradict thee.

Make use of gentle and kind words when thou reprovest any one, for thou wilt thus effect more than through those which are harsh and overbearing.

Love all, but love them not on thine own account, but for God.

Let not any one imagine that he loves God, if he cherishes an aversion in his heart towards his neighbour; for so the words of St. John teach: "He who loves not his brother whom he has seen, how can he love God whom he has not seen?"

Love solitude, and fly, as much as you can, unnecessary conversation with seculars; for God says in Holy Scripture: "I will lead her into the wilderness and there I will speak to her heart."

Do not judge and prize virtue according to the talents or the position of the person who exhorts you concerning it, but according to that which it is in itself. For God can speak to us through every man, and he who is wise will learn gladly from every one, be he ever so simple.

Do not have a divided heart, for in that case you will be left by both God and man.

It requires greater strength of soul to yield than to use many words of dispute; because it is harder to nature to fight with self and one's own inclinations than to fight with other people.

Do not be easily offended at the doings of others, since thou canst not know what is their intention; but accustom thyself to put a good construction on all thou seest and hearest.

Be compassionate and merciful towards the poor, and generous also if thou hast the means, and do not call them beggars.

Although the conversion of souls is very pleasing to God, yet He loves the perfection of each one so greatly, that He wills not that any one should commit even the smallest sin, were the whole world to be converted thereby.

If thou art obliged to punish any one, do it so that she be led to improve, and not thereby be embittered.

Take away from no one what he loves, unless thou givest him instead something he loves still better.

Zeal for souls is more highly to be prized in our state than visions and ecstasies; for zeal is necessary for us, but in these others a deceit of the evil one is easily hidden.

Ours ought to be endowed with the zeal of Apostles and the recollection of spirit of hermits, to attend at the same time to both their own and their neighbour's salvation.

We ought diligently to endeavour to give a good example to every one; for if all men are bound, in virtue of the command of Christ: "Let your light so shine before men, that they may see your good works and glorify your Father who is in heaven," to lead an edifying life, how much more are we, whom God has called to extend His honour, and to guide our neighbour to salvation.

It is a greater grace to help to save souls than oneself to suffer martyrdom.

III. How we are to behave towards ourselves.

Do good, and do it well.

Do what thou doest; that is, apply thyself diligently to the work thou hast in hand, to perform it carefully and perfectly.

Undertake no employment which thou canst not hope to complete with honour.

Sursum Corda!

Thou wilt never be tranquil and live contentedly, so long as thou placest thy inclinations inordinately upon some one place or person.

Wherever thou findest thyself remember that not the place, but the practices sanctify.

Virtue is only hard to those who hold it to be such.

Timid persons will never ascend very high in the path of virtue, nor work anything great in the religious state; on the other hand the presumptuous will not persevere to the end.

To those who do not willingly stay at home, going abroad is dangerous.

Whoever is not content with what is commanded him is unfit also for other employments.

Those who wish to do what they ought not, will afterwards have to do what they wish not.

A selfish person thinks only how she can enrich herself, and only with great difficulty will she do what is useful or profitable to others, unless she hopes to derive from it some honour or advantage, to which she eagerly aspires.

If anything is commanded thee which thou canst and oughtest to perform thyself, do not make use of the help of others.

Whatever falls to thee to do, that perform as much as thou canst faithfully and diligently; but be not too anxious as to how it may turn out, nor whether it will be hazardous or not, but commit it to the good God.

Do not begin what you have to do rashly and over-hastily; but weigh all well and thoughtfully, that you may not afterwards have to repent of it.

He who trusts too much to himself will often fail, for God sometimes lets the proud fall that they may learn what they are.

It is more difficult to bring a man to himself who has the appearance of virtue, than to convert a great sinner. He is on this account in greater danger as to his salvation; for it is of such a one that God has spoken the fearful words, "Because thou are neither cold nor hot, I will begin to vomit thee out of My mouth."

A religious should account no offence as little; for from him who has received much, much will be required, and he who does not avoid small faults will soon fall into great ones.

He who will preserve himself quite pure and spotless must fly occasions of evil; for no one can touch pitch and not be soiled.

Be careful not to give scandal to any one; for thereby not only is God offended but also thine own and thine neighbours' souls are injured.

Never look upon thyself as the conqueror unless thou hast overcome thyself.

Be diligent to root out thy vices, but not to hide them.

Sursum Corda!

As long as we live in this valley of sorrows we shall stumble and fall; therefore spiritual weapons are at all times necessary to us, that the enemy may not overmaster us.

He who would be rich in virtues must neglect no opportunity of exercising them.

He who would command well must first have learned to obey well.

If thy opinion is desired in any matter, give it frankly, then; push it no further, and do not trouble thyself what the end will be.

Be discreet and not over-hasty in thy speech, nor run from one subject to another, but finish the first before thou beginnest another.

Do not be so talkative that thou canst not remain silent about anything, but must immediately impart it to every one.

To say what is not in thy heart is deceit, and to say all which is in thy heart is folly.

Love and speak the truth at all times.

Show thyself as thou art, and be what thou showest thyself.

Do not appear ignorant to please one who is learned, nor refuse to learn from every one, for God loves simplicity but not ignorance.

It is a sign that the love of the world is not wholly put aside when persons speak much of their relations; ours ought therefore carefully to avoid doing so.

Such a similarity should prevail among *ours*, not only in our way of life, but also in our outward demeanour, speech, and in our manner of intercourse with our neighbour, that he who has seen one may imagine he has seen all; for harmony and uniformity are the greatest ornaments of our calling.

Edification both as to demeanour and clothing should be especially attended to out of doors; and therefore all should take care to go out in neat and not in torn garments.

As a thirsty man swallows eagerly whatever he receives to drink, so he who thirsts after perfection drinks in with joy every admonition, be it bitter or sweet.

Ours should seek after true and heroic virtues, not after consolations and sweetness, avoiding all unnecessary, curious questions or such as are not serviceable to perfection; and they should complain to no one who cannot help them.

Ours should take care to banish far from them all inordinate sadness, and show always a cheerful temperament.

A Superior ought not to be soft-hearted and allow herself to be persuaded by all, else many disorders will arise in the House.

In our calling, a cheerful mind, a good understanding and a great desire after virtue are necessary, but of all these a cheerful mind is the most so.

Ours will never live contentedly, if they do not diligently endeavour to have but one will and one intention with their Superior.

Sursum Corda!

If any one gives us a reproof, we should receive it with a thankful heart, and not think that this or that person has out of some grudge complained on us and hence behave ourselves in an unfriendly way towards her; for this would be to turn wholesome medicine into poison.

Whoever has received from God a good nature—that is, good natural qualities and inclinations—ought not to act contrary to them, but only direct them to a good end.

Gather for thyself in thy youth a great treasure of virtues and good habits, which in old age may prove thy support and thy consolation.

Let not anything disturb the peace of thy heart, not even thy sins. But if thou committest one, humble thyself before God, and say: "O Lord, I have acted now like myself, for my nature is to sin; do Thou then, O kindest God, act like Thyself, and forgive me; for Thy nature is always to have mercy and to forgive, therefore permit not that I should live out of Thy favour." In this way thy fall will procure for thee a higher step in virtue.

He who would do no evil must also do nothing which would be the cause of it in himself.

Let no day go by in which thou dost not heroically conquer thyself.

Do not be pusillanimous when the honour of God is concerned, but say with the Royal Prophet, "I will speak of Thy testimonies before kings, and not be ashamed."

Thy word ought to be of as much value as the work itself; do not therefore be over hasty in thy promises, but be faithful in keeping them.

The ways of virtue endure no standing still; he who does not go forward, goes back.

It is very beautiful, but is seldom seen, when the young are devout, the old patient, and the sick joyful.

Whatever uprightness thou hast, so much hast thou of other virtues also.

Do not put aside thy resolutions when thou canst fulfil them; but remember that thy everlasting happiness may hang upon the present moment.

If thou art reproved, without thy discerning thyself guilty, think, that if what is not just happens to thee now, thou mayest well have merited it through past failings; therefore thou oughtest not to excuse thyself unless thou art asked, in which case acknowledge the truth with simplicity.

A heroic spirit is a great advantage to virtue, therefore happy is he who has received this gift from God.

Faithfulness is not so much to be praised in great as in little things, as we may perceive from the words of our Lord Himself, who says in the Gospel: "Well done, good and faithful servant, because thou hast been faithful over few things I will place thee over many things; enter thou into the joy of thy Lord."

Sursum Corda!

The best satisfaction for past faults is a humble diligence in the fulfilment of the next duties which follow.

We ought to forsake the world, before it forsakes us; for it would be a poor gift only to offer to God what the world cares not for.

Vain fear and inordinate love are the bane of the female sex.

Mortification is necessary to everyone; for without it neither in the world nor in the religious state will any live peaceably with others, much less will any one attain to a high perfection. For the Kingdom of Heaven suffers violence, and it is only taken by force.

We ought to learn from St. Aloysius to perform every work with as great a perfection and fervour as if it were the last of our life; for by that means he received from God in a few years a reward such as others have not merited in many.

Make use of every opportunity which the good God gives thee for thy spiritual progress; for He does nothing in vain and without a wise object. Therefore He will require of thee a strict account for every moment of the time which thou misusest.

If thou feelest in thyself a desire to perform a virtuous work very profitable to the greater honour of God, but hast no opportunity of fulfilling it, rejoice if others bring it to pass instead of thee; for if God is served, what does it matter from whom He will receive the service?

Never wilt thou attain to perfection, if thou appliest not thyself fervently to prayer and dost not strive to live in the presence of God.

Whoever is much disquieted over his faults, shows that he trusts too much to his own strength; therefore God permits such failings, that he may learn to know himself rightly.

Whatever distracts and disturbs thee inwardly comes not from God; for the Spirit of God always brings peace and serene repose with it.

Be not changeable, but remain steadfast in the way of virtue; for not he who begins well, but he who endures to the end, shall be saved.

If we diligently please God during our life, He will not fail to console us on our death-bed.

Strive ever so to live that thou mayest be at all times ready to die; for where the tree falls, there it remains lying for all eternity.

ALL TO THE GREATER GLORY OF GOD.

THE TIME OF MY LIFE

INTRODUCTION

In 1821, Frances Teresa Ball set off from the Bar Convent in York, England to establish an independent branch of the Institute of the Blessed Virgin Mary near Dublin, Ireland. This thriving community in turn spread around the globe, establishing missions in India, Africa, Australia, Spain and Canada. Though still loosely affiliated with the rest of the Institute, this branch called itself the Sisters of Loreto, after the Marian Shrine in Italy where Mary Ward used to pray. One of its best known members in modern times was Agnes Gonxha Bojaxhiu, better known as Mother Teresa, who joined the Sisters in Ireland in 1928 before being sent to India a year later. Witnessing the extreme poverty of the people there led her to establish the Missionaries of Charity.

Well may you wonder how all of this relates to Mother Mary Loyola. During her tenure as Mother Superior of the Bar Convent from 1883-1891, Mother Loyola took advantage of improved means of communication to strengthen ties with the Loreto branch of the IBVM. In later years, as her writings made her well-known around the world, the students of Loretto[1] Academy in Niagara Falls, Canada

---

[1] The original spelling was "Americanized" in the houses established in North America.

were no doubt excited to find the following guest article published in their journal, *The Loretto Rainbow*, in July 1930. Here we can see that at age 85, after having been bedridden for 7 years, Mother Loyola's mind was still as active as ever, and her words still as inspiring.

THE TIME OF MY LIFE

In its April number, "The Rainbow" gives us an interesting prize essay, "What it Means to me to be a Loretto Girl," which starts with a frank bit of biography.

"It was from a home"—the writer tells us—"where I had never felt that I was in any way undesirable in anyone's eyes, that I passed into school life with the great wish, conscious or unconscious, to be popular and to get all I could out of everything shown or given to me." There must, then, have been many a conflict before she could declare herself "one of the happiest, if not the very happiest girl in Loretto Niagara." How the change came about, we are told:

"I've given up my desire to be popular, for a more deserving one; I have tried to be considerate to the other girls, a thing unthought of before, and with these higher aims have come real friends and happiness. I thank Loretto with all my heart for those first few months spent with her. They brought me to a realization of facts and prepared me somewhat for the world and its ways. And although that realization caused me some temporary sorrow, I can now work with an assurance which comes from the knowledge that determination for real achievement is better than all the popularity in the world... Ten years or even five years from now, where shall I be? I don't know... No one knows. But whatever I do that is good (and I must do something good), it will be because Loretto has helped to give me my chance."

The writer of this essay must not provide the text for a sermon. But the resolve: "I must do something good"—the conviction, of course, of all Loretto girls—recalls some words in the Apocalypse on which it would be hard not to dwell for a few moments.

Encouraging the soul which desires to do great things, Our Blessed Lord says: "He that shall overcome I will make him a pillar in the temple of my God." It is a promise and a reward. A pillar in the temple of God may support an altar in the sanctuary, or, in the porch, may serve simply as an introduction to the church. In any capacity its office is an honour to be envied. St. Paul speaks of "James, Cephas and John" (as) "pillars," and to this honourable office the Church is now inviting her layfolk with an insistence never, perhaps, equalled in the past. She not only invites; she implores. We are to be—each in place—her "living stones" erect ourselves and helping to support the weight of her ever-increasing burden.

We live in days when the humblest lot and the narrowest sphere may provide conditions for the boldest endeavour and the widest influence; an age of astounding exploits, when to gain the results of experience there are those amongst us who go all lengths and bring about contrasts and changes which at length fail to startle us. A Protestant Archbishop deplores not only empty churches, but "the want of the spirit of adventure in the youth of the present day." Surely exceptions here hardly justify the reproach. Boys and girls are venturesome to a degree hitherto undreamt of. As to the ventures, there may be two opinions, but it looks as if daring in some form or other is to be one of the characteristics of the country.

To prove the efficiency of the British light areoplane, a girl of twenty-two takes a lone journey of nearly ten thousand miles by air from Croydon to Australia, encountering for the first time unknown perils by land and water, over tropical seas and forests, through storms and darkness and unexpected climatic conditions during nineteen and a half days and nights. Another adventurer chooses the sea and swimming contests for the display of her powers. And yet another traveller, this time a man, preferring to feel the solid earth beneath his feet, starts on a globe-trotting tour from Rome to Cape Town, walking alone, through Switzerland, Germany, Belgium, Poland, France, Spain, Portugal, Morocco, Algeria, Egypt, and Abyssinia, arriving after four years of travel at his destination, twice stricken down by black-fever, and killing five lions and two elephants on his way.

In the discharge of her divinely-appointed commission, the Church more than keeps pace with the adventurous spirit of the age. Universal in time as in place, she is at home in all these spheres of adventure and labour. When time and speed are considerations, her sacraments are borne by air over mountain, plain and sea. The first aeronaut, born

Sursum Corda!

in 1685, at Santos, Brazil, is portrayed in the new Brazilian stamp to be used for the Brazilian air lines. As instances of her familiarity with the sea, we need only recall how her missionaries were among the first pioneers to encounter its perils in their quest for souls. Aboard the "Lutzow" on her way to the Eucharistic Congress at Carthage, an Archbishop celebrated every day and about a hundred priests tried to say Mass on the portable altars set up in various rooms on the boat.

And what about the very young, the little ones so dear to Christ? Pius X bade us prepare to find children saints. From the earliest Christian times they have never been wanting; and even in "the glorious company of the Martyrs" they are among the most glorious. In our own times it is truly "out of the mouths of infants" that God is perfecting praise. At the age of three, Thérèse of Lisieux, at four, Nellie Aherne of Cork, "Little Nellie of Holy God," entered consciously upon their upward path. And to name but one more, Guy de Fontgalland, who died in 1929, is becoming known all the world over and there is talk already of miracles and the introduction of his cause.

Small pillars these in the temple of God. But how beautiful, and how strong; else would they not be there. The promise of Our Lord is to conquerors. Combat and victory are required of all who have come to the use of reason.

We have been thinking of ambitions—more or less deserving—as a characteristic of the youth of the present day. Ambition is not in itself reprehensible. It is the very life-blood of youth. We may almost say of it, even in its least noble forms, what the Church says of life in the Preface of her Mass for the Dead: "Not taken away, but changed." We live by our desires. From the beginning God has shown His appreciation of noble desire. "Because thou art a man of desire I am come to shew it to thee," said the Archangel to the prophet Daniel whom he was sent to instruct as to the time of Christ's Coming and Passion. The loftiest lives earth has seen have sprung from desires. Every man has, or at one time had, his ideals as to what he would wish to be and the life that should be his. Two disciples of St. John Baptist, drawn by the charm of our Lord's Person and words, timidly followed Him, for awhile in silence. Then their desire took shape: "Master, where dwellest Thou?" Its reward was the invitation: "Come and see," which brought Andrew and then Simon Peter, his brother, their vocation to the Apostleship.

Our ambition may be self in one or other of its many shapes—comfort, ease, excitement, whatever enjoyment we can reach for the satisfaction of the senses. Or it may be God for His own sake, and for His sake our own and our neighbours' salvation; not merely passing pleasure, but rest to our souls, the solid happiness which is satisfying and lasting, to be found by falling in with God's designs for us. He made me for a distinct purpose, not for honours or for wealth, because He knows that none of these things nor all of them put together, can satisfy the soul of man. It is too vast to be filled with anything of this world or any good less than God, because it was made for Him alone.

Sursum Corda!

God is love. It was not enough for Him to be Absolute Beatitude in Himself. His happiness must overflow and be the beatitude of intelligent creatures. Therefore He created us in His own image and likeness. Because of this likeness we must find our happiness where He finds His own—in Himself. We are made "to know Him, love Him, serve Him and be happy with Him. Happiness is not to be found elsewhere. We can no more do without Him than we can breathe without air.

Men say they feel no need of God; they are satisfied with earthly enjoyments. It may be so; these may suffice them—for a time. The body has cravings which the gratifications of sense may appease. But the aspirations of the soul, created to the image of God, are vast beyond conception, and not to be satisfied with anything of this world. Its needs have an intensity to which no need of the body can compare. Within it is a void which creatures can never fill. We do not feel this now, but we shall prove it hereafter. Separated from the body in the next life, the soul has an all but infinite desire of God, a desire which as long as it remains unsated, causes pain all but infinite. Unless the soul corresponds to the original, to the likeness of which it was made, it can never be satisfied. Unless it finally possesses God it must fail of the end of its creation and be for ever miserable. There will be a hunger and thirst which nothing can satiate or slake in time or in eternity. Therefore God has so prepared my path that all upon my way may bring me to Him. He gives each one of us something to do for Him in this life and He has taken care to make us capable of doing it.

This career for which He has specially fitted us we name our "calling" or "vocation." It must be of great importance for us to find out what it is, not only because it is God's will, but because it is the supreme need for us. Nothing is at its best unless it is being used for the purpose for which it was intended. Consequently we are only likely to be at our best when we have found the calling for which God created and fitted us.

But how am I to know precisely for what God intended me? Sometimes I am drawn in one direction, sometimes in another; which is His will? As soon as I know it my main desire and ambition will be to follow it.

"To the Lord was His own work known from the beginning," Holy Scripture tells us. And not known only, but lovingly prepared as for "most dear children." Can He, then, be less interested in it than we are ourselves?

Think how that girl flier, soon to be on her way home from her perilous journey, must have prepared for it. How she must have cared for what was to be her only and inseparable companion on her air-course of nearly ten thousand miles. She was flying one of the smallest of our aeroplanes, and a second-hand machine at that. We are told that she made herself thoroughly acquainted with every part of its structure, knowing it would depend on her alone to provide for all its needs. Yet no affection for it blinded her as to its true character. Her very interest led her to estimate at their

Sursum Corda!

real value its good points, its defects, and its limitations. Startings and landings, and smooth running, the provision of fuel, risks and repairs, bad weather under appalling conditions, mischances of many kinds—for all these contingencies it must be prepared. She had qualified for an engineer's license as well as a pilot's, and had studied as far as possible the route her plane would follow. No care for its safety, no cost, no labor could be too great—it must not, it would not fail her.

And can we think our Heavenly Father will be unmindful of the work of His hands, from all eternity the object of His loving solicitude, the soul equipped to the least detail for the purpose He has designed, that all might be ready when its time should come?

The world followed the flier with admiration not unmixed with anxiety when, as she neared the goal, the daily record of progress brought by wireless failed for a while. When the glad news of her arrival in Australia reached her anxious family, and her father was asked what recognition of her wonderful achievement would be most acceptable to her, he suggested a new aeroplane. "Not," we can imagine someone objecting, "if this should involve the sacrifice of the tried and trusted companion of her venture. To that she would never consent. Dear to her almost as her own life; as a living human presence; an understanding faithful friend; in hours of perplexity and anguish her only earthly counsellor and resource—she must cherish it as her companion to the end."

The Time of My Life

Surely He who has not failed us in the past will not fail us in the future or turn a deaf ear to the humble, persevering prayer that only asks to know and do His will?

"You know not what you ask," was the answer of our Lord to the two apostles whose ambition had prompted their request for the first places in His Kingdom. How often He must make the same gentle reproach to us! We ask for trifles which would be in no way helpful to us, and perhaps hardly ever call to mind the vital matters on which our eternity depends. To take an instance: Do the generality of us ever give a thought to what will be our main concern when we come to die? We leave to those about us, possibly strangers, the care of providing along with spiritual helps, the dispositions we shall need. The Church, we hope, will fortify us with her sacraments and prayers, into the import of which we have never thought it worth our while to inquire.

However this may be, there is another vital question which every well-instructed Catholic must surely believe calls for constant and earnest prayer till it is settled: "What am I going to do with my life?" In other words: "What is my vocation?"

To many this word simply means religious life, and they turn away as from a subject that doesn't concern them. This is a mistake. The word simply means a call to some lawful career in life for which we are suited and by means of which we may save our soul. If we restrict it to the Religious Life, it indicates not an order to be obeyed like the Commandments, but a choice offered as a greater good, which (except in quite exceptional circumstances) we are free to accept or to decline. "If thou wilt enter into life keep the Commandments," said our Lord—to all. "If thou wilt be perfect," He said to the young man whom He loved for keeping the Commandments, and to whom as a mark of special love He offered as a counsel a further union with Himself. It was with disappointment rather than with displeasure that he watched the eager questioner going away sad. Unless, indeed, we take "appointment" and "pleasure" to indicate the distinction between command and counsel, between obedience to what is required, and the generosity that would offer what is more acceptable. This is what the child must have meant who, being asked if she had a devotion to the will of God, answered: "I don't know that I have; I prefer His good pleasure." "In My Father's House," Our Lord tells us, "there are many mansions." This is not saying that perfection is for those only who are willing to sell all and follow Him. Numbers who are treading the ordinary paths of life may be following Him more closely than are many in the Religious State. The question for each of us individually is: "What does God want me to do with my life?" For many of us the question is answered by the circumstances in which we find ourselves. These are God's choice for us and so long as they remain inevitable we must accept, them, agreeable or trying, as His will, and therefore capable of being made subservient, not to our salvation only, but to our perfection.

If the choice be left to ourselves, the only way to a safe decision is prayer, consideration, and, where available, prudent advice. Reading, too, may indicate by certain signs the kind of calling suitable for ourselves. The matter is a momentous one and we can hardly begin too early to make it a subject for patient, persevering, and trustful prayer, in these thoughtless times especially when acts of self-committal are so reckless and so common. We must be in our guard against precipitation on the one hand and unnecessary procrastination on the ether. "Which is God's calling for me, that alone will be fully successful for the accomplishment of His purpose?" Prayer for light to find it will help me, natural temperament may incline me, for grace often builds on nature; a calling—not necessarily the most distasteful and arduous—might be one to which my talents, qualifications and inclinations could be put to their fullest use.

And here we may call attention to a book by Father Bede Jarrett, O.P., written specially for the young who are at the parting of the ways. An unfounded apprehension nearly deterred him from writing "The Space of Life Between." "I was rather afraid of young men," he says: "they seemed to me so wonderful and even magnificent that I never thought they would pay attention to what I wrote."

Happily the friend to whom he confided his misgivings met them by saying that those whom he feared to approach were "extraordinarily shy and were only too pleased if anyone paid attention spiritually to them; they were the most forlorn folk in the Kingdom of God, too self-conscious to speak, too sensitive to religious ideals to want to escape religion, too tempted to move simply with the sacraments, too perplexed always to see their way."

It is impossible for anyone knowing nothing of American girls to say whether they share in any respect the accessibility discovered in a section at least of our English youth at the close of their college course. But there can be no harm in drawing attention to a book which many who are nearing the school-leaving age will probably find both interesting and helpful. A chapter on "The Priesthood" provides useful hints for those who think they may be called to the Religious State.

I may perhaps find it useful to tabulate on paper the results of my inquiries, but over all will be the silent, persistent desire of God making its still voice heard in my heart as to that "more acceptable" Will of His to which I desire to conform my own. St. Paul speaks to his converts in Rome of "proving what is the good, and the acceptable, and the perfect will of God." And David's loyal heart cries: "Make the way known to me wherein I should walk, for I have lifted up my soul to Thee. Teach me to do Thy Will, for Thou art my God. Thy good spirit shall lead me into the right land." (Ps. 142)

Prayer and trust in God is our great resource. From all eternity our path in life, with the action of our free-will upon its choices, has lain before Him, distinct in all its details.

Will He not watch over it with a solicitude for which we have no name? Will there be any prayer to which He will listen more readily than to the earnest petition: "Thy Will be done on earth as it is done in Heaven."

The simple dependence on the Holy Spirit in which the early Christians lived is very striking. They turned to Him confidently as to a personal friend always present, protecting them, directing their plans, and so associating Himself with them that the Apostles could say: "It hath seemed good to the Holy Ghost and to us." If we are weak, "the Spirit helpeth our infirmity." If "we know not what we should pray for as we ought, the Spirit asketh for us with unspeakable groanings." If in difficult circumstances where the interests of God are nearly concerned, we fear the result of our words, our Lord promises: "The Holy Ghost shall teach you what you must say."

To be guided by the Holy Spirit, we have to follow the Will of God where we know it. Often it is not clear to us, but we are only held accountable for what we know. If we make good use of the light we have, God will give us more, and lead us to the fulfilment of His designs. In our doubts the Holy Spirit would have us consult enlightened persons. Thus He sent St. Paul to Ananias.

Some people are self-sufficient or impetuous and will neither seek nor listen to advice. They start with vehemence on a path of their own choice, come to grief, and then begin to ask for counsel, perhaps ask it of God. But it is too late. They are so committed that they cannot go back. We must mortify this impetuous self-will. "He is the best servant," says St. Augustine, "who does not desire that God should say the things that he wills, but who desires himself to will the things that God says." Before we ask to know the will of God, let us, to the utmost of our power, submit our will to His, saying, "Give me Thy Spirit to teach me. My heart is ready, O Lord, my heart is ready—what wilt Thou have me to do?"

To follow the direction of the Holy Spirit is to follow an unerring Guide. In such dependence we may live in great repose of mind, relying upon His care of us, which will be greater or less according to our recourse to Him in need and our fidelity in obeying His promptings. He is ever ready to assist us in all that regards the designs of God over us. I should never take any step of importance without seeking light from God. But when the results of a decision may be felt throughout eternity, I must beware of counsellors whose views go no further than this life. Well-meaning they may be; untrustworthy they can hardly fail to be in matters beyond their province. To discern the path of duty and the Will of God amid the illusions of self-love and the conflicting interests that assert themselves, often calls for supernatural insight in a high degree, and points to the need of an enlightened guide. Our only safe course—above all when our state of life is the momentous question to be decided—is to turn for guidance to the Holy Spirit, and by earnest prayer and unreserved abandonment of ourselves to His good pleasure deserve to be led by Him. All life long we are choosing. A wrong choice may in some cases bring us misery in this world and in the next. Whose counsel will be always safe, always what is most for our good, will secure us against mistakes for which we should be grievously sorry later? What friend can never lead us astray because He can never be mistaken? Only our God. And just when we reach the age when our choices are most important, He comes forward and offers Himself to be our Friend all life long, to bring us safely through all its dangers to a happy eternity.

And so we end—with prayer. Thus by the blessing of God shall we find our way to Him; realize His purpose for us and the ideal of our early years "to do something good," at least by the example of a thoroughly Catholic life. So shall we be able to give of our best to God; to be "living stones" and "pillars" in His Temple; and—standing by His grace to the end—erect ourselves and upholding many, deserve to be admitted at last to His Presence for a happy eternity:

"To live for God and then to die—that done, all is done."

ADDITIONAL WORKS WRITTEN BY MOTHER MARY LOYOLA

How to Help the Sick and Dying (1889)
First Communion (1896)
Mass Before First Communion (1896)
Confession and Communion
for Religious and Those who Communicate Frequently (1898)
The Child of God *or* What Comes of Our Baptism (1899)
The Soldier of Christ: Talks Before Confirmation (1900)
Coram Sanctissimo: Before the Most Holy (1901)
Forgive Us Our Trespasses: Talks Before Confession (1901)
First Confession (1901)
A Simple Confession Book (1901)
A Simple First Confession Book (1901)
A Simple Confirmation Book (1901)
Hail, Full of Grace: Simple Thoughts on the Rosary (1902)
Questions On First Communion (1903)
A Simple Communion Book (1903)
Welcome! Holy Communion: Before and After (1904)
Credo: A Simple Explanation of Catholic Doctrine (1905)
Jesus of Nazareth: The Story of His Life Written for Children (1906)
Home For Good (1907)
Holy Mass (1907)
Heavenwards (1910)
The Children's Charter: Talks with Parents and Teachers
on the Preparation of the Young for Holy Communion (1911)
The Little Children's Prayer Book (1911)
Why Must I Suffer: "A talk with the toilers" (1911)
Abba, Father (1912)
Ita, Pater (1912)
On His Majesty's Service: "A talk with our wounded" (1916)
Blessed Are They That Mourn (1917)
The King of the Golden City: an Allegory for Children (1921)
With the Church, Volume I: Advent to the Ascension (1924)
With the Church, Volume II: The Ascension to Advent (1928)
Trust (1928)

www.ingramcontent.com/pod-product-compliance
Lightning Source LLC
Chambersburg PA
CBHW030131170426
43199CB00008B/36